Catholicism
and
Secularization
in America

Catholicism and Secularization in America

EDITED BY
David L. Schindler
Essays on Nature, Grace, and Culture

Louis Bouyer
Louis Dupré
Walter Kasper
Michael Novak
Glenn W. Olsen
David L. Schindler
Kenneth L. Schmitz

Our Sunday Visitor Publishing Division
Our Sunday Visitor, Inc.
200 Noll Plaza
Huntington, Indiana 46750
❋
COMMUNIO BOOKS
Notre Dame, Indiana

This work is a joint project of Our Sunday Visitor and *Communio:
International Catholic Review*, Notre Dame, Indiana. With the
exception of short excerpts for critical reviews, no part of this book
may be reproduced or transmitted in any form or by any means,
electronic or mechanical, including photocopying, recording, or by any
information storage or retrieval system, without permission in writing
from the copyright holder. Write:
Our Sunday Visitor Publishing Division
Our Sunday Visitor, Inc.
200 Noll Plaza
Huntington, IN 46750

International Standard Book Number: 0-87973-450-7
Library of Congress Catalog Card Number: 89-64273

PRINTED IN THE UNITED STATES OF AMERICA

Cover design by Rodney Needler

450

Contents

Preface

Most of the papers of this volume were presented in essentially the same form during a recent conference on "Nature, Grace, and Culture: On Being Catholic in America," which was sponsored by *Communio* with the support of Our Sunday Visitor Foundation and the Office of the Provost of the University of Notre Dame. There are three additions: the introductory chapter highlights the meaning of secularization in America as an issue of the relation of nature and grace, and thereby indicates the background concern which led to the conference. The comments by Archimandrite Boniface (Luykx) and Father Romanus Cessario were offered during the discussion period at the conference, and they seemed pertinent and significant enough to warrant inclusion in the volume. Finally, we include the document on faith and inculturation produced by the International Theological Commission chaired by Cardinal Joseph Ratzinger, because of its obvious relevance to our theme and because it serves to fill out the context of the discussion undertaken in the various papers.

Joel Barstad and Karen Kretschmer carried through the final preparation of the papers for publication.

David L. Schindler
Editor in Chief
Communio: International Catholic Review

Introduction: Grace and the Form of Nature and Culture

David L. Schindler,
University of Notre Dame

Henri de Lubac saw it clearly long ago. The problem of nature and grace is not an arcane matter suitable only for in-house academic squabbling among theologians. Rather, the problem reaches to the heart of what it means to be Christian. Is relation to God fundamental or merely extrinsic or "accidental" to human existence? In what sense? What follows with respect to all the other relations which make up human existence: man's relation even to him- or herself, to the economic and political order, and the like? What de Lubac saw so clearly was the inescapability of these questions: our practice—thinking, doing, making —will carry an answer to them, whether we are aware of that answer or not.[1]

De Lubac himself was at pains to retrieve the perspective of the Fathers of the Church, which he saw to require a direct if paradoxical relation of grace and nature: grace orders nature from the beginning of nature's existence and from the deepest depths of nature; grace is nonetheless not a requirement or implication of nature, but is rather an utterly gratuitous gift which calls nature radically, indeed infinitely, beyond itself. God calls and thus orders man from the depths of his being to God; and God is thereby more deeply related, more interior, to man than man is to himself. At the same time, the God who so orders is infinite and thus one in relation to whom man as a finite being can exact no claim whatsoever. As Augustine sums it up so beautifully in his *Confessions*, God is deeper than our inmost reality and higher than the topmost heights we can reach (Bk. 3, Ch. 6).

In a word, the transcendent God is immanent; the immanent God is transcendent. The transcendence and the immanence of God are directly, not inversely, related.[2] Elimination of the simultaneity of transcendence and immanence, in either direction, would release the tension which triggers the restlessness at the depths of human being. It is because God has made us for himself, and thereby has already reached into us, that our hearts are restless until they rest in God (*Confessions*, Bk. I, Ch. 1).

From this ordering of nature to grace, of man to God, there follow at least two characteristic features of holiness: transformation and eschatology. "Transformation" tells us that we must allow the relation to God which fundamentally orders us to penetrate our being ever more fully, to the end of transfiguration. "Eschatology" tells us that we must remain aware that this process of transfiguration is first a gift, always ecstatic (always takes us out of ourselves), and never complete short of the next life. Holiness in other words is a matter of allowing the transcendent God to "immanentize" himself ever more deeply in us, even as that "immanentizing" turns us ever more radically outside of ourselves, indeed calls us infinitely beyond ourselves to the infinitely transcendent God. Holiness thus excludes both a "supranaturalism" which would miss the immanence and hence transforming presence of God and a "naturalism" which would miss the transcendence and hence eschatological call of God. The former misses the *penetration* of God into nature; the latter misses the penetration *of God* into nature. The result in either case is secularization: a nature without God, a nature not ordered from within its depths to God.

Here then we can see the wonderful unity in the lifework of Cardinal de Lubac on nature and grace, atheism, retrieval of the Fathers, and the like. Regarding the relation of nature and grace, de Lubac insisted from first to last on a (*de facto*, not *de jure*) unity simultaneous with distinctness, and thereby never confused unity with identity, or distinctness with separation.[3] If in his earlier work he emphasized the unity and in his later work the distinctness, that was only because the theological context had changed so dramatically. In the name of the transcendence of the order of grace (and indeed to protect the integrity of nature in the face of the emphasis of Protestantism), much of post-Tridentine theology had drawn such a sharp line between nature and grace that nature and its activities were effectively left to themselves: to their own integrity and resources as natural. On the other hand, in the name of the immanence of the order of grace, of God, much of post-Vatican II theology so absorbed grace into nature that nature and its activities were in effect no longer seen as requiring radical transformation in relation to God, as needing judgment first from beyond themselves.

What de Lubac perceived was that both of these theologies led to

11

secularization: the dualistic theology following Trent, as it were, to a "conservative" form of secularization; the reductionistic theology following Vatican II to a "liberal" or "progressive" form of secularization. What de Lubac perceived, in other words, was that neither of these theologies was capable of meeting the crisis of modernity in its deepest roots — which lay in modernity's driving impulse to order the world without God.

Thus it is easy to see the connection between de Lubac's work on nature and grace and his work on atheism. Ordering the world without God can take "hard" and "soft" forms. Atheism can be theoretical and thus resolute. But atheism can also be practical or lived: a matter of a practice which pushes God to the margins or private gaps of culture. De Lubac's studies indicate where a civilization will be led which persists in building itself in a way which denies, implicitly or explicitly, the internal and fundamental ordering of man to God.

It is easy likewise to see the reason for de Lubac's return to the Fathers of the Church. Here, in accord with the truest Catholic spirit, he found the resources for the organic view of the nature-grace relation which was required to meet the challenge of the atheism, the secularized world-without-God, of modernity. It is in this context that we can also begin to see why, in a move which has puzzled many, de Lubac saw fit to emphasize the simultaneous significance for the twentieth century of the work of Hans Urs von Balthasar and Pierre Teilhard de Chardin.

Both Balthasar and Teilhard worked to overcome the extrinsicism of much of post-Tridentine theology, that is, while insisting on the primacy of grace. In an important sense, Balthasar and Teilhard both taught that grace is a form, which, because it is that of the trinitarian God, is thereby the form of love. One might say that Balthasar, perhaps more clearly than any other person of our time, has shown how, *in* Christ and his Church, this trinitarian love has taken on a christological, marian, and ecclesial form. And one might say that Teilhard, perhaps also as much as anyone else in our time, has shown us how, *through* Christ and his Church, this trinitarian love has opened onto the cosmos: giving the cosmos itself (already and not-yet) the christological, marian, and ecclesial form face of love.[4]

The point here is to suggest neither that de Lubac was uncritical of Teilhard nor that there are not tensions between the theology of Balthasar and that of Teilhard. The point is merely to underscore that, despite

12

criticisms and recognizing these tensions, de Lubac nonetheless saw that common to the two theologians was an affirmation of the primacy of the form of Christ: an affirmation, that is, of the form of Christ as providing the deepest order for nature, from the beginning of nature's existence. In this way de Lubac saw Balthasar and Teilhard as profound exemplars of the patristic perspective which he himself was laboring to retrieve and, again, which he saw as alone capable of meeting the challenge of modernity.

The ideas sketched here in the name of de Lubac help to identify the central concerns of *Communio* in its founding (de Lubac himself assisted in that founding) and, more immediately, in its decision to organize the conference whose fruit is the book before you. The theological insistence of *Communio* from its origin has been upon the primacy of grace, not in any merely vague sense of transcendence, but in its trinitarian form as given in and through Christ and his Church. From this insistence there follows a concern for transformation: a concern to see and criticize nature and culture — thought, action, and production: all of being — in the light of grace. The papers which follow take up various aspects of the meaning of grace in relation to nature and culture. My purpose in this introductory chapter is to try to bring out the fuller implications of what is presupposed in our thus giving such prolonged attention to the theological dimension of the problem of inculturation of faith. Is it possible now to say more about the sense in which the theology of nature and grace just sketched is a matter of importance for Catholics in contemporary America?

There is a peculiarly American way of turning issues into matters of *praxis*. That is, the question of truth often slides off immediately into the question "What difference does it make, practically?" In the present context, which concerns the inculturation of Catholic faith in America, this inclination toward *praxis* takes a particularly sharp form. Preoccupation with a theology of nature and grace, in the face of the serious problems which confront us, can seem a little like fiddling while the city burns — or in any case like a dissipation of energy into arid channels. The real issues, the life-and-death issues, concern how our theology turns up in social and political and moral terms. From the Left: What does it all matter unless we overturn the patriarchal or otherwise unjust structures of the Church and society? Indeed, the traditional mode of theologizing already presupposes those structures, and therefore taking up theology in

13

this mode already gives away what must rather be contested. What does it all matter while we mindlessly continue the arms race? If our economic policies do not eliminate or seriously reduce poverty?

Or again, and from the Right: What does it all matter as long as we can get Americans to practice more morality, and indeed to acknowledge a transcendent source for morality? As long as we can stop the practice of abortion, shore up the nuclear family, build a strong national defense, and free the forces of the market enough to provide the poor with the material necessities of life? As long as we can merely succeed in getting Catholics to apply the traditional formulas of Christian faith to their lives?

The issues focused by these questions are of course hardly trivial. My reason for recording them is not to suggest that they are trivial, but merely to direct attention to their *form*. In our culture these issues are typically taken to be first ethical in character.[5] Or, insofar as the issues concern the public order, they in turn become primarily sociopolitical: How do we as Christians make our ethics effective, particularly now in a pluralistic society? What I wish to suggest in contrast here, in the name of the work of Henri de Lubac (and Hans Urs von Balthasar), is that these issues, all of them, are first religious and theological in character. These issues, in other words, are matters of *religious form* before they are matters of practice — or rather, they are matters of practice only as already, anteriorly, given a religious form.

The question to which I wish to direct attention, then, bears at once on form and on religious form. Now we can begin by defining form as a pattern of intelligibility or a logic (*logos*) and a spirit. When we suggest that our practice already presupposes or is a form, then, what we mean is that that practice will involve a pattern of intelligibility or a logic; that it will be invested with a purpose; and that it will be carried through from within some sort of "spirit," which is to say with some definite sense of interiority or lack thereof. We mean, in other words, that that practice will already involve an ontology (or, if you will, an onto-logic) which is inclusive of a spirituality. But we have suggested further that the form of practice will be fundamentally religious in character. To get at the fuller meaning of what is thus entailed when we suggest that problems of practice are already problems of a form — and thereby of an onto-logic and a spirituality — which is first religious, we must look again at what is implied in the theology of de Lubac and Balthasar.

As we have seen, de Lubac — in a radicalism which Balthasar says is merely a retrieval of the radicalism of all great Christian thinkers[6] — argues that human nature exists (*de facto*, not *de jure*) only as already *related* to the God of Jesus Christ. And as the work of Balthasar himself brings out so beautifully and profoundly, this relation is not, as it were, merely a movement but (also) already a form. Relation to the God of Jesus Christ already orders nature and thereby gives nature a new form — a shape, a pattern of intelligibility, a logic, a "face." To be sure, one can never emphasize enough that this form is pure gift, in no way required by our nature or able to be claimed by our nature. And this form of God, already given in creation through Christ, is fully actualized only by means of participation in the Church which is the body of Christ and indeed, finally, in the unrestricted communion with God which can occur only in the next life.

But what nevertheless follows from this theology is that nature is never neutral with respect to religious form. Nature is never without a form, an implication of order, with respect to what is ultimate. And thus the practice—the activities and productions—in and through which we extend nature into a culture are likewise never without a religious form. Any claim that nature — and the practice which actualizes nature — is neutral would imply that nature is or has an integrity in and of itself apart from God, or that nature's relation to God is merely extrinsic or external. Or, if recognizing in some sense that nature has a direct relation to God, such a claim would nonetheless still imply failure to see that that relation is not only a movement but also carries a form.

In sum, then, when we say that our practice is a matter of religious form before it is a matter of ethics and politics, of morality and social justice, we mean that such practice will never be neutral with respect to religious form. Concretely, the practice of morality and of social justice will be different depending on whether that practice is consciously developed from within or outside of, as only extrinsically related to, the religious form given in grace.

But all of this remains abstract. We have said that nature and its practice are not neutral with respect to the religious form given in grace. Can we now say more about what this implies, concretely, for the form of our practice? We turn to a summary statement from Balthasar: "... the love of God comes and implants itself into this threefold *fiat* [the Son's consent to the Father, Mary's consent, and the Church's consent]. . . ;

15

within [this *fiat*] the Son's mission is formed, and within this the Church's mission and within this again, the Christian's mission; while it is for the sake of the whole plan, that we have the whole structure of creation, with its innumerable individual forms in time and space. For the creation, the forms of nature, have developed and opened themselves in spirit and in love to the unending fruitfulness of grace, receiving their final form from above so that everything natural is reformed, recast and reorientated. The archetype of this whole development is found in the way Christ's human nature stands out—ecstatically—in relation to his divine person, from which he draws his human existence; the mission he receives from the Father forms not only his office and destiny as Redeemer, but the essential traits of his individual nature. He assumed a human existence in order to offer it entirely to God for the sake of man and the world, in order to unite God and man by dissolving, 'emptying' himself, so that through the resurrection he might receive the nature he had sacrificed (and the world) back from the Father, transfigured and eternal, to place both eternally in the hands of the Father."[7]

Further, then, Balthasar goes on: "Every Christian must ratify [this] consent [the threefold *fiat* of Christ, Mary, and the Church] fully throughout his life in all that he is and does, and must try, however ineffectively, to approximate it existentially."[8] In short, the Christian must "put on the form of Christ's life."[9]

These statements are nearly inexhaustible in their richness. We as Christians, and indeed in some way already as humans, are ordered to God in Jesus Christ, are thereby called to put on the form of Christ. Our call to God is a relation to God, which relation in turn is not only a movement but a form. What is that form? First of all, of course, the "what" is a "who." The form, as the form of Christ, is thereby one of love; and the "what," thus, is love. But the point is that this love is revealed first of all *in* the person of Jesus Christ, *is* Jesus Christ. In Jesus Christ we find the form or logic of love, because Christ *is* that logic. Christ is the meaning of love as love is incarnate in Christ. All that we can and must say as Christians about the form of our "natural" activities and productions, of our practice, is thus found here: all that we are and do and make must take its bearings from the *form* revealed in Jesus Christ, and, therefore, from the love whose form is given Jesus Christ.

And, as Balthasar says, the archetype for this whole development is given in the hypostatic union: Christ's distinct human nature has its existence only in relation to, in unity with, the divine person. Christ's mission *as human* is from the Father. Likewise our mission — because and insofar as we are *alteri Christi*, Christs by participation and adoption — is from the Father in Christ. What is that mission? Kenotic and agapic love. We must empty ourselves for God and for all others in God, in order then to receive everything that we are and do and make back again, now transformed and transfigured in and through this relation of self-emptying, radically other-centered, love. In a word, as Balthasar himself sums it up in the words of Teilhard: "All of our work must finally lead to forming us into a kind of sacrificial or receptive material, to be transformed in and through the divine flame."[10]

Religious form, then, as understood in the work of de Lubac and Balthasar, is the form of Christ: form as Christ's love; Christ's love as a form. This is the Christian call to holiness: to put on the form which is Christ who is love. But before we turn to consider further what is implied for the form of ethical and political practice by the form of Christ's love, we need to recall what we suggested earlier: namely that the lack of the form of Christ's love shaping our practice will signal, not the mere absence of that form, that is, in a way that would imply neutrality, but, rather, the presence of a form which will just so far be weighted differently from that given in and by Christ's love. To put our question adequately, then, we must first ask what is the form which, concretely — given the horizon of our contemporary culture — is, alternatively, most likely to shape our practice. Can we say more about the form which practice in fact takes in our culture, to prepare us to say more, concretely, about the differences between this form and the form required by Christianity as understood by de Lubac and Balthasar?

In answer to this question, we can perhaps best begin with the conventional understanding of "rights." A "right" as conventionally understood — as understood in the liberal tradition which has been a dominant force in America[11] — is a claim which the self has on the other. The supposition is that the direction of obligation is from the other toward the self. The form or logic of the liberal understanding of rights, in other words, is self-centered.[12] That logic presupposes a primitive externality of relation between the self and the other, which in turn makes the self the center of relation.[13] A right in this context, then, merely expresses the kind of obligation which results from this self-centricity of relation —

that is, an obligation first of others to me. Even when this right is extended to all selves, the direction of obligation—the obliged relation—remains self-centered. What happens is merely that that self-centricity now becomes universalized.

The practice of abortion which is widespread in America illustrates well this inherent logic of relation carried in liberalism. A logic which makes the self, that is, in its constitutive or ontological separateness from the other, the center of action and thereby the center of obligation, leaves vulnerable precisely those selves who are least able to act for themselves and thus to make demands for themselves. An unborn human being is a self who is vulnerable in just this way. (This is unfortunately what opponents of abortion often fail to see. That is, opponents of abortion who would make their case in terms of conventional "rights" language fail to see that this language leaves intact the deeper logic which is precisely what has made America open to legalized abortion in the first place.[14])

But in any case my concern here is merely to illustrate how the conventional appeal to "rights" reveals the *form* or the *logic* of American culture. That logic is one of a self-centricity which presupposes a primitive (ontological) externality of relation between the self and others. Such a logic is the heart of what is called liberalism.

Another way of characterizing the form of our culture is, as Balthasar suggests, in terms of the machine.[15] The link between the form of liberalism and the form of the machine is externality of relations. What the language of the machine brings out is the preoccupation with power (understood in terms of physical force or displacement of physical bodies) and technique, and control or manipulation, which results from such externally conceived relations. Or again, the language of the machine indicates the materialization of relations, in a Cartesian sense of matter: things and persons are approached as though they had only an "outside" as it were.

Whatever one may think of it in other respects, the book—and now film—*The Unbearable Lightness of Being* provides a striking if disturbing illustration of what this means. Tomas, Tereza, and Sabina begin to develop their relationships during the time surrounding the events of Prague in 1968. When the tanks move into Prague, they all leave for Switzerland, Sabina eventually going on to America, Tomas and Tereza returning to Czechoslovakia. The point of the film — and the point to which I wish to draw attention — is that the *form* of the relationship of

18

Tomas to Tereza is the *form* of Prague which in turn is the *form* of Geneva. Tomas's promiscuity, the tanks of Prague, and the ugly consumerism of Geneva are all forms of the machine, of mechanistic materialism. Sexual relations hollowed out into their material shell become lustful manipulation. Political relations hollowed out into their material shell become brutal power. Market relations hollowed out into their material shell become hedonistic consumerism — and the music and architecture governed by the laws of such market relations become noise and harsh ugliness. Tereza sees the connection between the tanks of Prague and Tomas's promiscuity; Sabina sees the plastic of Geneva. What they both see (in varying ways and to different degrees — none of them adequate, I dare say, to a genuinely Christian sensibility) is that being has been hollowed out into its surfaces, and they find its lightness unbearable.

In short, what I wish to illustrate here is that the lust, power, and consumerism which often characterize the patterns of relations in contemporary culture have in common the *form* of a machine. It is simply that the machine in each case is put in the service of a different function: pleasure, so far as it concerns relation to oneself; control and manipulation, so far as it concerns relation to the other.

Now my assumption is that most Christians have noticed the negative features of our culture, as these are manifest in abortion, consumerism, and patterns of lust and power. My primary concern here in any case is not with those Christians who, sleepwalking through the twentieth century, have not yet noticed these negative features. My question, then, bears on how Christians should respond to such features.

I now return to the concern for morality and social justice mentioned above. I have already suggested that appeals to morality and social justice, insofar as they are made in conventional terms, and hence in terms of the *form* of our culture, will just so far miss the *form* which is given in grace. What I now wish to propose is that these appeals will be absent or lack the form given in and by Christ's love, by virtue of the *presence* of the form given in and by liberalism and mechanism. Such social-ethical appeals will likely succeed in eliminating some of the grosser patterns of lust, power, and greed in our culture, to be sure. What they will nonetheless leave intact — that is, insofar as they fail to challenge the conventional terms of our culture — is precisely the deeper logic of self-centricity and externality, and the consequent reliance on technique and control and manipulation, which are implied in liberalism and mechanism — and indeed which are what dispose the culture in the first place to its grosser patterns of lust, power, and greed.[16] What these appeals will leave unchallenged, in other words, is precisely the deeper *form* of our culture which is exclusive of the *form of love* — of the love called for by the gospel of Jesus Christ.

It is, of course, not possible here to attempt an exhaustive description of the concrete differences between these forms. But it should nonetheless already be clear that the fault line between them lies in what is meant by relation. Or rather, the issue is relation, but what must be kept clear, once again, is that relation is not only a movement or a matter of will but also a matter of form or logic and hence (also) a matter of the mind.

Above all, then, a practice which would be truly Christian requires *transformation*, a putting on of a new form, the form of Christ. On the one hand, a justification of structures which would be faithful to Christianity involves *forming* them *from within* in and into the love of Christ. On the other hand, a justification or "righting" of the will likewise involves, essentially, an informing of the will in and through the love of Christ, which is to say, giving to the will itself a form. If Christian transformation in the former case requires overcoming the externality characteristic of a mechanistic culture, in the latter case it requires overcoming the moralism proper to a liberal culture.[17] But this initial principle can be stated still more sharply: if externality and moralism (will exercised simply *outside* of and therefore also *without* the form provided by intelligence) can be said to have their paradigm in Descartes; and if the Christian form of love, as has already been indicated above in the words of Balthasar, comes into being only from within the *fiat* of Mary and the Church, then we can say that the most basic distinction here becomes that between a Cartesian and a marian-ecclesial form of relation and action.[18] Six comments in conclusion will help indicate in some measure the nature of the Christian's involvement with the world as mediated by these different forms.

1. Christ, as the form of love, does not replace other forms — the forms of nature and culture. Exactly to the contrary. Christ, as love, is utterly generous: a love formed within the *fiat* lets be, indeed makes be. At the same time, Christ, as the *form* of love, orders and thus orientates all natural forms, from the beginning and from their depths, precisely to the end of transformation and transfiguration in him (in love).[19]

Thus grace neither replaces nature (a truth usually recognized by Catholics) nor leaves nature untouched (a truth all too often overlooked by Catholics).[20] And what holds true for nature holds true for the culture which is the fruit of nature. On the one hand, Christianity does not replace human culture, and all of the human competences required in and by that culture.[21] On the other hand, a human culture which does not permit itself to be formed in and by Christianity will not be neutral; rather it will merely take on another form. And again, the present circumstances of the West suggest that our alternative form will be Cartesian, in its liberal or mechanistic variety.[22]

2. The love which is the inner condition and form of all Christian action and production is not a principle which we ever possess or control, and from which we can then deduce programs of action.[23] Rather, as Balthasar insists, we do not so much organize in terms of that principle as it "organizes" us.[24] In fact, that "principle of organization" is precisely a love which, in the paradox that is the heart of Christianity, takes the form of the Cross, of kenosis, of self-emptying gift. It follows that authentically Christian action can never be triumphalistic, that it must always proceed in and with the self-abandonment and humility characteristic of the love of the Crucified One. Alternatively, action marked by rigid concern for management and mastery, and by self-assertion, is just so far indicative of a form more like that carried in mechanism and liberalism.

3. The paradox indicated here must never be minimized. The form of love which Christians are called to put on in all that they do and make represents on the one hand the most "natural" of claims: that is, it is the form which comes from within the deepest depths of human nature. At the same time, this form of love comes to human nature utterly gratuitously, from utterly beyond human nature, and it thereby indicates a complete reversal of what is natural. It follows that Christian discipleship will always be scandalous: Christians must always seek to help human beings to the fulfillment of their nature, but they must do so in awareness of the paradox that this fulfillment can only take the form, finally, of a Love which is Crucified. In this light, the liberal version of "rights" becomes a much too pale version of fulfillment.[25]

4. Christian action is always a matter first of "being taken through grace into God's action,"[26] within the *fiat* of Mary and the Church. Such action therefore will always have an essentially receptive and contempla-

tive dimension. Alternatively, an action which proceeds from within a Cartesian form will typically be more activistic, more disposed to harshness, to control and manipulation, indeed even to force and violence — all of which features are a function of approaching relations externally and mechanically.

In sum, where an action mediated by a marian form will be marked by interiority and thus by the gentleness of movement which is first from within, an action mediated by a Cartesian form will be marked by extroversion and thus the forcefulness of movement which is first from without.

5. Though it would of course be ideal if the Christian form of love could fully penetrate all of our human organizations and actions, finitude and the weight of sin make this impossible in this life.[27] We have not here the heavenly city. Nonetheless, our participation in the form or mission of Christ permits no merely passive resignation.[28] As Christ is the one sent forth as Incarnate Love, so are Christians sent forth to incarnate love. As Christ is for this world as from and for the Father, so are Christians for this world from and for the Father in Christ.

In a word, an ethics inspired by Christ's love will always be open to both worlds, to this world, but always in anticipation of the world to come. This means that Christian ethics can never be dualistic or monistic: can never be reductively transformational, or eschatological to the exclusion of transformational. Again, the issue here is best seen in terms of form: the Christic form of love, unlike a Cartesian form, is incarnational *in* its transcendence and transcendent *in* its incarnation.[29]

6. Finally, then, the Christian's engagement with the world demands prudence. We as Christians must work *with* others in our society even as we must bear witness to our form as Christians;[30] and working with others in our society, which is today largely non-Christian, means that we must in some ways and sometimes compromise. We cannot force Christian ethics on non-Christians.[31]

The issue here, then, concerns the pluralism of modern culture. Working with others in a pluralistic society entails finding some common ground with them. Finding such common ground is the intention of all forms of what may be called "natural law" ethics. The principle which governs the sort of "natural law" ethics acceptable to the understanding of Christianity outlined here should already be clear: dialogue between Christians and non-

Christians is both possible and necessary, but only as already within the grace — and hence form — of Christ.[32]

This principle, then, has a double edge. On the one hand, it does not eliminate the common ground required for a natural law ethics. On the other hand, it does demand that that common ground be understood in terms, not which are neutral, but which are properly given only from within the analogy of faith. Once again, then, in accord with the theology of de Lubac and Balthasar, nature — and nature's laws — have an integrity as natural, but only concretely and historically, as already weighted either toward or against the finality given in grace. The common ground for which the Christian seeks in his natural law argument, therefore, is and can only be within the concrete history of the dialogue partners. Indeed, what needs to be underscored here is that the demand for a neutral form of natural law argument, for a form of natural law which would seek a common ground outside of the history of the dialogue partners, is as a matter of principle a demand for a liberal form of natural law argument.[33] It is a demand for exactly the sort of abstraction of form which is characteristic of Cartesianism.

It bears repeating: on the reading of Christianity sketched here in the name of de Lubac and Balthasar, nature and nature's laws have integrity to be sure; but they have an integrity which from the beginning is (*de facto*, not *de jure*) relative or relational to the God of Jesus Christ. They have integrity: it follows that the Christian need not make Christ explicit in every appeal to nature and nature's laws, nor should he or she attempt ever to account for nature reductively in terms of Christ. Nature and nature's laws have an integrity which is relational: it follows that the Christian should not, even for a moment, pretend, in his appeal to nature or natural law, that he is uninfluenced by grace, by the faith given in and by Christ, or that nature does not have its final end in Christ. Rather the Christian must give himself over to an accounting for nature in all of its integrity, *even as* he knows in faith that all such accounts can receive their deepest and final intelligibility only in Christ, only in love as Christic form. It thereby becomes incumbent upon such a person to show how any and all accounts of nature — or any aspect or activity thereof — which do not show forth the form of love, which are not open *from within* to integration in and by the trinitarian love of God revealed in Jesus Christ, are inadequate, *precisely as accounts of nature*: for precisely nothing of nature, no aspect of nature, is what it is except as ordered

23

to and thus in some significant sense already formed by this trinitarian love of God.[34]

With this, then, we return to the considerations with which we began this chapter. Henri de Lubac recognized long ago what was at stake in the nature-grace controversy. A true understanding of and challenge to the secularization of the modern world can begin only when one understands that nature is given as ordered from its depths to religious form — to the form, that is, which, concretely, is the love of the trinitarian God revealed in Jesus Christ and received into Mary and the Church by the Holy Spirit. But now we can see better the radical implications of the work wrought by de Lubac. There is and can be — in the concrete historical order which is ours — no nature or natural laws which are neutral of religious form. The claim which would make nature neutral of religious form merely succeeds thereby in giving nature the religious form of liberalism. This holds true also for the *praxis*, the appeal to social justice or morality, which would claim to proceed in innocence of religious form.

But the point here can be put more radically still. When we recall de Lubac's work on Nietzsche and other such thinkers, we become aware that the liberal claim that nature and hence culture is neutral of religious form is in fact one of the forms the death of God can take. It bears emphasis: liberalism is one of the *forms* of the death of God. It is the West's way of pushing God to the margins of culture, and thereby of turning questions from their depths to their surfaces. Indeed, we might summarize what we have written here in the name of de Lubac's work by saying that the god of the West has not really had the courage to die; he has merely become a liberal.

The present outline of a theology of form makes no pretense of having resolved the many complex issues involved in the discussion of Christianity in relation to American culture, particularly in their political and economic dimensions. But this has not been my purpose. My purpose rather has been to try to show where discussion of these issues must *begin*: and that is from within a religious form, and thereby from within an ontology (onto-logic) which is already and in principle a matter of spirituality.[35] My purpose thus has been to try to indicate the deeper form or logic of the prudence required to deal with political and economic practices and structures in a way which would be faithful to Christianity.

24

But the point is that this purpose has been set by a definite theology of nature and grace. And that was why the *Communio* conference was held. The authors of the various papers presented here take up different aspects and implications of the nature-grace issue; and in some cases they have widely differing views. But what the papers collectively serve to do, and what they were meant to do, is to bring into relief the centrality of the nature-grace question for discussion of Christianity and culture. In that I think they succeed.

Notes

1. The classic text of de Lubac here is of course *Surnaturel* (1946). This work was later expanded into two volumes: *The Mystery of the Supernatural* (New York, 1967), and *Augustinianism and Modern Theology* (London, 1969). See also his *Brief Catechesis on Nature and Grace* (San Francisco, 1984), and *The Discovery of God* (New York, 1960). Finally, see the important article by Francesco Bertoldi, "The Religious Sense in Henri de Lubac," *Communio* 16 (Spring, 1989), 6-31.

2. Cf. the statement by Kenneth Schmitz: "We may say, then, that, when said of the divine, the two terms 'transcendence' and 'immanence' designate one and the same relation in reality. They do not differ *in re*, but only *in mente*, in definition. The distinction of terms is a concession to the human mind as it deals with the real relation of creature to Creator" ("Theological Clearances: Foreground to a Rational Recovery of God," in a forthcoming volume in *Studies in Philosophy and the History of Philosophy*, ed. by Eugene T. Long [Washington, D.C.], p. 24 [typescript]).

3. The pertinent formula here is given in the terms of Chalcedon: "*inconfuse*" and "*inseparabiliter*." That is, this formula, which applies to the relation of human nature and divinity in Jesus Christ, provides an analogue (in the sense clarified by the Fourth Lateran Council) for understanding the relation of nature and grace in human beings.

4. See the articles on Teilhard by Jean Daniélou and de Lubac which are reprinted in *Communio* 15 (Fall, 1988), 350-360.

5. For example, even the Right's—legitimate—concern for traditional

doctrine can quickly slide off into a matter simply of willful adherence to or application of that doctrine, as distinct from a matter also of growing into the form revealed in and by that doctrine. But what this means will become clear only as we develop the meaning of "growing into the form."

6. Hans Urs von Balthasar, *In Gottes Einsatz Leben* (Einsiedeln, 1972), p. 75.
7. *Love Alone* (New York, 1969), pp. 101-102.
8. Ibid., p. 103.
9. Ibid.
10. *In Gottes Einsatz Leben*, p. 76 (quoted from *Blondel et Teilhard de Chardin, Correspondance commentée par H. de Lubac*, 1965, 43, Vgl. 91). Balthasar suggests that these words are the meeting point of Blondel and Teilhard — and de Lubac.
11. My intention is not at all to suggest that this is the only understanding of rights available in America. It is merely to suggest that the liberal understanding as I describe it has been prevalent — and that it will be recognized as such by those who have experience of American culture.
12. In technical terms, it presupposes a subject-object logic. The point, in other words, is not that the subject is necessarily egoistic in psychological terms, in terms of intention or motivation. The point rather is that the subject, even if altruistic in intention, is nonetheless — insofar as there is presupposed a liberal horizon — still self-centered as a matter of logic. Within liberalism, that is, the self as individual self, the self in its separateness from the other, functions too exclusively as agent, and thus as the center of action.
13. See preceding note: even if there is a *psychological intention* of altruism, the liberal horizon still leaves intact a *logic* of self-centeredness.
14. In connection with this suggestion, see Stanley Hauerwas, *A Community of Character* (Notre Dame, 1981). Hauerwas brings out well how the conventional, liberal terms of ethical arguments taken up by Christians invariably, though often unwittingly, undermine the positions Christians wish to defend. See especially Chapter 12 for a discussion of how this is the case with respect to the abortion issue. Vigen Guroian's *Incarnate Love* (Notre Dame, 1987) provides a helpful perspective which is also pertinent to the general point here.

15. See, for example, *Test Everything: Hold Fast to What is Good* (San Francisco, 1989), pp. 49ff.

16. Cf. here the words of Balthasar: ". . . Whenever the relationship between nature and grace is severed . . . , then the whole of worldly being falls under the dominion of 'knowledge,' and the springs and forces of love immanent in the world are overpowered and finally suffocated by science, technology and cybernetics. The result is a world without women, without children, without reverence for love in poverty and humiliation—a world in which power and the profit-margin are the sole criteria, where the disinterested, the useless, the purposeless is despised, persecuted and in the end exterminated—a world in which art itself is forced to wear the mask and features of technique" (*Love Alone*, pp. 114-115). Or again: "St. Paul was never tired of emphasizing that even the highest values of individual ethics were undermined without the love of God: love alone can fulfill the law, being its epitome (Rom. 13:10; Gal. 5:15)" (*Love Alone*, p. 105).

17. By moralism, I mean that tendency in a liberal culture which assumes that the human good can be adequately realized in terms simply of the will, and thus in a way which does not require the good's taking an incarnate or public *form* in the culture. The moralism of liberalism, in other words, expresses itself in the privatization — because it is hidden: without form—of the good.

18. For a discussion of how ecclesiology and Mariology must form Christian action, see *Love Alone*, pp. 95ff.

19. The form of agapic love, in other words, is to gather up and transform the sexual eros, the form of the family, of private property and the like (*Love Alone*, p. 110). See also in this connection Balthasar's *The Christian State of Life* (San Francisco, 1983), pp. 105-119. One could usefully recall here St. Thomas's teaching that charity is the form of the virtues.

20. One might appropriately say here that only a marian form can both let what is other be while being in direct (not merely external) relation with what is other. Only from within a marian form can what is other both have integrity as other and have that integrity in relation. In contrast, a Cartesian form forces what is other either outside of relation or, if into relation, then just so far into a relation of control and—in the limit—absorption. In short, only a marian form can truly incarnate and thus give shape, that is, with the generosity which then gives birth.

21. Cf. *Test Everything*, pp. 52-53.
22. It becomes interesting here to recall an acute philosophical insight of Alexis de Tocqueville in his classic *Democracy in America*. Tocqueville says that Americans are Cartesians, that is, in their individualism. He links this individualism with the further American principle of equality, and then shows how the two principles together make American culture particularly vulnerable to a kind of tyranny of the majority (see Vol. II, Pt. 1, Chs. 1 and 2; and Vol. I, Pt. II, Ch. 7). That is, individualism insists that each person should autonomously work out his or her own views on important questions of truth and goodness. But the principle of equality then immediately levels out all such views: because no one individual's view can be taken in advance to be better than that of other individuals. The result is that there is no built-in defense against the majority, against what the greater quantity of individuals sees as true or right. The result, in other words, is a peculiar vulnerability to mass opinion. Mass opinion becomes the — now tyrannical — tradition of those who would have no tradition. A tradition which tells individuals that they are or can be free of a tradition is likely to be particularly tyrannical in its control of such individuals, precisely because these individuals now believe that they are autonomous, presuppositionless—that is, formless—individuals. It is for this reason that Tocqueville can make his justly famous claim: "I know no country in which, speaking generally, there is less independence of mind and true freedom of discussion as in America" (Vol. I, Pt. II, Ch. 7).

It seems to me difficult to exaggerate the importance of what is indicated here, in view of the present circumstances of our culture. The denial of a tradition—of a public orthodoxy and form—in our culture is but an expression of a Cartesian and liberal tradition and public orthodoxy. The claim of a neutral public square is to be found only in a public square which is already and just so far Cartesian and liberal. But the problem of course is that it is precisely the Cartesians and liberals — the majority — who are the last to recognize this.

It seems to me that no compelling argument about the relation of Christianity and culture in America can be made which does not take account of the paradox recorded here. In addition to Tocqueville, the work of Michael Polanyi and Roberto Unger and the recent work of Alasdair MacIntyre are helpful in seeing various aspects of this paradox.

23. *In Gottes Einsatz Leben*, pp. 76-77.
24. See *Love Alone*, p. 105; pp. 108ff.
25. See, for example, in this context, Balthasar, *A Short Primer for Unsettled Laymen* (San Francisco, 1985), pp. 61-65; 68-71.
26. *Love Alone*, p. 94.
27. *In Gottes Einsatz Leben*, pp. 92-93.
28. Ibid., p. 93.
29. "The form of Christian love in the sign of Christ is indivisible; it can never be subjected to a sort of division of labour, some Christians specializing in the transcendent aspect (which is then called 'eschatological' or contemplative), others specializing in the immanent aspect (the active life, turned towards the world). Any hint of that dichotomy tears the image of Christ in two and makes it unrecognizable and incomprehensible in both aspects" (*Love Alone*, p. 109f.).
30 *In Gottes Einsatz Leben*, pp. 97-101.
31. Cf. ibid, pp. 93ff.; and *Test Everything*, pp. 52ff.
32. *Love Alone*, pp. 122-123.
33. Cf. the statement of Alasdair MacIntyre: "Where the standpoint of a tradition cannot be represented except in a way which takes account of the history and the historical situatedness, both of traditions themselves and of those individuals who engage in dialogue with them, the standpoint of the forums of modern liberal culture presupposes the irrelevance of one's history to one's status as a participant in debate. We confront one another in such forums abstracted from and deprived of the particularities of our histories.

"It follows that only by either the circumvention or the subversion of liberal modes of debate can the rationality specific to traditions of enquiry reestablish itself sufficiently to challenge the cultural and political hegemony of liberalism effectively" (*Whose Justice, Which Rationality?* [Notre Dame, 1988], pp. 400ff.). Or again: "The contemporary debates within modern political systems are almost exclusively between conservative liberals, liberal liberals, and radical liberals. There is little place in such political systems for the criticism of the system itself, that is, for putting liberalism in question" (p. 392).
34. I take this in a broad sense, to include the claim that the Christian is committed in advance, precisely as Christian, to a non-mechanistic account of *physis*, of physical nature. This means an account which is inclusive as a matter of principle of activity which is not forceful so

much as generous and from within (that is, of formal and final activity, and effective activity which is now transformed). On this see the important work of Kenneth L. Schmitz, which seeks to rehabilitate a sense of interiority and immateriality in nature: for example, *The Gift: Creation* (Milwaukee, 1982); and "Immateriality Past and Present," *Proceedings of the American Catholic Philosophical Association* (1978), pp. 1-15. See also my paper in the present volume, and my "Beyond Mechanism: Physics and Catholic Theology," *Communio* 11 (Summer, 1984), 186-192; "Catholicity and the State of Contemporary Theology," *Communio* 14 (Winter, 1987), especially pp. 430-437; "Theology, Science, and Cosmology," *Communio* 15 (Fall, 1988), 270-273; and "The Foundations of Morality," in *Act and Agent*, ed. by George F. McLean et al. (The Council for Research in Values and Philosophy, 1986), pp. 271-305.

35. See Balthasar, *A Short Primer*, pp. 61-65; and p. 133: "The maxim of action, of *ethos*, always needs a *logos* that precedes it and gives it its meaning. In Christ, the eternal *Logos*, God's Word of meaning for the world and for mankind, has come among us bodily. By giving full meaning to human existence, he has also given the true maxim of human action; he lived this maxim, even more, he has proved identical with it."

More generally, see my discussions with George Weigel in *Communio* 14 (Fall, 1987) and 15 (Spring, 1988); and with Richard John Neuhaus in *The Thomist*, January, 1989.

Nature, Grace, and Culture:
On the Meaning of Secularization

Walter Kasper, University of Tübingen

Introduction: The Issue

The discussion of the relation between nature, grace, and culture is one of the most consistently debated issues among twentieth-century Catholic theologians. Since the turn of the century with its so-called Modernism and Americanism, this topic has occupied theologians of the post-conciliar Church, raising recurrent questions about the relation between nature, grace, and culture.

We may initially view this as mere monkish squabbling or the kind of in-house academic game that only tangentially affects the life of the faithful or the concrete problems of life. Far from it! The message of grace is at the heart of the Christian faith; Christianity revolves around it. (The New Testament is filled with images and concepts which are used to proclaim the message of the appearance of the grace of God through Jesus Christ: life, light, freedom, peace, joy, justification, redemption, reconciliation, new creation, gift of the Holy Spirit, and many more images and concepts.)

The real question is: How does this central concept of the Christian faith relate to our modern and frightfully secular culture? How does it relate to our everyday experiences and those social, economic, and political issues that confront us on a daily basis? How can we keep the message of salvation alive in a world that is characterized by the experience of destructive forces? How can we speak of reconciliation in a world that is not reconciled but is deeply alienated? What is the meaning of the message of grace for the Church and our culture on our way into the third millennium?

If we translate these concrete issues facing every Christian into the abstract language of theology, we are immediately confronted with the question about the relationship of nature, grace, and culture. Nature, as understood here, is what something is on the basis of its origins, its genesis, and its birth (*natura* > *nasci*); and what it can achieve and reach on the basis of the innate powers of its essence. Culture is a basic component of this nature, since culture is the sum of all those achievements — good or bad — of which we are capable because of our natural disposition, be it through our physical, technical, artistic, or mental efforts. Culture is therefore not just some esoteric affair, it represents the concrete, historical, and constantly changing sphere of human life. In contrast, grace cannot be inherited biologically or sociologically; grace cannot be manufactured by employing scientific, technical, political, or even ethical or ascetic means. Grace is God's freely given gift that leads us and our world to a perfection that exceeds our wildest dreams and wishes. Grace is ultimately not "something" given by God, but is God himself in his free self-communication to man.

But if grace is something wholly new, how are we to make it experiential and understandable in our natural and culturally determined and largely secular life? How are we to distinguish it from something imaginative, a projection, a consoling ideology, or an unworldly utopia? How can we have an answer ready for people who ask us the reason for our hope (1 Pet. 3:15)?

The present crisis facing Christianity in the West does not touch merely on some peripheral concerns; rather, it specifically addresses this very question. We are dealing here primarily with a crisis of relevance. We hear daily that the dogmatic teachings and, even more, the moral rules of the Church no longer reach a large segment of believers. They appear to offer answers to questions that are no longer asked. Nonetheless, the crisis of relevance represents merely the superficial side of the problem. It has long since led to a much deeper identity crisis within the Christian churches. The question is no longer *how* the Church will be able to reach the modern, secularized world; rather, the question is *what* constitutes Christianity as such. What can Christianity, *must* Christianity, say to the modern world? Does it have something of its own to say, something unmistakable?

The first part of this paper will deal with the question about Christian identity. To be sure, one never possesses identity of itself or for itself; one possesses identity only in relation to others. That is why I will discuss in the second part the theological challenge of modern secularization. Finally, there will be discussion of the significance of the Christian nature-grace problem for our modern Western culture and a new Christian humanism.

I. The Relation between Nature and Grace as an Essential Feature of Christianity

The question dealing with the position of Christianity within the present cultural situation is a specifically Christian question; it is tied to the question of Christian identity. It would never have occurred to any ancient philosopher to inquire about the place of Greek religion within the Greek *polis*. We are familiar with the statement of Thales of Miletus: "There are gods everywhere." The gods symbolized the numinous depths of nature; myths were a legitimation and a sanction of the *polis* as well. Whoever questioned this, questioned both the cosmic and the political order, and was accused of being a public menace, a demagogue, and a despicable enemy of the state. Such impiety was punishable by death. Socrates and the early Christians were to suffer its consequences.

Therefore, the fact that the Bible distinguished fundamentally between God and the world on its very first page in the so-called priestly account of creation was truly revolutionary in the eyes of ancient Oriental and Greek and Roman cultures. It was only the Bible that understood God as wholly divine, and by the same token, the world as worldly. As a result of this process of demythologizing, Israel was consistent in its efforts to describe its existence not in terms of natural virtues — as was the case with other nations — but as a result of divine election from among all other nations. Early Christianity continued this line of thinking and radicalized it. One does not become a Christian because of birth or affiliation with a certain nation or culture; rather, one becomes a Christian as a result of God's free grace and a consequent faith that freely responds to God's election. Tertullian says: "*Fiunt, non nascuntur Christiani*" ("Christians come to be, they are not born").

This unique position in antiquity broke open the unity of worldly and religious order. The duality of nature and grace became part and parcel of Christianity, affecting its very essence.

The distinction of nature and grace broke open the harmonious view of man and the world in classical antiquity. It presupposed a new view of God and man. In biblical terms, God no longer is the depth dimension of reality; rather, he is the living God who faces the world in sovereignty, who addresses the world in underived freedom, and who turns to man with unfathomable goodness. Man, who was created in the image and likeness of God (Gen. 1:27), does not experience fulfillment in anything worldly; he does so only if God by his free grace accepts him into his communion. As the image of God, man is hunger and thirst beyond anything found in the world. St. Augustine said: "You made us for yourself and our hearts are restless until they rest in you."

This new and revolutionary definition of the relation between God and world pitted early Christianity against another powerful contemporary spiritual movement, that is, Gnosticism. Gnosticism also questioned classical Hellenism's harmonious view of the world; it, too, thematized the alienation and homelessness of man in this world. In contrast to Christianity, however, Gnosticism derived from this a radical dualism between God and world, spirit and matter. As a result, the biblical understanding of nature as created by God was radically challenged, resulting in a "mortal" conflict with early Christianity which had to affirm continually the duality, inherent in faith, of God and world, nature and grace, while simultaneously and clearly refuting Gnostic dualism.

The epoch-making achievement of the Fathers of the Church of the second and third centuries, such as Irenaeus, Tertullian, and others, was to maintain the unity of creation and redemption while emphasizing their distinctness. In so doing they laid the foundation of a new synthesis, one that was essentially richer in tension and more dynamic than the world picture of antiquity that rested harmoniously in itself. No longer was reality a cosmos that rested and revolved in itself, in which there is nothing new under the sun; rather, reality was now understood as history between God and man which tends beyond itself toward communion with God, which man never reaches by himself, but which he can only receive as a gift through God's gratuitous self-communication.

Gregory of Nyssa had already shaped this new view into a kind of definition of the essence of Christianity. In agreement with the whole patristic tradition of the Fathers, he stated that "Christianity is assimilation (*mimesis*) to divine nature." This definition has been frequently criticized as Platonic and as proof that Christianity had undergone Hellenization at an early state. It nevertheless has a good biblical foundation. Martin Buber termed the imitation of God the "central paradox of Judaism." Jesus himself is completely embedded in this tradition when he requires in the Sermon on the Mount that we be perfect just as our heavenly Father is perfect (Mt. 4:48; cf. Lk. 6:36). Consequently, St. Paul can require us in his epistle to the Ephesians to "become imitators of God" (Eph. 5:1). This is not meant primarily in ethical terms; rather the point is participation in the divine nature (2 Pet. 1:4).

So far as formulae are concerned, this pronouncement may be unique within the New Testament. Still, against the background of St. Paul's theology, its central significance becomes evident. According to St. Paul, we are accepted by God, through the Holy Spirit, as sons and daughters in accordance with the image of the one Son of God. In the final analysis, Gregory of Nyssa's definition of Christianity expresses the driving force that stands behind the Christology and pneumatology of the creed (*symbolon*); God has become man in order that man might become God. Hans Urs von Balthasar again made theology aware of this "wonderful exchange" (*admirable commercium*) of God and man as the innermost core and the fundamental form of the Christian message of salvation.

It is no mere accident that this definition of the essence of Christian existence would be ultimately clarified by Christology, for Christology attempts to conceive the highest possible union of God and man without erasing their differences. The fourth general council at Chalcedon (451) succeeded in doing so by devising the famous formula that the divine and the human natures are both "unmixed and undivided" in Jesus Christ.

The liberal historian of dogma Adolf von Harnack showed nothing but disdain for this formula. Today we know more precisely why this formula was anything but a compromise. We are dealing here rather with the highly reflective concepts derived from the Neoplatonic theory of emanations. By means of these concepts, one could conceive of a union that was instituted "from above," a union, however, that did not absorb the lower, that is, that which derives from it, but sets it free and releases it into its own. Indeed, the One that diffuses itself permits the dependent other to participate in the fullness of its existence, thus becoming one with it. On the other hand, there is a qualitative difference between the reality of the One that exists *per se* and the reality that exists by mere participation. Thus union by participation at the same time gives rise to qualitative difference. The One and that which is derived from it are at once "unmixed and undivided."

Clearly, this Neoplatonic formula could be applied to Christology only by way of an analogy, since the hypostatic union of the two natures in Jesus Christ is simply unique. This is why it can be used only analogously as the paradigm of the Christian understanding of the world. The path to that understanding was indeed long. Christianity in late antiquity and the Middle Ages was deeply influenced by Augustine, the great genius of Western theology. Augustine's passionate soul was so radically shaped by his yearning for God and eternal peace in God that there was no room left for an integral significance of natural values. Augustine accepted these only as means and a passage for reaching the eternal goal. According to Augustine, only God is to be enjoyed (*frui*), that is, only God is to be loved for his own sake; everything else is merely to be used (*uti*). The medieval subordination of secular to spiritual authority followed basically from such a passionate theocentrism.

It was not until Albert the Great and Thomas Aquinas at the height of the Middle Ages that distinctions were proposed within this all-encompassing theocentric order. Within this theocentric order — both ordained by and directed toward God — these men attempted to think through the relative integrity of the world. Their insight was not accepted in their age. Late medieval nominalism once again exaggerated the omnipotence of God to the point of arbitrariness. This was bound to generate reactions. Regardless of the painfulness of these disputes, we are today in a position to appreciate their cathartic effect, since they made possible an authentic Christian world-view. That is why we consider Albert the Great and Thomas Aquinas as precursors of a renewed understanding of the relation between nature, grace, and culture, of a view which only now, after the storms of modern secularization — in post-modern fashion, as it were — has a chance for success.

II. The Challenge of Modern Secularization

Beginning with the Renaissance and humanism in the fifteenth and sixteenth centuries and even more strongly since the period of Enlightenment in the seventeenth and eighteenth centuries, a new way of looking at things has forced its way to the fore. People grew weary of Augustinianism and the demands of Christian asceticism. A new appreciation of the world and a new piety of the world became popular; in fact, a spirit of this-worldliness gained ground. On many occasions, this led to hostility toward the Church, to anticlericalism and secularism in modern Europe. In those countries shaped by Reformed Christianity — including the United States — the Christian doctrine of predestination was frequently secularized and interpreted as the basis and incentive for worldly, especially economic, success.

The emergence of the modern age involved a complex process. We must therefore beware of oversimplification. We are dealing here with a process that did not unfold in linear fashion; each movement was accompanied by powerful countermovements. Descartes' *idea clara et distincta* is juxtaposed to Pascal's *logique du coeur*, Enlightenment to Romanticism, and revolution to restoration. Contemporary postmodernity therefore stands in the best modern tradition. There has never been modernity without a critique of modernity. If we were to look for a common denominator among these various currents, we can see it in the anthropological turn. God is no longer the reference point; it is rather man who defines and determines the whole of reality. The ideal is no longer the deification, but the humanization, of man.

This modern humanism springs from motives which must be taken seriously. It was an attempt to overcome the late medieval separation of God and world through a new unified way of thinking. This seemed all the more necessary when nominalism all but equated the Christian view of divine transcendence with the notion of an arbitrary God who did not release the natural order into its own, but who appeared to suppress it. From this point of view, the modern period must be understood as a rebellion of human dignity against a supranaturalism and a suprarationalism that had become repressive. This is why one attempted to construct the unity no longer theocentrically, "from above," but to conceive it "from below," in terms of the rational nature commonly shared by all human beings. As a result, "nature" became a critical measure even for religion and Christianity. Accordingly, Revelation is meaningful only insofar as it serves to promote humanity. The title of Kant's religio-philosophical treatise, *Religion within the Limits of Pure Reason Alone*, typifies this new position.

It has become customary to describe this development as secularization. This, too, is a complex and highly ambivalent concept. In Max Weber's terms, it constitutes the removal of magic from the world. The world is no longer merely a derived entity and an appearance of the divine; rather, it advances to an existence of its own that must be understood in terms of its own essential laws. Thus it became the worldly world. As already mentioned, this development has biblical roots. Of course, if it is carried through radically, it changes into its opposite. For if the world is everything, then the world has become absolute in a new way, that is, the world has become deified. This can be accomplished through pantheism as well as through materialism and atheism. Consequently, man must now accomplish on his own what was previously the task of religion. Consistent with this way of thinking, the ideas of religion, particularly those of Christianity, were reinterpreted in secular terms and assigned new functions. This applies in a particular way to the biblical idea of salvation history that was now remolded into utopias and ideologies of salvation, especially in the form of the modern belief in progress. Christian transcendental hope, that is, "vertical" transcendence, now turns into the "forward" transcendence of the modern belief in progress.

Karl Marx believed that to the degree that secular alienations are removed, religion will become superfluous and disappear. This turned out to be merely wishful thinking. There is no place where religion is more alive today than in those regions that are dominated by Marxist ideology. Also in the West, religion has returned in many different forms. Sociologists in the United States have rightfully replaced the thesis of the gradual dying out of religion with that of a persistence of religion.

Hegel already recognized that to the degree that religion disappears from the external world it retreats into the interior in order to erect its temples and altars in the heart. As a result, secularization did not cause the death of religion; it led rather to the alienation between a secular and monotonous cultural world and a kind of "Sunday existence" represented by religion. Religion did not cease to exist; it did, however, become but one sector of modern life along with many others. Religion has lost its claim to universality and its power of interpretation, and has become particular, at times even a form of a subculture.

To be sure, not only religion, but man himself has become homeless in the modern world. Wherever man loses the all-embracing unity of all reality that used to be articulated by religion and cultivated by liturgical celebrations, the individual human being becomes homeless and without support. Max Weber referred to this function of religion as theodicy, that is, meaningful explanation of life and reality, particularly in view of the experience of suffering and evil. The new secularized ideologies of salvation met with remarkably little success in providing satisfactory theodicies. Thus, while modern society has banished religious theodicies from consciousness, it has also failed to remove those experiences that demand them. People are still plagued by illness and death; they still experience social injustice and exploitation. The lack of convincing answers leads to a subliminal fear that this splendid façade could ultimately hide the gaping void of nothingness.

This loss of meaning also affects the institutions of freedom that have been created by the modern world. These ultimately evolve from a religious, or more specifically, a biblical source. The idea behind human rights, the idea of the unconditional dignity of every individual person, was first conceived by the Judeo-Christian tradition: it is rooted in the idea that man is the image of God. It signifies that every human being reflects something of the nobility and glory of God. As soon as this religious justification for the dignity of every human being no longer exists because the idea of God has been discarded, the institutions of freedom which modern Western culture prides itself on will lose their most fundamental legitimation. The result is a cultural crisis within Western society. Such a crisis develops whenever the fundamental values that underpin a culture are no longer convincing. We experience not only a scarcity of external resources, but resources of meaning as well.

The concept of the dialectic of the Enlightenment has become common knowledge. What is meant is that the Enlightenment now faces the same predicament into which it had sought to push religion and had partly succeeded in doing. It destroyed its own foundations to the degree that it divested itself of its religious and Christian roots. The Enlightenment ceased to be a viable force to the extent that Christianity came to an end. The death of God became the proclamation of the death of man. Thus we now experience the destruction of modernity at its own hands. Not only has Marxism reached its limits with its breathtaking reconstruction (*perestroika*); even our Western civilization has reached the "end of the modern age" (Guardini's *Ende der Neuzeit*).

This situation should not make theologians gloat or feel gratified. Indeed, modern secularization has also jeopardized their foundation. On the other hand, the modern age has unfolded many human values that are ultimately rooted in Christian ideas—particularly human rights—more so than was possible during the Middle Ages. This precludes any dreams about a restoration. Neither can we uncritically baptize the modern development and simply refer to it as a secular realization of Christianity, as did the theology of secularization advocated during the fifties and sixties that merely followed the Hegelian philosophy of history. This would lead to an ideology of mere adaptation and to a bourgeois Christianity. By underscoring the suppression of marginal peoples and cultures, of women and nature, liberation theology correctly pointed out the negative aspects of modernity engendered by the dictatorship of the autonomous subject. Still, we ought not indiscriminately to denounce modern Western society with false theological radicalism nor discredit the modern institutions of freedom as a matter of principle. Such a method could quickly lead to ideological totalitarianism. We must accept our situation as a challenge, with all its positive and negative aspects.

What this means is that we must undertake a new evangelization, including a new inculturation of Christianity. When confronted with this task we ought to be inspired by the courage and the faith of the Fathers of the Church and the great Scholastics who detected in their contemporary cultures seeds of the Word (*logoi spermatikoi*), the Word which they proclaimed in its fullness. In our situation which is shaped, among other factors, by the spirit of Christianity, we should be able to discover even more such points of contact. To be sure, just as the fruit that drops off a tree will rot and become poisonous, so will the modern secularized forms of Christianity that emancipated themselves from their Christian roots. Therefore, a "discernment of spirits" and a creative transformation will be necessary. A glance at Third World countries can be challenging for us. Still, it would be rather naïve to believe that we could simply adopt their ways in our very different cultural situation. We must discover ourselves and tread our own path into the twenty-first century. One point is clear. The battle against Christianity and the Church may have appeared necessary for establishing the orders of freedom in past centuries; today Christianity is a condition of survival for the many positive values in our order of freedom and our Western culture.

III. The Crisis of Post-Conciliar Theology

Theology encounters the crisis of modern Western society precisely at the moment when it experiences a deep crisis of its own. Unfortunately, much of contemporary theology can therefore give us only little help in fulfilling our task.

Catholic theology initially responded in almost entirely negative terms to the challenge presented by modern secularized culture. In contrast to the great Augustinian and Thomistic traditions, we no longer

40

possess the strength required to integrate the new culture critically and creatively into the Christian view. As a result, the natural order has been juxtaposed to the supernatural order more or less without any connection. The great commentator on Thomas Aquinas, Cajetan, was probably not responsible for this dualistic and separatist conception concerning the determination of the relationship between nature and grace; still, he was its authority and guarantor. It fully matured in the thought of the great Baroque Scholastic Suarez. We encounter it in its completion in the nineteenth century in the equally important neo-Scholastic Matthias Josef Scheeben.

As Henri de Lubac has convincingly proven, the teaching on the two orders, the natural and supernatural, represents an innovation when compared to Augustine and Thomas Aquinas. This system, which is loosely called the two-story system, combined more or less extrinsically the natural order in a form that corresponded to the modern sense of life, with the freely given grace that is essential to the Christian message. It was content to note that the two orders did not contradict each other. An inner (immanentist) relationship was rejected for the sake of the gratuitousness of grace. By way of analogy, the relationship of Church and state was understood as a relation of two perfect, that is, autarchic, societies with goals of their own, each equipped with the means to achieve these goals. Without wanting to do so, this distinction favored a humanism without God as well as a Christianity that had become alienated from the world and man and as a consequence no longer had anything to say to them. In this way, the Baroque and neo-Scholastic understanding of the relation between nature and grace was one of the sources of modern secularization.

So-called Modernism and its offshoot, Americanism at the beginning of this century, sensed the gap that had opened between the Church and the modern world; they strove to reconcile the two. No matter how justified this concern was, its execution was nevertheless insufficient. The antimodernist declarations of the Church rightly condemned the attempt to use modern philosophy of subjectivity and an immanent theory of development to close the gap. While criticism of the attempted solutions was justified, the pronouncements of the magisterium were blind to the underlying legitimate concerns. The first round of discussions in our century met therefore with unsatisfactory results on both sides.

It was Maurice Blondel who suggested, in the midst of the modernist crisis, a solution beyond immanentism and extrinsicism. Like de Lubac and Rahner, Blondel adopted a specifically modern point of departure. He began with man and showed how the dynamism of human striving aims beyond everything finite and conditioned toward something unconditioned and absolute; in every act that affirms the finite as finite the infinite is also affirmed as the one thing necessary. Thus human dynamism aims at "something" that transcends its own abilities. It consists in the disproportion between the original stimulus of our volition and the desired goal, between object and thought, between achievement and willing. This human paradox, as de Lubac was to call it, can be resolved only if man surrenders his self-will and surrenders completely to the absolutely free initiative with which God himself turns to man. The idea of the supernatural, that comes from without, corresponds to man's inner self, to the "yearning of this heart for an unknown Messiah."

All in all, this new synthesis of the so-called "*nouvelle theologie*" corresponded to the Thomistic teaching of the *desiderium naturale* of man. De Lubac sought to buttress this new theology with his admirable knowledge of theological tradition. Like Balthasar and Rahner, he appealed to Scripture, according to which everything is created through Jesus Christ and in him (Col. 1:16ff.). That is why there is no area of reality that is not directed toward Jesus Christ or most deeply shaped by him. In the concrete order of history, there is no *natura pura*. Not only non-Christian religions, but also modern culture, literature, and art reveal multiple traces that refer to Jesus Christ and are fulfilled only in him. In the words of the Second Vatican Council, Jesus Christ is therefore "the goal of human history, the point where all endeavors of history and culture converge, the center of mankind, the joy of all hearts and the fulfillment of their desires." Thus a new synthesis appeared to have been found in a second round of discussions during the middle of our century.

The crisis of contemporary Catholicism consists in part in the fact that these ideas were discredited after the council. The sixties and the beginning of the seventies were characterized in the West by a new wave and push of the Enlightenment. Everything supernatural was conceived and criticized as empty consolation, as ideology and projection. People complained about the lack of experience in Christian faith and opted for the concretization, intelligibility, verification, and praxis of grace in this world and in this life.

In his later writings, Rahner sought with all his might to pick up this

42

development and to integrate it. His principal argument was: since in God's plan of salvation everything is ordered toward Christ and since God desires the salvation of all mankind, man who exists within a historical context has always been touched by grace. Grace is an existential that characterizes man. All of world history is ultimately salvation history. Therefore, he who accepts his existence ultimately affirms also Jesus Christ. According to this way of thinking, the *proprium* of Christianity does not lie on the level of events, but on the level of consciousness. Christian faith articulates reflexively what is universally given in an anonymous manner.

This much disputed, though ingenious, theory of anonymous Christianity, which I have only been able to recount briefly, permitted a twofold further development. In one direction Karl Rahner paved the way for Western liberal theology, in the other for the radical liberation theology of Latin America.

Western liberal theology proclaimed the end of the old supranaturalism. Experience and "experienceability" became the criterion of the message of salvation. Where the thesis of the end of the old supranaturalism was thought through radically, the end of a transcendental view of God was proclaimed. It is thus understandable that the Church as sacramental form of mediation between God and man was called into question and that the Catholic priesthood, the value of celibacy, and monastic life had to face a fundamental crisis. The crisis of the "supernatural" is the root of the Church's present crisis in the Western world.

Liberation theology justifiably criticizes secularist liberal theology as a bourgeois ideology. It, too, is concerned with overcoming supranaturalism; it, too, emphasizes the unity of history over and against the old dualism. The *desiderium naturale* may now be heard in the cry for liberation among the poor; grace is the answer to the yearning of the world for liberation and happiness. Work for changing the world is part of the redemption of the world; the struggle for justice is also a struggle for the kingdom of God. The Church constitutes the reflexively Christified part of the world, that is, the place where grace is reflected; it no longer represents a sacrament for the world, but a sacrament of the world. Its goal is the topical realization of the Christian utopia of man and society. (Thus, the familiar Augustinian distinction between the City of God and the City of Man was dropped. It can be shown that the roots of this political messianism lie in the *religion civile* of Jean-Jacques Rousseau, Saint-Simon, and Lammenais, and in Ernst Bloch's philosophy of hope, which proposes Marxism as the heir of Christianity.)

No matter how great the differences between Western liberal theology and radical liberation theology may be, they nevertheless share a common denominator in their common struggle against ecclesial supranaturalism and its hierarchical understanding of the Church in which they frequently form tactical alliances and play into each other's hands. But what about the singularity (*hapax kai ephapax*) of Jesus Christ which is so central in Scripture? Will they be able to preserve the newness of Jesus Christ of which Irenaeus spoke? If this newness is abandoned, the relevance of Christianity is destroyed. Once identity is lost, relevance is lost as well. Only the one who has identity can have relevance.

IV. Suggestions for a New Christian Humanism

There is only one way out of this crisis: we must reflect back on our roots. The *ressourcement,* the return to the sources of Scripture and tradition, is the necessary prerequisite for an *aggiornamento,* for making theology and the Church relevant in our world today. An authentically Christian humanism is the answer to the challenge of secularization and the crisis into which contemporary humanism has slipped through the absence of God.

The Second Vatican Council laid down the most important guidelines for this Christian humanism. Over against all old and new forms of dualism, it proclaimed the unity of God's plan of salvation and Jesus Christ as the center and goal of all reality. All things were created in Jesus Christ, through him and for him (Col. 1:16), and everything will be brought together again under him (Eph. 1:10). Thus, what was revealed to man through Jesus Christ, who is both God and man, was not only the mystery of God: but in Jesus Christ God revealed man to himself, and revealed to him his highest calling. The rift between the faith one professes and one's daily life, therefore, is one of the grave errors of our time.

In his apostolic letter *Evangelii nuntiandi* (1975), Pope Paul VI goes one step further. He writes: "The rift between the gospel and culture is undoubtedly the drama of our epoch, just as it was the drama of other

44

epochs." That is why he demands that the "drama of a humanism without God" (H. de Lubac) be confronted by an integral humanism and an integral understanding of liberation. This humanism proceeds from the primacy of the spiritual mission of the Church; without this primacy the Church would become the victim of ideologies that are alien to its nature and mentalities that are dependent on the times, or even particular group interests. Nevertheless, the mission of the Church is not limited to the areas of religion and the heart. Its mission is to permeate man in his entirety and in all his dimensions and to do so from the center of its message.

Evangelization and inculturation necessarily belong together. This does not only apply to the Third World; rather, the unity of the two is also a program for the churches in the Western world. They must not be satisfied with the existing dualism of Church and secular culture, nor must they adapt to the secularized world: they must seek to penetrate it anew from within.

Together with its efforts to overcome dualism, the council also turned its back on integralism. It emphasized the distinction between God and world, creation and redemption, Church and culture, Church and politics. It taught that there is room within the order of salvation for a rightly understood integrity of earthly realities as these possess their own laws, their own truth and goodness, all of which can be recognized step by step by human reason. According to the council, it is precisely the recognition of God's transcendence that assures the transcendence, that is, the freedom of man. Because the gospel binds only in the moral sphere, conscience, it liberates in purely worldly spheres and in the questions of concrete cultural and political formation.

The relative integrity of the world does not stand in opposition to the unity of God and world, of creation and redemption. Because of its complete dependence on God, the world remains also infinitely different from him who is totally independent. Every similarity is matched by an even greater dissimilarity. If this difference collapses, then we will necessarily arrive at a deification of the world and an absolutism of secular values — be they race or class, money or national unity, or the high yet limited values of a certain culture — which enslave people and lead to hostility among them. Only if the world remains merely world, that is, if it remains a relative reality, will man become free in the world and will people become open to others beyond all barriers of culture and interest. "The truth will make you free" (Jn. 8:32).

Thus unity in Jesus Christ is unity in freedom. Grace understood as the personal communion with God presupposes the person; it is personal communion based on the free decision of faith. Instead of *"gratia praesupponit naturam"* we ought to say *"gratia supponit personam."* To me this seems a better and less ambiguous formulation, for if we speak of a natural human desire for God and communion with him, such a statement seems to imply natural necessity and questions the gratuitousness of grace. Things change when we include the term "person." The person is essentially ordered toward recognition and acceptance in love; however, love can never be necessitated, neither can it be demanded as a right. While love is necessary for man, it is unenforceably free: only as a gift is it the fulfillment of the person. It unites by setting free: love says "I want you to be."

Thus, by integrating modern humanism into a more all-encompassing christological perspective, the council adopts in a positive way its impulses of freedom, while protecting it against destruction at its own hands. At the same time, the council clearly states that such a Christian humanism cannot be a harmonious system, or an unbroken transition between Church and culture. Concrete reality is not simply open toward God in the manner of advent, but closed because of sin. Concrete man is specifically *homo incurvatus,* man turned into himself, whose encrustations can be broken only by conversion. Therefore, the council speaks of Christ having paved the way for a new life through his crucifixion and resurrection. To remove the reality of the Cross from the relationship between nature, grace, and culture would contradict the gospel; it would reflect a frightful loss of reality that ignores the negative experiences and catastrophic sides of life. Only by incorporating the Cross and the resurrection into the foundation of a new Christian humanism will we be in a position to join the Second Vatican Council and say: "Christ enlightens the enigma of pain and death that would overcome us without the gospel."

In the light of the christological formula of Chalcedon, Karl Rahner summed up the christological view of reality. The unity and difference between God and man do not grow in inverse proportion, but in direct proportion. The greater the unity with God, the greater the integrity and the freedom of man. From the perspective of the Cross and the resurrection one must formulate more clearly: in the measure in which man abandons his sinful and self-destructive attempt at autonomous self-determination and self-realization, that is, in the measure in which he turns around and honors God, he discovers his true life. Irenaeus of Lyon already proclaimed: "The glory of God is mankind fully alive."

Blaise Pascal once said that plurality without unity is chaos and unity without plurality is tyranny. We can apply this also to the relationship between nature, grace, and culture: a one-sided emphasis on unity, immanentism, and ecclesiastical integralism suffocates freedom and leads to spiritual and ecclesiastical totalitarianism. Still, any one-sided emphasis on plurality and differences, on the dualism and extrinsicism of nature and grace, Church and world, leads to secularism; secularism, however, is incapable of providing the world and culture with unity, direction, and meaning. It ultimately leads to self-destruction and nihilism. Just as Jesus Christ alone is the salvation of the world, so the christological paradigm "unmixed and undivided" proves to be the only adequate solution to our problem.

V. Three Concrete Conclusions

In conclusion let us inquire into the concrete implications of the Christian "world formula" for a new Christian humanism. I will limit myself to three points.

1. This formula is a statement about the essential character of man and his orientation toward absolute values. If man is created in the image of God and if this image was renewed through Jesus Christ, then — as the Fathers correctly conclude — man can find his fulfillment only in God. As Basil formulated it: "The ultimate desire is to become God." Thomas Aquinas says the same thing when we read: "God alone satisfies us."

It is all but impossible to communicate this truth to modern pagans, for as the question is put, what reasonable person still wants to become God these days? However, if we reduce man to the level of earthly needs, he will lose his dignity. (Nietzsche's caricature of the "last human being" will then be correct. "The most despicable of men who has lost his capacity to despise himself." "What is love? What is creation? What is desire? What is death? — thus asks the last human being, and blinks." Nietzsche, therefore, knows: "If there were gods, how could I stand not being a god!'') According to Jean-Paul Sartre: "To be human means to strive to be God; or shall we say: man ultimately is desire to be God." To abandon this desire would be tantamount to the abolition of man. For man infinitely transcends man (Blaise Pascal).

By means of this theological definition of the essence of man, theology defends the humanism of antiquity as well as Christian humanism against its destruction by modern humanitarianism. Humanism acknowledges the happiness (*eudaimonia* = *beatitudo*) of man in virtue, that is, in the moral realization of good that makes an unconditional demand on man and his freedom. On the other hand, humanitarianism interprets happiness as the greatest possible gratification of the needs of the highest possible number of people; it strives to minimize pain, suffering, and privation while at the same time maximizing pleasure and instant gratification (the so-called quality of life!). Modern humanitarianism replaces the good life with long life and a life of pleasure. It is devoid of unconditional values that demand courage, sacrifice, privation, indeed even heroism under certain circumstances; all that is left is the calculation of happiness that — as illustrated by the deplorable debate about abortion — even relinquishes the humanistic idea of the unconditional value of every human being and ends in a primitive consumer mentality.

Thus, as we approach the end of modernity, we realize that the idea of the dignity of man feeds on religious prerequisites that cannot be guaranteed by a secularized civilization. Modern society depends for its own sake on the message of God as the basis and purpose of life and also as a gratuitous possibility to realize the true and good life. That is why Christianity is one of the conditions for the survival of the positive cultural heritage of modern humanism.

2. A civilization of love is the model of a culture renewed by Christianity, a model that follows from the relation between nature and grace as described above. Indeed, grace does not merely presuppose nature; it does not merely heal and affirm nature, grace perfects nature in ways that excel all natural things by leading to communion with God through Jesus Christ. In this way, the indeterminate open mystery into which man points with the entire dynamism of his human existence reaches its eschatological and definitive specification in Jesus Christ. In Jesus Christ, the new Adam, God revealed to man the final meaning of his human existence. By revealing himself as self-giving love, he reveals

the final meaning of his existence to man created in the image of God: human existence finds fulfillment as pro-existence, as existence for others. Love is the final meaning of existence.

This theological message has concrete and practical consequences. Pope Paul VI described the resulting goal as a civilization of love. In *"Justitia et Pax,"* a document published by the papal commission after the 1971 synod of bishops, the implications for a Christian interpretation of human rights are made clear. The issue in the document is the relation between justice and love. It states that Christian love does not replace justice; rather, it includes the demand for justice. The minimum requirement of love that unconditionally accepts every human being consists in giving everyone his due. However, what is due and proper to everyone is in the final analysis not thing-like. The person demands unconditional acceptance by other persons. Thus justice attains its content and fullness solely through love. Pope John Paul again deepened the understanding of the interior relationship between justice and love in his encyclical *Dives in Misericordia* (1980). He showed that a justice that merely gives *things* to which the other has a claim does not correspond to the personal dignity of man. Man is recognized fully in his dignity only if he is recognized and accepted in himself and for his own sake: only love and mercy give man his due. Right and justice remain cold; the greatest right can turn into the greatest injustice (*summum ius, summa iniuria*). Love, therefore, is the fulfillment of justice. Only a civilization of love is a truly human civilization.

Love is more than a vague feeling and a superficial emotion. Love means overcoming the individualism and egoism that is so typical of our Western civilization; it means adopting an attitude of solidarity; it is the genuine answer to the misery in today's world. While love and mercy cannot be codified by laws, they can and must inspire the concrete order of law and justice and transform society from within. Herein lies the specifically Christian contribution to the realms of economics, culture, and politics, We must clearly demonstrate that solidarity and mercy are inalienable components of the humanness of human society.

3. The relationship between nature, grace, and culture also shapes the basic pattern of ecclesial renewal. The newness and gratuitousness of grace implies that grace is sacramentally mediated through words and signs, as well as through officially appointed witnesses. The Church as the universal sacrament of salvation is, therefore, an essential element

within the theme of nature, grace, and culture. The Church must demonstrate, after the manner of a sign, what the proper relation among these three entities is. The Church itself is a complex reality that grows together from a human and a divine element. Its human form must reflect the message of the grace and mercy of God; it must be a Church with a human countenance. However, it must also represent the newness and underivability of grace; it must preserve its own identity and project a profile of its own. Only in this way will the Church be in a position to become a sign of Christian freedom and an instrument for freedom in the world.

What this implies is that the Church must never become part of any specific social, political, or cultural system or, worse, adopt its ideology. The Church is connected to its contemporaries through its message: to this extent it must know and take into account the mentalities that prevail in any given culture; the spirit of the age and the mentality of a certain culture can, however, serve only as points of departure and contact, but never as a measure. Only the gospel can be the measure for the Church. This does not entail any sort of sectarian narrow-mindedness. It is precisely because of the Church's acceptance of the transcendence of the message of grace that it can be the guardian and the defender of the transcendence of the human person. In doing so it clearly demonstrates that the person of man is never just an element within a specific system; it has its dignity rather from its direct orientation toward God. Because we are all sons and daughters of the one Father in heaven, we are all brothers and sisters in spite of all our cultural differences. By preserving its freedom vis-à-vis all social systems, the Church preserves its universality and catholicity that overarches nations, racial differences, and class distinctions. Precisely in its otherness the Church becomes both the symbol and the beginning of a new brotherly and sisterly humanity.

It is not the task of the Church to usher in a new social order. The Church does not have the necessary means, nor is that its mission; however, the Church can put up signs; doing something right, in the manner of a sign, is often the best contribution to the solution of a problem. New measures are introduced and new possibilities are revealed. In the past, the establishment of religious orders frequently offered exemplary responses to the issues and challenges of the times. Nowadays, new communities are emerging everywhere within the Church, suggesting a new spring after a lengthy period of winter.

In our Western culture, rooted as it is in human dignity and freedom, it is particularly important for the Church to emphasize Christian freedom. This cannot be done through theories and words alone; Christian freedom must be realized above all within the Church. An atmosphere of freedom, trust, and also mercy must characterize the relation among the faithful, among the various Church offices and the faithful, as well as between the magisterium and theologians. The relation of nature and grace must also lead to a culture of freedom, dialogue, consideration, tolerance, and love within the Church. St. Paul reminds us of this when he says that we are to practice the truth and love (Eph. 4:15).

Modern secularization is a challenge. Retrospectively speaking, it could also be a grace if it affords us a deeper understanding and more extensive realization of what is properly and specifically Christian. To be sure, the *proprium* and *specificum* of Christianity is never particular in the manner of a sect; it is universal and catholic in the original sense of the word. It is the foundation of a new synthesis of nature, grace, and culture, and its goal is a new humanism in a postmodern third millennium.

Note: This paper was the keynote address for the *Communio* conference, "Nature, Grace, and Culture: On Being Catholic in America," Notre Dame, Indiana, May 8-11, 1989, and is reproduced here as it was delivered, without benefit of footnotes.

Nature and Grace: Fateful Separation and Attempted Reunion[1]

Louis Dupré, Yale University

We cannot but marvel at the surprising continuity which links the Christian order of grace with the ancient concept of nature. It was a concept determined by ideas current in Rome at the end of the Republic. Among them the Stoic ones dominated. They had already made their impact upon such biblical writings as Ecclesiasticus and the Book of Wisdom. One essential difference was, of course, that, for Christians and Jews, nature depended on God both for its essence and existence, thereby losing much of the self-sufficiency and even of the inner teleology which the Greek *physis* had possessed. On the other side, however, it derived a new sacrality from its total dependence upon a divine Creator. To sustain its existence God had to be *immanent* in nature without coinciding with it.

More and more Christian theologians, especially in the Greek-speaking world, came to express that divine immanence in the language of Neoplatonism. What attracted them in Plotinus's and Proclus's theory is that the One (which Christians identified with God) remains *present* in its emanations while nevertheless transcending them. Thus nature also *represented* God and granted the mind a means for becoming united with him.

The doctrine of representation laid the basis for a theology of the image, the oldest and most durable one in Christian mysticism. As God's own Word, the uncreated Image of the Father holds God's presence in itself. All of nature, linked to the generation of the Son, could be viewed as an image of the uncreated Image and serve as a symbol of God's presence.

The most successful attempt to integrate nature and grace according to the Neoplatonic scheme we find in that anonymous theologian of the sixth century, who for a millennium was identified with the Denys whom St. Paul is reported to have converted on the Areopagus in Athens. Combining the theology of Proclus with that of the Alexandrian and

Cappadocian Fathers, he presents the entire cosmos in an ascending scale of beings that participate in a totally transcendent divine nature. Placed in a supreme position on that scale, human nature—elevated in grace—mediates the divine presence throughout the cosmos, thereby bringing it to its divine destiny. In the human person the entire world becomes "graced" and sanctified. To interpret this universal sanctification as a barely Christianized rehabilitation of the Greek idea of a divine cosmos would be a serious error. As Christians conceived it, nature depends entirely upon a source *transcendent* to nature as such. This crucial distinction caused a dynamic tension between divine activity and created order. But at the end of the Middle Ages it would lead to a static dualism of two separate orders of reality.

Early Western theologians, generally less daring in their speculation, developed a practical, more than a mystical, theology. Even in the more speculative Augustine, the image of God in the soul at first appears to be no more than a psychological, external analogy with the Trinity. As one God exists in three persons, the one soul functions in three faculties. But in describing this function Augustine's theory approaches in the order of acting the Greek theology of deification in the order of being. In focusing its mental powers of loving, knowing, and remembering on the one divine Object, the soul's merely external similarity with the triune God becomes transformed into an internal presence. Thus, in the process of knowing and loving God, the psychological image becomes converted to that Image which is God's own immanence.

Yet another trend in Augustine's theology moved in the opposite direction. Stirred by polemics with the Manichaeans first, and later with the Pelagians, Augustine ever more strongly stressed how much nature had been wounded and even incapacitated. The medicinal aspect of grace, always prominent in Latin theology, thus tends to freeze a living relation into a semi-independent entity. Thus Augustine planted the seeds of two doctrines that would, in different ways at the close of the Middle Ages, introduce a theological dualism. In one, redemption superimposes a new order of reality upon nature. The other, reacting against the inconsistency of such a dualist vision and its implied worldliness, stresses the intrinsic corruption of nature to a point where grace, no longer able to transform it, turns into a substitute of nature. Thus grace, which earlier had penetrated the order of nature, came to be viewed in one case as an addition to it — a "supernatural" reality; in the other, as extrinsically

53

imputed to, or substituting for, nature. Theology thereby lost much of its potential for intrinsically affecting culture. Instead of shaping its very substance, as it had done in the past, it became reduced to a science among others with a method and object exclusively its own. Other sciences henceforth could freely ignore it, and for the most part amply availed themselves of the opportunity by going out of their way to avoid any contact with potentially hazardous theological issues.

It was some time during the thirteenth century that we perceive the first signs of an opposition between nature and grace. The Aristotelian Scholastics considered the order of nature the formal object of a rational investigation in its own right. While Albert and Aquinas clearly subordinated this semi-independent realm to that of theology, the Averroist Aristotelians in various degrees detached the study of nature from that of revelation. With the condemnation of the theory of "double truth" the powers of Averroism were roundly defeated. Yet the more fundamental problem in incorporating Aristotle's philosophy into Christian theology remained its different concept of nature. In Latin theology *nature* had referred to human nature in the concrete context of grace. Thus St. Augustine calls the original state of justice "natural" — an expression that would be seriously misunderstood by Baius and Jansenius. Even as late a writer as Duns Scotus still posited the existence of a "natural" desire toward a "supernatural" vision. Aristotle's concept of nature, however, followed a strictly immanent teleology in which the end had to be strictly proportionate to the available (human) means. Aquinas, perceiving the restrictions of this Aristotelian concept of nature for the interpretation of life in grace, conceded that nature contained some immanently human teleology — Aristotle's ideal of virtue and contemplation in the good city — yet this defined only a part of human destiny and had to be subordinated to the transcendent, Christian end.[2] His later followers, especially in the sixteenth century, were less cautious. Accepting Aristotle's principle concerning the proportion of ends to means they denied that *nature* was capable of any "supernatural" desire or end at all. Once this idea of *pure nature*, a by-product of late medieval nominalism, gained entrance in Thomist theology, it would avail itself of Aristotle's philosophy to justify itself.

In Aquinas there had been no question of a supernatural order "added" to nature. For him, the term "supernatural" referred to the *means* for attaining the one, final end for which our natural powers no longer suffice.[3] God himself is called *agens supernaturale*, not to separate the order of grace from that of nature, but rather to distinguish the order of the Creator from that of creation (in which nature and grace appear together). Nature itself thereby becomes the effect of a "supernatural" agent. The term *supernatural* would not begin to refer to an order of grace separate from the order of nature until in the sixteenth century man's "natural" end came to be conceived as distinct from his revealed destiny. Thus, St. Thomas's sixteenth-century commentator, Sylvester of Ferrara, interprets his master's position as if it separated the reality of nature from that of grace. If God were man's "natural" end to be acquired only in a "supernatural" way, he argues, we would have a conflict that is not *conveniens* between nature and its goal.[4] Yet for Aquinas nature is not an independent reality endowed with a self-sufficient *finis naturalis*. Still, one feature of St. Thomas's theological construction could, and eventually would, threaten the marvelous balance of its complex unity. It had nothing to do with the acceptance of the Aristotelian apparatus, but everything with the too exclusively medicinal interpretation of grace in the Latin tradition. Rather than considering the Incarnation a decisive but by no means discontinuous moment of a divine self-communication that had begun with creation, as Scotus was to do, Aquinas saw it essentially as a divine response to remedy the effects of the fall. Without the fall the Incarnation would not have occurred.[5] To such a fallen nature grace was no longer a supernatural means whereby man was to attain his "natural" ends in the order of God's vocation. The fall had wounded nature itself to a point where it had acquired a false sufficiency. To remedy this, redemption had to set up a *new* end that would initiate an order of grace distinct from that nature, yet not separated from it.

Yet another idea of thirteenth-century Scholasticism would, at a later stage, become instrumental in separating nature from the divine altogether. I am referring to a particular causal interpretation of the relation between God and creation. The idea of causality had always played a part in linking the world to God, for the Ancients as well as for Jews and Christians. Yet comparing the nature of this causal relation in modern thought with that of the classical and medieval one, we note a major difference in the degree of immanence of the cause in the effect. In Plato's *Parmenides* the psychic cause of motion remains entirely within the effect. So do the combined causes (the *synaitiai*) of the cosmos in *Timaeus*. To them Plato adds the efficient causality of the Demiurge. But this mythical unification of all other causes ought not to be understood as containing the primary meaning of Plato's idea of causality. Indeed, all the important functions which later philosophy assigns to efficient causality Plato ascribes to *participation*. Aristotle's notion of causality in its fourfold aspect continues to reflect a similar immanence. Natural substances contain the source of motion and change within themselves, and the concept of nature (*physis*) itself refers to the intrinsic principles of substantial motion and rest. Yet, significantly, the causal relation between God and all lower beings appears no longer as intimate as it had been in Plato's theory of participation.

Misunderstanding Plato's metaphysical principles as physical entities out of which the Demiurge fashioned the world, early Christian theologians anxious to stress the *creatio ex nihilo* had almost exclusively emphasized the efficient causality in God's creative act. Aristotle's theory of the Prime Mover had seemed to confirm their position. But never had they claimed exhaustively to explain thereby the intimate, permanent presence of God to the finite being. Only after Aristotle's philosophy had become accepted for the articulation of Christian theology did the more extrinsic conception of efficient causality come to determine the relation between God and man altogether. St. Thomas continues to hesitate between Plato's participation and Aristotle's efficient causality for expressing the relation between God and the creature.[6] In the *Summa Theologiae* we read: "Being is innermost in each thing and most fundamentally present within all things, since it is formal in respect of everything found in a thing. . . . Hence it must be that God is in all things, and innermostly."[7]

Nonetheless, when it comes to defining the nature of this divine immanence, Thomas concludes that it must consist in a relation of causal dependency. This explication by means of Aristotelian categories somehow appears to give less than what the "innermost presence" promised. How much Aquinas here sacrifices to the Aristotelian conception becomes evident in the rest of the passage: "An agent must be joined to that wherein it acts immediately, and touch it by its power; hence it is proved in the *Physics* (VII, 2) that the thing moved and the mover must be together. Now since God is Being itself by his own essence, created being must be his proper effect; just as to ignite is the proper effect of fire."

Here the Aristotelian category of efficient causality proves inadequate for describing God's presence to his creation. Nevertheless, participation in Thomas's thought continues to balance efficient causality. Moreover, Aristotle's efficient causality essentially differs, precisely by the immanence of the cause in the effect, from the later mechanistic conception.[8]

Despite these tensions, the Thomist concept of nature still continues to receive its definitive interpretation from the order of grace. Independently of grace it is an abstraction, or as Rahner called it, a residual concept (*ein Restbegriff*)[9] that must be understood through its dialectical counterpart. Being thus tightly linked to the order of grace the question of what human nature by itself would be able to accomplish becomes meaningless from Aquinas's theological perspective. To be sure, following Aristotle St. Thomas also uses a purely philosophical concept of nature. But this object of rational reflection, unsupported by revelation, has nothing in common with the *natura pura* which sixteenth-century theologians abstracted from the concrete reality of the fall and redemption. Aquinas's philosophical *nature* is not a nature without grace, but human nature as we concretely find it, when considered independently of what revelation teaches about grace. It possesses a transcendent openness to grace and, some Thomists would claim, a *desiderium naturale* toward a fulfillment in grace.

The solidity of the Thomist synthesis appears in the vision of the cosmos — both natural and transparent of grace — that continued to inspire poets and artists throughout the thirteenth century. The majestic construction of nature and grace, of cosmology and theology, of politics and philosophy, which Dante erects in *De Monarchia* and assumes throughout the *Comedia* shows the creative and enduring power of that Christian Aristotelianism which Aquinas had first conceived. If the synthesis showed any weakness as compared with that of the Greek Fathers and Augustine, it consisted in what its authors must have considered its strength, namely the distinctness of its various components. Precisely because of its neat conceptual separation this distinctness would, at the slightest shift in emphasis, harden into a base-superstructure dualism. This is of course what happened once the distinction between nature and the supernatural developed into one between two separate orders of being. Aquinas's genius had kept this separatist tendency in check. But it appeared almost from the start among less moderate proponents of the Aristotelian synthesis, such as Siger of Brabant, or Boethius of Dacia who reduced the synthesis of Christian revelation with

Aristotelian philosophy to a mere juxtaposition of two orders of being without even a proper concern for their compatibility. Aquinas correctly regarded those extreme Aristotelians whose sources were so close to his own as the greatest threat to his synthesis. He emerged victorious from the battle with these antagonists. But the trust in the viability of his project had been shaken. In 1277 Michel Tempier, the archbishop of Paris, condemned some of the crucial Aristotelian theses. The resistance against Aristotle's philosophy concentrated on the *Physics* and the *Metaphysics* — the *Logic* and *Ethics* had been accepted without major problems — because these treatises provided the basis to separate philosophy from theology. Precisely in this separation we detect one of the decisive factors that contributed to the distinctness of the modern age.

Even so, Aristotle's philosophy was neither the immediate nor the sufficient cause of the separation of grace and nature into two orders of being. As Thomas had proven, they could be kept in perfect harmony within an Aristotelian synthesis. What prevented the Aristotelian concept of nature from becoming an independent entity in Aquinas's synthesis was, I suspect, its marvelous flexibility, the strong allowance for change which that concept contained. Nature functioned essentially as a matrix of development, not as a fixed entity. In different ways nature remains wide open for change. Changes may come from the situation created by the fall or by the new direction given by grace as well as from human progress and refinement. "The just and the good . . . are formally and everywhere the same, because the principles of right in natural reason do not change. . . ; but materially they are not identical for everywhere and for all men because of the mutability of human nature and the diverse conditions in which men and things find themselves in different circumstances and times."[10] The significance which the state of innocence assumed in St. Thomas's discussion indicates how much the concrete condition — with grace or without grace — was on his mind. Yet none of these fundamental distinctions necessitated for Thomas the admission of a *pure* nature as a separate entity distinct from grace. The real separation, foreshadowed by a few Averroist philosophers, was essentially achieved by those who had led the resistance against Aristotelianism — the nominalists.

The nominalist theologies which came to dominate the fourteenth and fifteenth centuries destroyed the intelligible continuity between Creator and creature. The idea of an absolute divine power unrelated to

58

any known laws or principles definitively severed the order of nature from that of grace. A nature created by an unpredictable God loses its intrinsic intelligibility in favor of the mere observation of actual fact. Nor does creation itself teach us anything of God beyond what this divine omnipotence has revealed in Scripture. Grace itself became a matter of divine decree unmeasurable by human standards and randomly dispensed. Detached from its transcendent moorings, nature was left to chart its own course. The rise of the supernatural signaled the loss of an intrinsically transcendent dimension in nature and the emergence of a profound distrust of that nature on the part of theology. The delicate balance was permanently disturbed. The distinction between God's *potentia absoluta* (what he can do, if he chooses to do it) and the *potentia ordinata* (what he actually does) had originated in the eleventh century and had become universally accepted to preserve the idea of God's total freedom in creation. Nominalist theology had extended its meaning by freeing divine omnipotence from any limits other than internal contradiction. The resulting increase in opposition between an unlimited divine power and a wholly contingent world order conveyed to distinctions which previously had been no more than rational abstractions a reality status they had never possessed before. Among them was the idea of a *pure* nature, that is, nature conceived without any supernatural destiny to be attained in the order of grace. As the term had been used in St. Thomas and in thirteenth-century Scholasticism, "nature" had been a theological concept: it referred to a concrete existing reality, either in the prelapsarian state of grace, or in the condition after the fall. As theologians commonly used it, "nature" was no longer human nature in its original state, but a *transformed* nature that had not remained untouched by sin and grace. Hence the original state of innocence could not serve as the norm, nor were such concepts as natural law based upon it.

The concept of *pure nature*, however, that emerged between the fourteenth and the sixteenth centuries overruled those distinctions elevating an abstract idea derived from the theory of God's *potentia absoluta* into all real entity. Though claiming to be independent of the historical stages of the fall and redemption which theology had traditionally distinguished, from a theological point of view, its very bracketing of those stages introduced yet another, albeit artificial, historical concept. When later ethical and political philosophies adopted this concept as a theologically neutral basis for speculation, they did, in fact, build upon a negative theological concept. Reformed theologians placing a strong emphasis upon the historical difference between the state of innocence and the fall understandably avoided a concept which struck them as theologically incoherent.

How ambiguous the concept was appeared in the opposite intellectual attitudes to which it gave rise. On the one hand nominalist theology (which via the idea of God's *potentia absoluta* had led to the concept of pure nature) led to the decline of natural theology. Since human reason could attain little insight into the relation between nature and an inscrutable Creator, it came to rely on the positive theology of revelation. To be sure, philosophical theology had never been severed from revelation. But Aristotelian Scholastics, most prominently St. Thomas in the *Summa contra Gentiles*, had nevertheless granted a relative autonomy to the natural sources of knowledge of God. Scripture itself seemed to support such an independence in the words of St. Paul: "His invisible attributes . . . have been visible, ever since the world began, to the eye of reason, in the things he has made" (Rom. 1:20). Though it would be incorrect to claim that nominalism had broken the link between the existing order of nature and the nature of the divine principle, it certainly had considerably weakened that link. Ockham had felt confident that the natural order proved the existence of a sustaining cause of the universe, but he found no rational support for claims about the nature or even unity of such a cause.[11] The actual order of the universe was the result of an inscrutable divine decree, rather a display of a rationality similar to our own. For positive information about God, believers had to turn to revelation.

On the other hand, once the concept of pure nature became detached from its hypothetic context (within the idea of a *potentia absoluta*) and acquired an assumed reality in its own right, it provoked a new, wholly unprecedented attempt to establish a science of God on purely natural grounds. If "nature" could be understood independently of revelation, so could the transcendent cause of that nature to the extent that it was actively operative in that nature. Natural theology came to occupy the same independent position vis-à-vis revelation which "nature" took with respect to what henceforth was to be called the "super-natural." The new branch of learning found, of course, strong support in the rediscovery of such ancient texts as Cicero's *De natura deorum*. We shall have to return to the unexpected significance of this phenomenon. While Protestant

60

theology had mainly adopted the more negative attitude of nominalist theology toward natural theology, Catholics by and large appeared ready to accept the idea of pure nature in support of the assumed continuity of nature throughout the historical stages of innocence, fall, and redemption. The polemics with Protestantism on this issue merely strengthened the roots of the new concept. Once the abstraction of an independent, quasi-autonomous natural order had gained access to theology, it rapidly spread to all schools. In the sixteenth century it entered the mainstream of Thomist theology — with such famous commentators as Cajetan. At that time the medieval synthesis of grace and nature came to an end. Once established, the relation nature-supernatural (as two quasi-independent entities) continued to hold sway over Catholic theology until the second half of the twentieth century. As late as 1950 the encyclical *Humani Generis* once again reasserted the gratuitous character of the order of grace by insisting that God could have created human nature independently of a "super-natural" vocation and implying that this nature could be considered an independent entity.[12]

We may well regard the early period of modern thought—from the fifteenth through the seventeenth centuries—as a prolonged attempt to recover the lost unity. This took different forms. The Reformation marked a return to the earlier, pre-"Aristotelian" Christian synthesis with, however, a hazardous emphasis on the late Augustine's conception of a thoroughly corrupted nature. The humanist movement, driven by a new confidence in nature, went in the opposite direction. Yet the naturalism of the early humanists had been inspired by a Platonic-Christian theology, still apparent in the later Michelangelo. The sympathies of important figures of the Reformation for classical humanism (Melancthon, Bude, Lefèvre d'Estaples), as well as the Protestant leanings of many humanists (Marguerite de Valois and much of the French court under Francis I, Justus Lipsius, the early Erasmus) shows the early compatibility of two movements which, despite a different inspiration, presented in fact parallel quests for a lost synthesis. As we know, both failed. Reformed theology expressed an awareness of man's *total* involvement in the drama of sin and redemption far more profound than the late medieval theologies with their dual vision of a supernatural order "added" to nature. Yet soon Protestant theologians returned, for different motives, to the kind of nominalist thinking of which they had fled the philosophical consequences. The very seriousness with which they stressed the impact of sin

— the *corruptio totalis* — resulted in a concept of fallen nature which grace itself would no longer be able to transform intrinsically. The "imputed" righteousness, while expressing a change in God's attitude, left nature right where it found it. Thus a separation not unlike the earlier one between nature and a supernatural order here emerged at a later stage. The gap between nature and what once had been its *own* transcendence remained as wide as it had been before. The Anglican divine William Law attributed much of the secularism of the eighteenth century to the extrinsic character of a forensic justification. In a few memorable pages of *The Spirit of Love* he rejects outright the notion of an "imputed" righteousness as well as the distinction between a natural and a supernatural order. Divine righteousness intrinsically transforms human nature. Yet since it had been first *received* at creation and then *restored* by a divine redemption, he is willing to call it *God's* righteousness, as long as we remember that God "calls us to own the power, presence, and operation of God in all that we feel and find in our own inward state."[13] Whenever it affects man's nature it is *eo ipso* "natural." Thus, "There is nothing that is supernatural but God alone; everything besides Him is form and subject to the state of nature. . . . There is nothing supernatural in it [Redemption] or belonging to it but that supernatural love and wisdom which brought it forth, presides over it and will direct it till Christ. . . ."[14]

Law correctly perceived that to reduce righteousness to an imputed quality had provided Deism with grounds for setting up a *natural* religion next to one so severely separated from nature. For Law, Christianity itself — basically founded in the nature of things, following the powers of nature, and responding to nature's demands — is the "one true, real, and only religion of nature. For a religion is not to be deemed natural because it has nothing to do with revelation; but then is it the one true religion of nature when it has everything in it that our natural state stands in need of?"[15]

I have referred to Law because he saw the problems created by a forensic theory after they had had occasion to grow up and contribute to the religious crisis of the eighteenth century, but also because he appreciated the more fundamental drive of the Reformation to restore the unity of nature and grace lost by the distinction between the orders of nature and the supernatural. Reformed theology had attempted to overcome the separation between nature and grace. Yet, in its theory of forensic justification, that attempt failed and indirectly the destructive separation.

A different attempt to recapture the lost unity of nature and grace was made by the early humanists. Humanist theology seldom receives the attention it deserves. Past interpretations tended to dismiss the whole movement as a return to classical paganism modified by some halfhearted compromises between an undogmatic Christianity and an adjusted Neoplatonism. I tend to take more seriously the effort of its religious writers to overcome the separation between nature and grace and to forge a tighter link between revelation and what experience or non-Christian sources teach us about the human condition. Some of the early humanists perceived the pre-Christian religious aspirations of ancient writers fully continuous with their Christian fulfillment. Marsilio Ficino rejects any separation between Plato's *eros* and the life in grace to which it aspires. His *Theologia platonica* reinterprets the Platonic desire toward contemplation into a Christian call to the harmony of grace. This total rethinking of love places the Florentine Platonist closer to the Greek Fathers than to Plato or Plotinus.[16] He supports this religious naturalism by reinterpreting the concept of *form* in an aesthetic sense which may be applied to God himself. "In the highest Being to be is to be 'formosus' and bright, indeed to be form and light."[17] God includes all forms without being restricted by any *"formaque fons formarum."* Thus Ficino converts Plato's theory of participation into a basis for a Christian aesthetics. He supports his innovation of transcendent form by the more traditional one of light which the Greek Fathers had attributed to God himself. The divine light which causes seeing— *"In lumine tuo videbimus lumen"*— is also the object of seeing, the sublime element in which form reaches perfection.[18] God the fullness of light is also the perfection of form. Ficino avoids the all too physical implications of identifying God with light and formal perfection by asserting the invisible quality of both this transcendent light and form. *"Deus ob nimiam lucem est incognitus."* The all too abundant light renders the divine form unknowable. But though unknown to the intellect, the warmth of this light makes itself all the more felt in the will.[19] Pico della Mirandola likewise asserts the priority of love: "As long as we dwell in this world, imprisoned in the life of the senses, it is through love more than through reason that we are able to grasp God."[20]

Pico and Ficino went far beyond the traditional "expropriating the spoils of the pagans." Rather than using the classical philosophers for spare parts in an exclusively Christian theology, they placed Plato and Plotinus on equal footing with the prophets. The assumption here is that creation remains fully continuous with elevation. Since the Christian revelation is true, it must be universally accessible, and that requires its full compatibility with the great teachings of antiquity. Revelation, far from being a restrictive norm is an ever expanding truth continuously acquiring new depth and meaning. This Platonic theory of form as a transcendental quality of Being would provide religious artists of the Renaissance with a justification fully to display the natural world which contained, in its very essence, an upward movement surpassing its own finitude. As Cassirer wrote, the Renaissance artist "must constantly unite what is separated and opposed: in the visible he seeks the invisible."[21] No one pursued this religious naturalism more consistently than Michelangelo who, though coming at the end of the Renaissance, perhaps most perfectly realized its ideals."[22]

And yet, the religious impetus of early humanism failed. In the end it did not succeed in fully integrating the disparate elements of which it built its synthesis. It was not only that pagan antiquity and Christian revelation intrinsically differed. They did, and any accommodation would have to be constantly reexamined. But, more fundamentally, the new source of meaning upon which the Renaissance drew, the priority of the human subject, implied an idea of *nature* that could not be made continuous with the order of grace. It was new, independent of ancient sources, and not directly assimilable.

A third attempt to restore the lost unity of grace and nature resulted in one of the most complex systems Western thought has ever designed. It was also one of the most elusive. Though attacked, criticized, and theologically condemned, it was never definitively refuted. The condition for its existence was created by the nominalist theology of God's *potentia absoluta*. This included the possibility of a *pure nature*, that is, a human nature without supernatural gifts, grace, or participation in divine life. Until the sixteenth century this fiction appears to have remained a mere working hypothesis for developing theories of grace. In the sixteenth century some theologians began to assume it to be a reality in its own right. It immediately gained great popularity and, when the leading Thomists as well as the most prominent Jesuit theologians (especially Molina and Suárez) embraced it, came to be almost universally accepted outside the Augustinian camp. No previous theory had more overtly

64

asserted the dualism of nature and grace which had been prepared for centuries but had never clearly surfaced.

The two Louvain theologians Baius and Jansenius clearly perceived how much the new conception deviated from a tradition established since Augustine. Baius attempted to consolidate that tradition by including the modern views of nature. His efforts to rebuild the lost synthesis ended in a peculiar mixture of a most untraditional "naturalism" and an equally new, anti-natural determinism. Jansenius, his admiring student and successor at the Louvain faculty, elaborated these insights into an enormously complex yet coherent system that he presented as St. Augustine's theology of grace.

On the basis of a well-known passage in Augustine, Baius denied that human nature had been fully formed until it received the *forma filiorum Dei* — the original state of justice which later Scholasticism in order to stress its gratuitousness had come to call "supernatural." Grace is a *demand* of nature, and God's image in grace is the natural image of the soul. In that original condition of nature "actual" grace is required only for acting, not for "elevating." Adam by his natural powers attains his divine destination. Thus Baius with one bold stroke unites what centuries had sundered. But the problems return with his description of the fall. Once the fall deprives man of his original justice, nature itself breaks down to a truncated reality. Since nature itself was *essentially* justified, the loss of that original justice affects its essence, rendering it intrinsically incapable of natural goodness. Even a habit of accomplishing one's duty becomes vitiated by a general orientation toward concupiscence rather than toward charity. The virtues of this fallen nature intrinsically committed to sin are but "*splendida vitia.*" Here we begin to feel the failure of Baius's attempt. The opposition between a nature that is either "naturally" justified or "naturally" sinful introduces a discontinuity that must inevitably result in a new dualism of nature and grace even more pronounced than the one it replaces. Whatever restoration grace will achieve cannot but result in a new reality diametrically opposed to the fallen nature.

Ironically, Baius's theory, based upon the anti-Pelagian writings of Augustine, came under fire for Pelagianism. In the state of original justice man by nature alone elicits salvific acts. The charge, directly opposed to Baius's own intentions, nevertheless shows up an unresolved ambiguity in his thought. The basic assumption about the original condition of the human race secretly shares an axiom of Renaissance Stoicism, namely that nature *must be perfect* in all respects. This optimistic principle is no more Christian in origin than Ficino's Platonism: it rests on a clear misreading of Augustine's text. The pessimistic description of lapsed nature directly follows from the disappearance of this "natural" justification. Despite the reversal of original sin, the general tone of Baius's theology remains basically within the optimistic Renaissance mood.

Jansenius's mood was different. Temperamentally tending towards emotional gravity and subject to the influence of the dour Abbé de Saint-Cyran, Jansenius gave a pessimistic twist as well as a greater consistency to his mentor's theses. Adam's state, he explains in his *Augustinus*, could not be called a state of *grace*, even though he did not *merit* its orientation toward a divine beatitude. God morally *owed* it to an intellectual creature to call it to the highest form of spiritual life. In its original state nature itself was grace. Adam needed no "grace" (symptomatically defined as what is *added* to nature) to be properly disposed for *willing (velle)* this end, only divine assistance for *being able (posse)* to act rightly toward its attainment. We, after the fall, require grace both for the *velle* (disposition) and the *posse* (the ability to act).[23]

Combining Baius's rigorous logic about a nature wounded in its very essence by the fall, with a pessimism of his own, Jansenius concluded to a determinism of damnation and, for the few elect, of salvation, in the present state of mankind. Since nature had been crippled, grace, rather than assisting it, had to substitute for it. Once the will has turned to *cupiditas* it can be transformed only by losing its *liberum arbitrium*, that means, by ceasing to function naturally. De Lubac dramatically expresses this conversion: "C'est sur les ruines de la nature, autrefois maitresse d'elle-même, que règne aujourd'hui la grâce de Dieu."[24] Instead of a dualism of complementarity, we have now a full-dressed battle between nature and grace. A destructive opposition in time has replaced their gentler coexistence in space. Jansenius overcomes the dualism he is combating by successively eliminating either one of the two elements of the synthesis: first nature exists without grace, then grace without nature. "Tantôt instrument aux mains souveraines de l'homme, tantôt force envahissante qui supplée toute activité naturelle et réduit celui qu'elle libére en un nouvel esclavage. . . ."[25]

Jansenism remains hard to refute on its own terms, even though we may clearly perceive its failure, because more than any other theological system it has consistently drawn the conclusion from the modern premises. To be sure, one can hardly fault Jansenius for denying any neutral ground between *cupiditas* and *caritas*. Yet the opposition between the two has become more rigid than when St. Augustine first formulated it. It is difficult to criticize the foundations of Jansenius's thought without in some way implicating Augustine himself. The tradition initiated by the Latin Father moved, from the start, in a hazardous direction. The medicinal concept of grace so exclusively emphasized in Western Christianity carries within itself the seeds of a dualism that, mixed with the right ingredient, would become explosive. Yet only the modern equation of the real with what is actually present to consciousness provided that ingredient. Without that equation Augustinianism would never have become Jansenism. In the medieval synthesis grace, being primarily a *habitus*, inserted into nature a mode of being. Reduced to a conscious intention — the *motivum caritatis* — it comes to stand independent of nature and exists as in a *vacuum*. A state that requires to be thus *actualized* at each moment becomes totally detached from the nature it is supposed "to heal" and turns into a substitute for it. The problem we encounter here anticipates in the theological order that of Kant's moral theory. The same insistence on actual intention and the same absence of context appears in both cases. The primacy of the subject found its way into theology before philosophy had fully formulated it.

All the attempts to regain the lost unity made at the dawn of the modern age failed. Meanwhile Christians have learned to live with the separation. As their world has grown more and more "secular," their faith has come to depend with increasing exclusivity on revelation separated from, if not opposed to, "nature." The total split which neo-orthodox theologians insist on making between the realms of nature and grace express a separation which *de facto* exists within the modern mind. To correct that distorted perspective it is not sufficient to be aware of it, for the distortion affects those who perceive it as well as those who don't. It is in this climate that some contemporary theologians — Henri de Lubac and Hans Urs von Balthasar foremost among them — have made a new effort against the modern tradition. What distinguishes them from their early predecessors is a thorough acquaintance with the patristic sources of Christian theology as well as with modern thought in general. In the preceding part of this essay, especially in the presentation of Baius and Jansenius, I have relied on some of de Lubac's analyses. In this final part I shall turn to Balthasar as my guide.

In *The Glory of the Lord* Balthasar states his case with all desirable clarity. Grace is not "added" to the Being of nature, as an accident; it is its very depth. "Out of those mysterious depths the object of theology breaks forth as the self-revelation of the mystery of Being itself; such a revelation cannot be deduced from what the creaturely understanding of itself can read of the mystery of Being."[26] Theology must build upon the natural mystery of Being. "A 'supernatural' piety, oriented to God's historical revelation, cannot be such unless it is mediated by a 'natural' piety of nature and a 'piety of Being' " (*The Glory of the Lord*, I, 447). In the tradition of the transcendental Thomism of Rousselot and Maréchal, Balthasar posits that, beyond its immediate object, the mind attains Being itself both as immanent and as transcendent. Yet he combines this "natural" theology with a negative one inspired by Dionysius and Nicholas of Cusa. Philosophy remains unable to define the nature of transcendent Being and even of adequately describing its relation to finite beings. It possesses only a relative autonomy, sufficient for rendering the realm of finite being intelligible in its own right, but insufficient for properly answering the ultimate questions which it raises itself. Precisely the simultaneous presence of a transcendently oriented naturalism and an intrinsic inability to achieve the union it initiates rebuilds the harmony of nature and grace that was lost during the last four centuries. Only if grace fully penetrates the very order of nature can finite form, rather than excluding the divine, express it. Revelation alone, interpreted by theology, conveys the "super-form" of the triune Deity that gives its definitive interpretation to nature, and to its philosophical interpretation. Thus Christ himself, the direct form of God in nature, becomes the ultimate norm not only for measuring the content of revelation, but also the "natural" forms of cosmos and history. The Christ form constitutes the final and decisive principle for theologically interpreting all created forms.

Balthasar does not deny the relative autonomy of those forms, but he assumes them into an aesthetic of grace which, while fully respecting their autonomy, nevertheless transforms them in its divine-human light. Nor is this light external to that form itself, as a separate, created grace: it is the light that radiates from the divine form itself. God's revelation in Christ establishes both its own content and the light in which the believer perceives that content. The light within which the believer apprehends God's manifestation in Christ originates entirely in the manifestation itself. The believer's response, his ability to see in that light, still consists of that light itself transforming his own vision. The believer assents "within the object of his faith" (*The Glory of the Lord*, I, 192), partaking in the eternal *yes* the Son speaks to the Father. The eye with which the believer sees God, as Eckhart forcefully expressed it, is the eye with which God sees himself.

For Balthasar, then, the experience of grace forms itself an essential part of grace. Where the modern Latin tradition since Suarez had lowered experience to a "purely" natural level, Balthasar returns it to the essence of grace. Only by building upon an experience *in* faith can theology regain both its original, mystical quality and its central position in culture. Instead of restricting the light of faith to a set of revealed principles which theology then systematizes into a logically coherent cognitive structure, theology constitutes a new experience, fully continuous with all other experience and transforming it from within. Though fulfilling the mind's natural aspirations, the *experience* of faith emerges from *within* faith, follows the standards of faith, and results in seeing the form *of* faith (*The Glory of the Lord*, I, 225-227). Faith conveys its own intrinsic necessity to the entire order of nature. Yet grace "imposes" its form without doing violence to nature. A divinely created nature manifests already in its own being God's eternal presence. Received *within* the form of nature, grace brings that form to completion by extending it to its ultimate archetype — God's triune nature.

Which religious believer would not wish to recover this religious vision upon which the entire tradition of his culture is based and which in Balthasar's majestic presentation may appear once again to lie within our reach? Why should the experience of faith not be available, today as in the past, to reshape our entire private and cultural experience? These questions, in my opinion, do not receive an adequate response from the incisive critics of modern theology that de Lubac and Balthasar were. It is not that they have not confronted the issue of modern atheism. Both of them devoted major works to it. Even after several decades *Le drame de l'humanisme athée* and *The God Question and Modern Man* remain fundamental texts. Yet I doubt whether they perceived the full consequences of their own pessimistic analyses for the viability of their alternative views. The direct experience of the sacred described by Otto,

Van der Leeuw, and Eliade, and whose possibility still underlies de Lubac's and Balthasar's theologies of reunification, is no longer universally available to faith in our modern culture. Though the experience of grace still exists, it has become exceptional, mostly secondary to personal reflection and deliberate choice. Of course, even today the believer decides for the acceptance of a religious world-view on the basis of *some* experience. Moreover, faith has at all times consisted of both experience *and* decision. What uniquely distinguishes our present situation, however, is the nature of this experience. Direct and self-interpretative in the past, it has now become ambiguous, open to a multiplicity of interpretations. The religious interpretation rarely has its ground in the experience itself. It is mostly mediated by a reflection and a decision which separate the experience from the act of religious acceptance which thereby comes at the end of a voluntary but by no means necessary decision.

This separation between experience and the act of faith renders the earlier synthesis of nature and grace practically problematic. For the experience is not the experience *of* faith. We rather seem to be dealing here with an ambiguous, more or less neutral experience, subsequently interpreted in a religious sense. Thus the separation between the orders of reality, a natural and a supernatural one, which de Lubac and Balthasar successfully attack in modern theology, has deeply entrenched itself in the modern experience from which it cannot be easily dislodged. Balthasar has attempted to resolve the modern tension by incarnating his theology within the various forms of aesthetic experience which Catholicism has produced after the great theological syntheses of Thomas, Bonaventure, and Duns Scotus lost their power. Artistic expressions of faith have endured right up to the present time. But what such recent expressions of grace as we find in Hopkins, Péguy, Bernanos convey by no means coincides with the direct experience of grace contained in the theologies of the Greek Fathers and Augustine upon which he erects his own structure. There we found harmony, union, a synthesis of grace and nature; here, especially in today's "religious" literature, we find mostly tension, doubt, a split between two orders which modern culture has separated into two opposite realities.

Our own proposal in the light of the modern situation and the absence of a strong, direct experience of grace would be modest — perhaps too modest. We would think that the synthesis is available only in a mediated, and hence indirect mode. Our atheist-oriented culture no longer admits the kind of universal union between nature and grace such as existed in the high Middle Ages. Most believers no longer "perceive" the sacred in persons, objects, and events closely connected with their relation to the transcendent. They rarely find the source of sacralization in the symbolic reality itself, but in a subject that determines what may function as a symbol of transcendence. Traditionally established symbols appear to be often reduced to instruments freely chosen or accepted according to strictly personal needs. Religion exercises its integrating function primarily by means of a personal decision to *adopt* a traditional doctrine and to *use* it for guidance and integration of the various aspects of social and private conduct. The *inward* turn *mediates* between what the believer directly and publicly experiences, and the religious meaning he gives to that experience. For that reason we consider only an internalized and indirect synthesis of grace and nature available to most reflective believers today.

Notes

1. This paper includes material published by the author in previous essays: "Hans Urs von Balthasar's Theology of the Aesthetic Form," in *Theological Studies* 49 (1988), pp. 299-318; "The Dissolution of the Unity of Nature and Grace at the Dawn of the Modern Age," in *The Theology of Pannenberg* (Minneapolis, 1988), pp. 198-221.
2. *Summa contra Gentiles* (hereafter *SCG*) II 4; *Summa Theologiae* (hereafter *ST*) I 3 aa 2 and 4.
3. Henri de Lubac, *Surnaturel* (Paris, 1946), Ch. V. The classical passage (cited by de Lubac) reads: "Opportet quod homini super-addatur aliqua supernaturalis forma et perfectio, per quam convenienter ordinetur in finem. . . . Homini, ad consequendum ultimum finem, additur aliqua perfectio super propriam naturam, scilicet gratia" (*SCG* 150 and 153).
4. Sylvester Ferrariensis, *Opera* (Venice, 1535), Vol. I, pp. 39-41.
5. *ST* III 1 a 3. This statement is counterbalanced, however, by the preceding articles which describe the fitness of the Incarnation on the basis of God's goodness and of man's "full participation in the divine nature" (*ST* III 1 a 2). The connection with sin appears to rest on a scriptural basis, the *modus loquendi Sacrae Scripturae*.

6. Cf. Cornelio Fabro, *La nozione metafisica di partecipazione secondo S. Tomasso d'Aquino* (Brescia, 1939) and L. B. Geiger: *La participation dans la philosophie de St. Thomas* (Paris, 1942).

7. *ST* I 8 a 1.

8. *If* God was to remain truly immanent in all reality, as religious thinkers had always held, in a mechanistic system of reality, this could mean only, as Spinoza perceived, that he had to be a *part* of the system, or, since this would conflict with the definition of an infinite Being, the *totality itself* in its originating aspect — *Deus, sive natura*, that is, *natura naturans*.

9. Karl Rahner, *Theological Investigations*, Vol. I (London, 1968), p. 302. "Certainly the philosopher has his own well-grounded concept of the nature of man: the irreducible substance of human being, established by recourse to human experience independently of verbal revelation. This concept may largely coincide with the theological concept of man's nature, insofar as without Revelation the greater part of what goes beyond this theological 'nature' is not experienced, and at any rate is not recognized *as* supernatural without the help of Revelation to interpret it."

10. *Quaestiones disputatae de malo* 2, 4, and 13.

11. E. K. Moody, *The Logic of William of Ockham* (New York, 1935), pp. 307-315.

12. On the modern history of the concept, cf. Josef Fuchs S.J., *Natural Law: A Theological Investigation* (New York, 1965), Ch. 3.

13. William Law, *The Spirit of Love*, Dialogue III, in *The Classics of Western Spirituality* (New York, 1980), p. 439.

14. Ibid., p. 444.

15. Ibid., p. 453.

16. In distinguishing love from *libido* Ficino places himself in the medieval tradition of courtly love in Italy represented by Brunetto Latini, Guido Cavalcanti, and Dante. Festugiere suggests a direct acquaintance with the theoretical *Flos Amoris* which circulated under Boccaccio's name.

17. "*Argumentum in Platonicam Theologiam ad Laurentium Medicem*" in Eugenio Garin, *Prosatori Lattini del Quatrocento* (Milan, 1952), p. 342. Garin translates *formosus* as *bello*, and *forma* as *bellezza*, thereby sidestepping the ambiguity but forcing the meaning.

18. "Lumen quod cumque videtur, nihil est aliud quam purae efficacisque

formae spiritalis quaedam amplificatio," "*Argumentum. . . ,*" Opera I, 695; Garin, 314.

19. "Deus ergo in summa intellectus cognitione quodammodo nox quaedom est intellectui. In summo voluntatis amore certe dies est voluntatis" (Garin, 344).
20. *Opera* (Basel, 1576), p. 250.
21. Cassirer, *Individuum und Kosmos in der Renaissance* (Darmstadt [1927], 1963), p. 142.
22. Having in his adolescence often been admitted to the Medici Academy where Pico and Ficino exposed their theories, he had over the years deepened a Neoplatonic aestheticism of form into a religious vision. In the light of this vision the artist had become ever more dissatisfied with the purely finite form. He had increasingly turned away from the too individual, personalized expression of sculpture and painting. On the religious quality of Michelangelo's work, cf. Rolf Schott, *Michelangelo* (New York, 1965).
23. Jansenius supported this naturalist interpretation of Adam's condition by an amazing interpretation of Augustine's expression of wonder at the even *greater abundance* of grace granted to the elect after the fall for keeping the path of righteousness. Cf. Henri de Lubac, *Surnaturel*, pp. 56-63.
24. Ibid., p. 69.
25. Ibid.
26. Hans Urs von Balthasar, *The Glory of the Lord*, Vol. I (San Francisco, 1982), p. 145.

Response to Louis Dupré

by Peter Henrici, S.J.,
Gregorian University, Rome

In response to Professor Dupré's learned and nuanced paper, with which I largely agree, I would like to add three complementary remarks: first, on the transition from medieval to modern thought; second, on Balthasar's theological project; and third, on the notion of secularization.

1. Discussing nature and grace, we are likely to forget that "nature" means for modern man, as it did for the ancient Greek, first of all the nature surrounding us, this complex of things and of facts, regulated by natural laws, that are the objects of the natural sciences. It is clear to everybody that at the dawn of modern ages there was a major shift in the understanding of this nature, a shift marked by the birth of modern science.

This shift presents two related aspects. Generally speaking, it is the transition from a closed cosmos to an open universe — to quote the title of a famous book.[1] Whereas for the Greeks and Medievals the world was a harmonious, well-ordered, and hierarchic cosmos, in which every being had its proper place, the modern universe is nothing but a set of single facts,[2] linked together by certain forces and common laws, whose overall unity must be sought (if anywhere) only in the scientist's mind. This radical change went on not only and not even primarily for astronomical reasons; it was prepared and made possible by the shift to nominalist philosophy and theology, according to which God the Creator is not so much producing an overall harmonious order of essences (reproducing his own divine ideas) but single beings, loved and willed for themselves. What divine plan and wisdom stands behind these freely created facts, no human mind can explore.

This nominalist world-view had its drawbacks for the conception of nature and grace. In the medieval cosmos every being had its own natural perfection, by standing in its right place; hence changes were either "natural," that is, leading to greater perfection by moving a thing closer to his appropriate place in the cosmic hierarchy, or "violent," that is, removing and alienating it from this position. Grace could be seen as that which favors the human person's "natural" move toward greater perfection; it was therefore in full consonance with nature, contributing even to its greater harmony. *"Gratia non destruit, sed perficit naturam."* On the contrary, in the modern, nominalist world-view that is not built upon a predetermined, harmonious essential order, it is hard to see what "greater natural perfection" could mean; grace, therefore, is considered as a free, gratuitous, and superadded gift of God, (not unlike his creative act itself) that helps a single being to overcome his imperfections. Strictly speaking, grace does not effect anything in the human being; it is only a mark of God's good will to consider humans righteous (the Lutheran forensic justification, already foreshadowed in the nominalist notion of *"acceptatio divina"*).

To this, a second more immediately evident aspect must be added. In the ancient cosmos all change or motion was teleological, occasioned and determined by an end, toward which it tends. Even the First Mover, God, is for Aristotle not an efficient but the final cause of the universe: *kinei hōs erōmenon*[3] — which finds an echo in Dante's "L'Amor che muove il sole e l'altro stelle."[4] Modern, mechanistic physics, on the contrary, relies on efficient causality and eliminates all teleological considerations. That is most evident in Galileo and Newton, where even the attracting force (gravity) is seen as an efficient cause (underlining the loss of a hierarchical cosmos by the Galilean relativity of motion and Newton's reciprocity of attraction). In Descartes, God himself became a "pushing" efficient cause that gave the initial *"chiquenaude"* to motion and keeps it going; and toward the end of modern times, Darwinism succeeded in eliminating the notion of teleology even from evolution, by substituting it with the utterly mechanical "struggle for life."

These rapid glimpses at the development of modern, mechanical science may help us to understand to what extent the modern mind relies on *efficiency*, whereas ancient and medieval philosophy was in search of *meaning*. For modern man, the more efficient something is, the better and more perfect it is.

No wonder, then, that in this context the theological concept of grace has undergone a radical change. Grace was conceived more and more as a kind of efficient cause (*"gratia efficax!"*); divine (pre)motion was no longer understood as a charming attraction, but as a moving force, which makes man achieve what he is not able to do by his own forces. Grace, therefore, did not so much add a supplementary divine, and indeed "supernatural" meaning to human life, as complete an inborn (by original sin) inadequacy of his nature and actions. The discussion about what man is able to achieve by his own forces became paramount in this kind of theology of grace, as well as the intricate problem of how divine and human effort (or "freedom") could combine—the historical debate "*de auxiliis.*" In this perspective it was unavoidable that finally everything that was attributed to grace seemed withdrawn from nature: nature and grace were looked at as competitors, quasi-hostile to one another; nor could it fail that in this competition grace, as the weaker part, was gradually eliminated.

Meanwhile in the patristic, and indeed biblical sense, grace is a moving force, not as added to and competitive with man's natural abilities, but as a kind of *attraction*, adding love, urgency, and joy to a person's natural striving and acting. This was the meaning of the Greek word *charis*, "charm": grace meant God's loveliness, charming us and making us fall in love with him so that in turn we may become charming for him. The other New Testament word for grace, *pneuma*, "spirit," had a similar meaning: God's spirit dwelling in us makes us take delight in God's command so that we may fulfill it spontaneously (cf. Gal. 5:16-26). Augustine's conception of grace as "*delectatio victrix*" gave to this same view a theological formulation: grace makes God's commandment look more attractive to us than are our own concupiscent strivings.

2. The renewal of Catholic theology at the beginning of this century started from a rediscovery of this older conception of grace. Maurice Blondel first rediscovered, on philosophical grounds, that human life is intrinsically oriented toward the longing for a supernatural gift, and that this longing constitutes its real and unique meaning. Stimulated by Blondel's impelling thought, Thomists then rediscovered St. Thomas's teaching on man's "natural desire for the vision of God" as the very constituent of our intellectual life (Pierre Rousselot, Joseph Maréchal), and from there they went on to a rediscovery of the true Augustinian theology of grace (Henri de Lubac). All these rediscoveries, however, remained anthropocentric, giving most of the attention to man's openness and longing for God. This anthropocentric theology found its most systematic and coherent expression in Karl Rahner's conception of man as "hearer of the Word," endowed with a supernatural "existential" resulting from its being called to beatific vision.

Hans Urs von Balthasar's theology originated from these rediscoveries. He underlines the importance of de Lubac's insight, that the concrete, historical human beings have but one supernatural end. Yet he rejects the (still very "modern" and subjectivist) anthropocentric setting of the aforementioned theologies, and tries to build up an objectivist theology, which we rightly may call "postmodern." God's grace, which charms and attracts us, is doing so by its objective, immediately perceivable "form" or figure (*Gestalt*), which is God's "glory," namely God making himself seen *as* God in a humanly perceivable and understandable appearance. Now, pure meaning or meaningfulness, immediately perceivable and experienced, is beauty — hence Balthasar's theological aesthetics, which is a theology of God's historical self-manifestation as God, a theology of the "glory," relying on a theology of eros, of man's being charmed by this divine revelation.

Since it is God's glory that manifests itself in the *Offenbarungsgestalt*, this revealing "form" or figure is absolutely unique, an intra-historical phenomenon that lies beyond all we could conceive or imagine about God, "the *economic* id quo maius cogitari nequit" as Balthasar once called it. It is Christ's loving descent and humbling, his obedience unto the cross and his descent to the realm of death, prefigured in the Old Testament by the humiliating obedience of the prophets.[5] It is still perceivable in the figures of the saints, in particular in the figure of "the Christian fool" at the beginning of modern times.[6] That is to say that this Christian manifestation of God's glory stands in strict contrast to all that the world would consider glorious, and by this contrast it reveals itself as the form of divine glory. There is no possibility, therefore, of gradual approximation to this unique form by other religious experiences; no triumphant "cosmic Christ" either, since the manifestation of God's love in this sinful world is the humiliation of God himself. Throughout his life, Balthasar has been in search of this divine form, trying to find it reflected in so many Christian (and anti-Christian) writers in his *Apokalypse*, but also in Christian art and in the overall human search for love and beauty. All these manifestations, however, must be measured by the unique form the gospel shows us: therefore, Balthasar's work is in all its parts a work of Christian discernment, and his polemic writings (like *Who Is a Christian?* and *Cordula*) have no other intention than to prevent Christians from obfuscating this unique, counter-worldly divine form with easy accommodations and coming to terms with secular patterns of behavior, particularly those of modernity (see Rom. 12:2).

3. At this point, some short concluding remark on secularization may be opportune. Secularization consists precisely in eliminating this visible and evident Christian otherness from public life. With secularization Christianity, though not ceasing of necessity to be Christian, ceases anyhow, by way of a kind of mimicry, to be evident, to be striking, and to be a scandal. It was against this depravation of Christendom that Kierkegaard fought at the price of his own life, and Balthasar, in this regard, feels deeply sympathetic with him. Kierkegaard's (and Balthasar's) main adversary, Hegel, presents us indeed with the best description of secularization I know, in a text of his very last years, which Kierkegaard evidently did not even know.

In a long addition to paragraph 552 of his *Encyclopedia*, Hegel discusses the relation between religion and the state, in order to conclude that "it was the foolishness of modern times, to try to change a corrupted social system, the Constitution and the laws of a State, without changing its religion, in other words to have made a Revolution without a Reformation." The reason for this statement is that the state, for Hegel, relies mainly on the civic sense of its citizens, and that this civic sense has to be rooted in religion. Yet the Catholic religion underlines and fixes God's otherness by all sorts of rites and institutions: A clergy separate from lay people, and from which the latter receive guidance, prayers by intercession of the saints, the veneration of relics and of the Blessed Sacrament, where "a material thing," instead of being destroyed and sublimated by eating it, is conserved and adored, and above all by a "holy" life-style defined by celibacy, poverty, and religious obedience. Such a religion, according to Hegel, is unable to foster civic sense, keeping people alienated from the divine which finds its worldly expression in the state. Hence Hegel's program for radical secularization: "The divine spirit must permeate the wordliness, staying immanent in it." Such immanence of the divine in the secular (secularization is always a divinization of something secular!) are for Hegel the socio-ethical structures (the "Sittlichkeit") of marriage, business, and loyalty to the state — a perfectly secularized "religious" triad, which, by the way, forms the groundwork of Hegel's *Philosophy of Right*.

If then we ask, what has to be done to counteract the modern trend of secularization, in order to make the Christian "form" more evident in our contemporary world, all we need is to read Hegel's statements in opposite sense. What Hegel sees as impediments for a true civic sense may be exactly what is needed to make Christian testimony evident in our secularized world, whose obsession is efficiency.

Notes

1. Alexandre Koyré, *Du monde clos à l'univers infini* (Paris, 1962).
2. "The world is all that is the case" (Wittgenstein, *Tractatus*, 1.1).
3. Aristotle, *Metaphysics*, 7; 1072 b 3.
4. Dante, *Paradiso*, XXXIII, 145.
5. Ibid., Vol. III, 2.1, pp. 209-282.
6. Balthasar, *Herrlichkeit*, Vol. III, 1, pp. 492-551.

Spirituality for the Coming Years

Louis Bouyer, University of San Francisco

What are we to expect as the possible developments of spirituality for Christians of our times, the last decade of the twentieth century?

Before trying to give some elements of a possible answer to the question, I must insist on the fact that, in opposition to what is too often supposed by too many Christians of today, clerical or lay people, religious or secular, there are a variety of spiritualities (plural) in Christianity. Basically, essentially, there is only one: the spirituality of the gospel, as it is expressed in the New Testament, and further developed through, first of all and above all, the traditional liturgy: "*legem credendi statuat lex supplicandi,*" as it was said in the *Indiculum de Gratia,* already in the early fifth century.

However, this one Christian spirituality, in its concrete application to varied situations, diverse in time and place and in forms of existence, has to take account of a great variety of possible problems. What I shall try to elucidate is the answers we are to give to the problems of the present generation, in order to make it realistic for the men and women who have to live in this context their own application of the spirituality of the gospel, the spirituality, in other words, resulting from what Jesus himself has taught, done, and, above all, manifested of what he was and will remain for all times: our Savior, the Son of God made man from our own fallen humanity, in order not only to rescue it but to associate us to the full reality of his unique sonship.

Again, of such a spirituality there cannot be an array of more or less independent varieties. Yet precisely here we meet with the first difficulty, a singularly grave problem of our times. From the time of the Church renewal which took place in the Romantic period, in connection with the resurrection of the religious orders after the French Revolution, it became a fashion for each of them to be distinguished from all the others, not only by its habit and its constitution, modeled generally on the different tasks they had made their own, but, first of all, by a special brand of spirituality, carefully distinguished from (and often explicitly opposed to) that of any other.

80

We must insist here on the newness of this fact. Of course, in the past, there had been plenty of rivalries and suspicion between these companies of would-be seekers of Christian perfection. However, this had not prevented even such a traditional order as the Carthusians, in the seventeenth century, under the leadership of their prior general, Dom Innocent Le Masson, from borrowing much of their inspiration from the Jesuits, whatever may have been the differences between their styles of life. But St. Ignatius Loyola himself, for his own part, had strongly encouraged his disciples to read Cassian, the greatest classic of the monastic tradition in the West, in spite of the fact that the Jesuits strove to be active religious and not at all contemplative monks. Many other cases could be quoted in the same line, until the end of the eighteenth century.

After that, not only such borrowings become exceptional, but, when they do, they are judged severely by the confreres of the culprit. This went so far that the Trappists of the nineteenth century, under the influence of their restorer, Dom de Lestrange, came to be very careful, not only to be different in all their ways from the black Benedictines, but even from the first fathers of Cîteaux: when Dom Anselme Le Bail, in the 1930s, launched a renewal of studies of not only St. Bernard, but William of Saint-Thierry, Guerric of Igny, etc., he was immediately looked at askance by the generalate, and, had he not lost his mind at the time, would certainly have been deprived of his abbatial dignity for his initiative. Similarly, in the English Oratory, when Newman founded a school in Birmingham, it was objected by Dalgairn that that was typical of the French, and not of the Roman Oratory from which the English had received the Philipine tradition (a reflection which would certainly have provoked the most pungent irony from St. Philip Neri himself!).

More recently, between the two world wars, in Belgium and in France especially, connected with what was then called "Catholic Action," it was insisted not only that a special form of spirituality had to be invented for the laity, having nothing to do with those either of the diocesan clergy or of the different religious orders, but soon that even this newly born variety should itself be set aside, in favor of carefully separated spiritualities for the workmen, for the peasants, for the bureaucrats, for the intellectuals, for the aristocracy, etc., etc., ad infinitum! And soon after the Second World War, at the time when a pastoral and liturgical movement was launched in France, I remember having heard a religious proclaiming that parishes were outmoded because it was impossible for a workman to go to Mass (*a fortiori* communicate) together with the director of his firm or any of the members of its executive board.

And at present do we not see somewhat strange developments of a spirituality for women, exhaling the most outspoken disgust for anything masculine? I am afraid that, for the younger generations, all such things already seem not only ridiculous but positively shameful, and, above all, totally un-Christian.

The movement in favor of "reconciliation" may have been too vague or too naïve in some of its forms, but it has certainly corresponded to an increasingly disseminated feeling, and it has helped that feeling to become explicit and fully aware of its own legitimacy.

Now, of course, once again, this is not a question of rejecting the need to pay attention, in the development of spiritual life, to the special problems raised by the different conditions of life in which Christians may find themselves, but the radical absurdity of trying to produce a special spirituality for every layer of the social order is now felt practically everywhere, except in some surviving little groups for which the slogan "openness to the world" means simply that they have made a private world for their own use, from which they cannot any longer get out.

Together with that common feeling after a return, not only to the center, but to that Catholic openness to whatever is good, essential, of a permanent value in the faith transmitted to us once and for all by the apostles of our Lord, we must mention what has been called, with some measure of irony, even if it is a friendly one, a "return of angels." In fact, it is more simply a question of the return of God!

What did we not hear, twenty years ago or so, of the urgent necessity of accepting the "secular city," and therefore substituting some horizontal Christianity for a completely outmoded vertical one! Not only Harvey Cox, but Bonhöffer, even Kierkegaard, were invoked as the great patron saints of that deliberately unspiritual kind of Christianity. The funny thing is that such a rage for openness to the world and even "conversion to the world," happened among the clerical tribe just at the time when the most secular, the most materialistic world ever known was suddenly and desperately seeking a way to avoid what, only too clearly, appeared to be moving more and more toward the concentration camp!

The unavoidable result was that, finding priests and ministers casting off a God whose death the theologians had solemnly announced, the new craving turned its quest elsewhere, to bastard forms of pretended Eastern spiritualities: Yoga, Zen, when it was not simply mescaline, soon followed by cocaine!

I remember, at the acme of that access of madness, while I was teaching at Brown University (Providence, Rhode Island), I had a colleague come from India, himself a very dignified as well as very learned Brahman. He was the best counter-poison to all the silly things told to the students by the great luminaries, at the time, of the post-conciliar theology. For he said to them: "First, all that stuff of pseudo-Oriental spiritualities offered to you is, to real Brahmanism or Buddhism, the equivalent of what I could get from a southern Italian witch concerning Christian spirituality. And even if it were not so, the genuine forms of Hinduism were conceived for people fully integrated in the world in which we live, while the modern, technological civilization has only too completely cut your ties with cosmic reality. The result for you, even from authentic forms of Yoga or Zen, can therefore be more probably schizophrenia than any type of what may be called religious experience" — a point recently confirmed to me by a California psychiatrist telling me: "Thirty years ago, the inmates of our lunatic asylums were generally alcoholics. Twenty or even ten years ago they were taking drugs. Now they tend mostly to be adepts of what they call Zen, Yoga, or Transcendental Meditation. . . ."

Now, at last, people are no longer expecting from us artificial kicks, but simply God, the one true God, the God of Jesus Christ. If they have ceased to frequent our churches, it is too often not because they rejected God but because they feel it is ridiculous to turn to priests who are ready to talk on any subject rather than their own specialty. The plain evidence of the fact is in the few churches where God, the God of Jesus Christ, is frankly announced and worshiped as he should be, and in the unexpected crowds which gather there, as soon as it is widely known. The most traditional monastic churches, especially, even when they have the dimensions of cathedrals, are too small to house the congregations of unknown people they see coming to them every Sunday.

Therefore, if there is something evident concerning the spirituality of the coming age, it is that it will have to be a spirituality in which the search for God, prayer, and a life dominated by Christian contemplation will again be taken seriously by a clergy who have ceased to be interested in anything except the things for which they have been ordained — but who, it must be frankly acknowledged, are still too often unprepared!

For twenty or thirty years, books like Dom Chautard's *The Soul of the Apostolate* were exiled from up-to-date clerical libraries, and the Catholic bookstores unanimously told the naïve pious Christian consumer that Dom Marmion's *Christ, the Life of the Soul* could and should no longer interest any man of our times. However, the few well-thinking or simply well-advised businessmen who have tried to reprint such books have been the first to be startled by their sudden new success. Whatever some of the liberal neo-conservatives may still think or say, it is clear that, if the Church has a future in the world of today, it is as the sign par excellence of the supreme reality, the supreme importance, of God.

To say this, to insist on this, is not in the least to forget that we cannot love God whom we do not see unless we love, as God loves him, our neighbor whom we do see. It means simply that what is first must be put first: we shall never love our neighbor as God loves him if we are not first interested in loving God for himself. Or rather, as St. Paul put it, it is only with the love of God, that love proper to God, shed forth in our own hearts by his Spirit whom he has given us that we shall be able to be such witnesses of that love.

Now this, of a necessity, implies that we should say something of the growth in the Catholic Church itself, in recent years, of the charismatic movement. Whatever may be said of the possible eccentricities of which it may have been an occasion, it cannot be denied that it has been, until now, the most powerful (and popular) development springing up since the Second Vatican Council for rediscovering the properly religious character of authentic Christianity. That the most important gifts of the Spirit are not the most visible was already a preoccupation with St. Paul. But he did not in the least diminish his insistence on the fact that the fundamental experience of Christians is an experience of the Spirit, working through the whole of our life, but starting with the interiority of its reception. It is what St. Augustine later would call: "God more intimate to myself than I myself can be!"

For my own part, I would say that the best promise for the immediate future of the spiritual life in the Church may be the growing and ever deeper, because more authentic, influence of the works and personalities of three modern Carmelite nuns: one canonized more than fifty years ago, but only recently discovered in her full reality, namely Thérèse of Lisieux; the other two beatified in recent years: Elizabeth of the Trinity and Edith Stein (Theresa-Benedicta of the Cross).

Thérèse's "little way" is in fact a heroic way open to everybody: a total surrender to God as the Father of Jesus, and of all of us in him, a surrender made even in total darkness. Elizabeth's message is that of a life lived entirely in a joyful praise of the Holy Trinity, through Christ living in our hearts by the Spirit, to the glory of the Father. Edith's vision could be described as an unflinching acceptance of the Cross of the Son as the way of our return to the Father, as of so many prodigal children, led, through the Spirit of annihilation of the egotist selfhood, into the infinite openness of the Godhead. And, for that daughter of Israel especially, it is clear that the only way to make such a spirituality our own was through full entrance into the perspective of that prayer of the Church of which the Mass is the heart and in and through which our whole limited being has to be surrendered to the Unlimited One.

Now it is enough to mention these three Carmelites of our own century — the last of whom actually died a martyr, and the other two quietly accepted a premature death as the consecration of their total offering to the will of the Father — in order to realize that such a return to a properly mystical view of Christianity (I mean, as Dom Anselm Stolz was the first to establish it: not a borrowing from Neoplatonism, but simply a life absorbed into the mystery of God's love manifested to us in the Cross of Jesus) cannot be separated from a return also to asceticism.

This word, "asceticism," must be understood in the sense it had let us understand just what was meant for the first monks of Egypt, who came immediately after the martyrs of the first three Christian centuries: a liberation from all the ties which imprison us in the jail of our modern and so comfortable but so flatly materialistic way of life.

Recently I came across an article written toward the beginning of this century by the English poet Francis Thompson. It was the first among many such articles calling for a positive Christianity, to be substituted for a spirituality based upon a negative, dolorist assumption of what would have been for a long time believed to be the heart of Christianity: the Cross. Thompson, himself having had a tragic experience of a life of hopeless poverty in the worst slums of London, could justly have called for a Christian recognition of the intrinsic goodness of creation — and, therefore, for a spirituality opening upon cosmic joyful praise instead of any contempt of creation and creatureliness — without minimizing the place of the Cross in any Christian life.

But what too many modern, sentimental, romantic forms of Christianity have mistaken for Christian asceticism, that is, a dubious kind of dolorism, has nothing to do with any Christian asceticism worthy of the name. As Father Lebreton has shown it convincingly in his book on the spirituality of the New Testament, authentic Christian asceticism has never been based upon a condemnation of creation, but upon the preference given to the Creator rather than to his own creation. Such it was in the first great renewal of Christian spirituality, for a St. Anthony and all the fathers of the desert, as they came to be called. Once again, it was simply a search for liberation: a liberation not from our human, created condition, but from our self-centeredness, nourished by a spirit of acquisition, of egotistical possession. Against that demoniac caricature of happiness, it is indeed the pure joy of the beatitudes, of the detachment of generous love!

It is true that, in opposition to the self-chosen poverty of the old monks, Catholics in general seem today to be persuaded that, if our forefathers could easily fast, prove independent of material comfort, reduce the time of their sleep in order to prolong that of prayer or of work, it was because they were much stronger than we are now. But all that talk on our supposedly more tender frame, more delicate bodies, unable to bear any kind of hardship without being in danger of some collapse, is a mere farce! All the specialists are agreed now that our ancestors, not so well fed as we are, were smaller, weaker in their constitution, and, as a result, not able to reach or even to approach our average length of life. Why, then, are we so afraid of doing now what so many generations of Christians have done as a matter of course?

In fact, even today all the good monks of the Eastern Church — and they are many, for they have known an extraordinary renewal of monasticism, taking place not only in Mount Athos, but in the Meteora, in the north of mainland Greece, as well as in Russia, and still more in the Coptic church — all these monks are still imposing upon themselves all the practices of an Anthony or a Pachomios.

And it is not only the monks, but all the Orthodox Christians practicing their religion, in Russia especially, where their number, among younger generations, is fast growing now, where during Lent, they submit themselves to austerities even harder than those known by our forefathers, as, for an example, the abstention not only from meat but also from eggs or milk.

I remember with what sweet irony Paul VI delighted to tell everybody the answer that the Coptic patriarch, Shonouta, himself the leader of the great monastic renewal in Egypt, had made to his question: "What difficulty do you see in acknowledging in the Catholic Church today the continuation of the Apostolic Church?" The patriarch had replied: "It is difficult for me to see how the Church founded by Christ could be a Church in which people pray so little and no one ever fasts!"

In fact, it was a Catholic, a Benedictine monk, the best specialist today in France of the study of primitive Benedictinism, Dom Adalbert de Vogüé, who, in a book on this question, confessed that, when for his own part he tried, in spite of poor health, to practice the fasts formerly accepted as prescribed in the Rule, together with rather intensive work, he discovered that not only had prayer and recollection become easier and more profitable, but his health itself, far from suffering from it, had never been so sound.

Will we not go back to the teaching of St. Leo the Great: that by economizing, by fasting, what we shall then be able to give to people poorer than ourselves not only will be of more help to our progress in prayer, but will also be a more effective form of Christian love?

Our recent liturgical revision has simply dropped from our Lenten prayers all mention of fasting, and nearly all references to penitence. Lent is a matter of sincerity, we have been told! Would it not be equally sincere, and more worth the trial, if we were to put our actions in agreement with our prayers, rather than our prayers with our inhibitions?

More generally, is not that ecclesiastical conviction, now stronger than ever in the post-conciliar clergy, that you will keep the Christian faithful in the Church only if you do not expect of them anything more than you would from any average nonbeliever, an insult to the Christian people? And what is more stupid than that illusion of all these so-called "religious" of our times, who persist in being persuaded that they will attract crowds to their vanishing institutions by telling the young among others: "Come, come to us: it is exactly as in the world"? Is it a matter of mere chance that the only orders which now attract not only as many candidates, but even more than they did in times past, are those which not only still wear habits and follow traditional ways, but whose silence, solitude, and simplicity of life are as strict as ever—notably the Carthusians?

Anyhow, what most powerfully attracts people, now as in the past, and now more than in a recent past is certainly not a dilution of Christianity, but a practice and an offer of the purest and the most basic expression of its spirituality, as it was ever found in the traditional liturgy, which illuminates the deeper sense of the Word of God itself. It was this conviction that led Vatican Council II to make its first text a declaration on what is the importance and the fundamental significance of the Church's liturgy, and especially of that liturgy restored to its full authenticity and made accessible to all, either by translations or needed adaptations, but above all through a rediscovery of its true nature and its full spiritual implications.

Now it must be honestly acknowledged that this document has not yet produced the effect it was intended to have. It has been too often misinterpreted or misapplied.

What people today, and not only the integralist, call "the new missal," most of the time has nothing to do with the missal approved by Paul VI, which very few have ever even had in their hands and almost nobody has ever taken the time to study attentively. They mean merely what they may have chanced to hear or see amid the infinity of the now-famous "creativity" of a clergy which imagines itself to be at the peak of progress, but which is more or less ignorant of the authentic tradition of the Church at prayer.

In fact, the main point in the revision of the missal was not only to reintroduce a richness of prayers representative of all the great lines of tradition at its best, but above all to restore to the People of God in its entirety all the variety and the richness of the Word of God itself.

And this was the object of another conciliar text, which dealt with the importance and proper interpretation of that divine Word in the Church. It is hardly an exaggeration to say that this other text has been passed by, as practically nonexistent. All that a noisy majority of scholars have drawn from it has been an alleged authorization to pay no attention to any of the prescriptions or condemnations of the former Biblical Commission, which was, to be sure, certainly more distinctively moved by its terror of innovations than by any effective contribution to a biblical initiation of the Christian people!

A retreat that I preached a few years ago to one of the bigger monasteries of contemplative nuns in northern America gave me a good opportunity to check the effect of such a situation. I had taken as the main theme of the retreat a subject that was very traditional in ancient and medieval monasticism: the *Lectio divina*, which meant a meditative reading of the Bible, within the framework of its use in the liturgy, and along the lines of the general interpretation drawn from this liturgical practice.

Apart from the very intelligent abbess and two or three others, I soon discovered that the community was simply infuriated by my choice of this theme. One half said to me: "To meditate on the Bible, in the light of the liturgy? But it is a thing entirely pre-conciliar! Talk to us rather about Zen, Yoga. That is the only possible future for contemplative prayer!" The other half was no more unanimous in their protest: "The Bible! Now, what has the Bible to do with the Catholicism in which we were all born and educated? Is it a Catholic book? Is it not rather the very book from which the Protestants have drawn all their heresies? And what could we do with a book filled with dirty stories, like that of the daughters of Lot? To think of good nuns meditating on this stuff!"

It must be said that such misunderstandings of the council have been only too much encouraged by those Catholic scholars who have seen in it nothing more than an authorization to adopt the most unorthodox interpretations of the Bible ever launched by Protestant critiques. I remember a lecture of the Anglican Bishop Robinson, given in Washington a few years before he died, on the Jewish Palestinian background of the Fourth Gospel, and therefore its certain antiquity. Immediately after he had finished speaking, it was an almost unanimous protest: "Did not Bultmann, long ago, establish the very late date of this gospel, its evident dependence upon Greek, and not at all traditional Jewish tradition?. . ." A few moments later, the good Englishman said to me: "Is it possible, indeed, that the Catholic Church might become the funeral home of Protestant theories now discarded, for purely critical motives, by all the best Protestant scholars themselves?. . ."

The fact is that among the freest, the most independant Protestant scholars in the last quarter of a century, simple honesty and competence have brought about a rediscovery of everything that could be described as "Catholic," already present in the most primitive trends of the New Testament literature, to say nothing of what could be said of the sacramental atmosphere of the Word of God in the Old!

If all the treasures of the biblical teaching and its living transmission and assimilation by the liturgical tradition of the Catholic Church were not now promptly made available to the average Catholic, then there would be no future for Catholic spirituality, because the Catholic Church would have practically renounced to fulfill its mission in our times, times in which it is needed more than ever if men are not to die of spiritual inanition. In order to avoid such a failure, we shall have — at last! — to go beyond what Cardinal Ratzinger not long ago called "the council of the journalists," and not stop any longer at the council of the "experts" who are only interested in imposing, instead of the views of the Church, their own pet theories. We shall have to reach (if it is not too late) that council of the bishops, which has ever been the only real one, but one so little divulged by the famous "media," which once more appear as instruments of disinformation rather than information!

I would willingly conclude upon these words, were it not of capital importance, after what has just been said, to formulate, at least, some of the special problems posed to any application of Christian spirituality to the conditions of the present time.

I see three main problems before us, all of which engage not only our existence as Christians, but also as of men having to live in a world which is not of their choice, which we certainly have some power and some duty to influence, but no way to constrain to make its own our ideal.

The first concerns what I will call the vocation of the laity in its relation to clerical or religious vocations, "religious" in the technical sense of the term; the second, problems of what has been called the liberation of women; and the third, the development of technology to be expected in the coming years.

In modern times, and beginning only in the second half of the Middle Ages, it has become customary simply to reserve the term "vocation" for the different forms of religious celibacy, either clerical or "religious," the call to married life being either ignored or carefully distinguished from "vocation" in a Christian sense. This was not the case in Christian antiquity. The first theological theorician of the monastic life, St. Gregory Nazianzen, in his great poem on *Arétè*, a Greek word generally translated by "virtue" — but which Werner Jaeger, in his great book, *Paideia*, has taught us to translate rather as "the life worth living" — sees things in a completely different perspective. For him, it is a question of two vocations much more complementary than mutually opposed. The monastic vocation insists on the necessity of the Cross for the full development of divine love in man. Christian marriage, for its own part, shows the fecundity, both natural and supernatural, of that love communicated to all men.

It is no less remarkable that we have many sayings of the fathers of the desert themselves insisting that "the perfect monk" may well be a man or a woman who is not technically a monk at all, but who has reached the perfection of charity in any way of life. At the Council of Nicea, it seems that it was a monk no less austere than Paphnutius who prevented the Fathers of the Council to impose celibacy on all the clergy at that time, because, he said, the pagans could be led thus to believe that Christian marriage itself was not holy.

No less important the fact that a pope, Nicholas I, prescribed to King Boris of Bulgaria that Christian marriage should be celebrated with the blessing of the priest applied to the mutual consent of the bride and the bridegroom, together with their solemn "*velatio* and *coronatio.*" This ritual, still observed by all the Orthodox Christians, and which was kept until recently by many very old Catholic rituals of the West, unfortunately has been disused everywhere that the new revised Roman ritual has been introduced. The more traditional ones supposed that every Christian marriage should be seen as an anticipation of the eschatological union of Christ with the Church. For our times, total separation of what has come to be called simply "sex" from any kind of faithful love is looked on as normal. Only the traditional vision of marriage can remedy such a fall of human sexuality below the level of even the normal animal one: certainly one of the most disgusting perversions of modern men and women!

Secondly, any effective liberation of women in the Church will fail if it tries to make of women pseudo-men. Such would be the case if women were allowed to exercise those functions which have always been acknowledged as proper to the males: the priesthood, as it appears in both the New and Old Testaments. Far from being the result of an influence of the ancient mentality (in biblical times there were, in all other religions, as many priestesses as priests), this was a distinctively biblical feature. And far from implying any inferiority of women, it emphasized their equality with men in the difference itself. For all of Christian antiquity explicitly saw in the consecration of virgins an anticipation in them of the glory of the Church of the last times, as in the widows or deaconesses devoted to all the motherly functions of charity in the Church. These "orders" were complementary to the masculine ones. These latter were only transmitters of the divine grace, the feminine ones constituted an anticipation of all the possible effects of that grace in redeemed humanity. Thus the Blessed Virgin Mary, as the perfect virgin and the perfect mother, was explicitly declared superior to the Apostles themselves, without needing their particular form of consecration.

Technology will pose a much more difficult problem for Christians in the coming years, especially in the field of spirituality. It was a basic principle of ancient monasticism that work, material work, to earn one's life in the sweat of one's brow, was the most elementary form of asceticism, without which all others would be unrealistic. Together with this ascetic aspect of work, Benedictine monasticism, especially, developed a more positive one: the idea that man's work is for perfecting the material creation, to humanize it in the best possible meaning, by becoming an extension of worship into the most utilitarian occupations of human life. From these two elements, a whole spirituality of work should evolve.

However, the developments of contemporary technology are creating, undoubtedly, a growing ambiguity. First, there is the terrific growth of pollution (in a few years, maybe, all the seas of the world will have become a threat for all forms of life, instead of its original place, and, already, something of that is seen as a near threat for the atmosphere of the globe itself); other developments more directly lethal for mankind are even more irreconcilable with such a Christianization of work. On this last point, something like the atomic bomb is not perhaps even the worst of these: more insidious, but even more immediately antihuman, is the tendency, more and more apparent, to make man himself just a piece of some monstrous engine, ever growing with less and less human justification; the next idol(!) which could prove a juggernaut, finally crushing man under its weight rather than serving him.

Here we can only say that an intense effort of reflection will have to be, and is already, one of the main duties of man, especially of Christian man. My last word is that we need an eschatological vision, probably one that is as far from the purely optimistic one tried by Teilhard de Chardin as from the utterly black one which appears at least as a temptation even to so deeply Christian a thinker like Jacques Ellul. But in this field it seems that nearly everything has yet to be done, while we can wait for it no longer lest it come too late.

Response to Louis Bouyer

by Georges Chantraine, S.J., Jesuit Faculty of Theology, Brussels

There is only one Spirit, the one who overshadowed Mary, who brought back to life Jesus the Son of God, and was given to the Church, the Body and Spouse of Christ. This Spirit, through Its gifts, raises up in the Church various missions for the sake of the world. All of these are exercised within the unique mission of the Incarnate Son of God and carry out that mission in such a way that Jesus Christ may today be present to man and recognizable to all those who do not close their eyes to his light.

The common defect of various spiritualities is not that they are diverse, but that they tend to forget this one unifying and sanctifying Spirit and the missions of Christians. This defect consists in withdrawing into an interior subjectivity without ecclesial or embodied dimension. In a recent colloquium on spirituality and the cinema held in Brussels, the participants agreed to separate all dogmatism and fundamentalism from spirituality, in order to make spirituality consist in an interiority encompassed by silence, with a consciousness subject to no other requirement than self-awareness. This consciousness of self would, then, offer the key to all possible revelation. The Sacred Scriptures are to be demythologized for the sake of allowing consciousness to see by its own light, which is regarded as its truth.

Under such a scheme, the traditional interpretation of Sacred Scripture is unthinkable and impractical,* for the Spirit is indeed present in the letter, as it is in history, and God who transfigured the entire history of the Old Covenant also transforms our Spirits in him whom he manifests as the Lord of History. Such a unity of the history of man and of the eternal present of God, of the letter and of the Spirit, is foreign to conscious-

---

*For this traditional interpretation does not describe the itinerary of consciousness, but, so far as is possible, it comprehends the history of the Spirit with the Son, sent by the Father.

ness in its search after interiority, which characterizes that which we have here called "spirituality."

It is appropriate to note here the objective connection between Christian forms of spirituality and non-Christian forms, whether they belong to the Orient or to the post-Christian West. To be sure, the intention of those who promote and practice Christian forms of spirituality are within the bounds of revelation and the teaching of the Church. However, because they center on subjective consciousness, they concentrate on what is purely human rather than on consciousness as transformed by the Spirit of Christ. Consciousness is the locus where the human spirit reveals both itself and its depths in the absolute. For this reason, some centers of spirituality, retreat houses, find it easy to adapt Christian spirituality to forms that draw persons into their inner consciousness, forms like Zen, Buddhism, Yoga, and Transcendental Meditation. In the West, these are almost always transposed into a Nietzschean mode of human self-mastery as a means of going beyond oneself.

The movement of the human spirit upon itself in consciousness is not in itself wrong. It can find its fullness in docility to the Holy Spirit. This inner docility leads to taking on the identity of Christ. The Holy Spirit leads our spirit in Christ to say, "Abba," "Father," and to know God such as he is in himself: Father, Son, Spirit. This experiential knowledge comes into play above all in liturgical celebration, particularly in the eucharistic celebration. It is there that the Church brings into play the spiritual understanding of the Scriptures. There the Church proclaims (through the mouth of each of the faithful who says "I believe") the Credo which sums up the Apostolic Kerygma and the dogmatic content of the Holy Scriptures. There all the adopted sons finally dare to say in the Spirit, "Our Father." Spiritual understanding of the Scriptures, Credo, Our Father, and sacrament are united in the eucharistic celebration and produce experiential knowledge (*connaissance*) of God, which is the Christian faith. It is not faith knowledge if these four elements are not united. And since it is a matter of celebration, therefore of an action, it is understood that the faithful ought to act conformably to their faith not only at the moment of the celebration but throughout the length of their lives, which ought to be one long celebration. Liturgical time makes actual this conformation of human duration to time and to the life of the risen Christ.

Several consequences follow from what has been said:

1. Catechesis finds its form in the liturgy; it rests on the Credo, the "Our Father" as the form of prayer, the sacraments and action in the Spirit according to the law of Christ. If the bond of these elements were to be loosened, catechesis would no longer belong to the liturgy but would become exterior to it; it would no longer prepare for it, and thus no longer lead the faithful to experiential knowledge of God, but at best to a spirituality tinged with Christianity.

2. The object of theology in each epoch is to lead all human knowledge and all men to that experiential knowledge which is brought about by the celebration of the liturgy. In order to do that, theology remains inside that celebration and receives as its proper light the spiritual understanding of the Scriptures which is given to the Spouse of Christ by the Spirit and of which the hierarchical Church is the sole authentic interpreter. Therein lies the liberty of the theologian.

3. In order to remain Christian, the liturgy reads the Holy Scripture from both Testaments — and from no other sources — according to spiritual understanding, and not according to the results of scientific exegesis. It organizes itself according to the faith confessed in the Creed, and, when such is required, proclaims the Apostles' Creed or the Nicene Creed — and not private compositions. The liturgy is an act of prayer offered to the glory of God, not a course, a conference, or a reunion of Christian sympathizers or affiliates. Finally, it is the celebration of God the Creator and Redeemer. It is the praise, the adoration, and the service in view of which God created man, which the only Incarnate Son rendered by his loving obedience even to the death on the Cross, which the Church, united with the Son through the Spirit, is capable of rendering in its turn. This idea of celebration extends itself almost limitlessly, so rich is its content. We sketch this out in three directions.

● Man is loved for his own sake and, correlatively, God has no other reason to create than for himself (God), out of the love with which God loves himself, or, we could say, his glory. The adoration by the Creature is consequently penetrated by gratitude, by thanksgiving; and, reciprocally, the thanksgiving is penetrated by adoration, as the Apocalypse shows. Adoration is not the silent groveling of him who annihilates himself before God who is, but a joyous exclamation, the ever-new canticle (Holy, Holy, Holy) of the Son, who acknowledges every obligation to the Father who has given all, because in himself he is. Being is consequently a gift, and it is distinct from him (God) who is. It is the gift through which that which is not participates in being and is deserving of God himself. Adoration filially acknowledged by the Christian thus supposes ontological difference and the analogy of being: the resemblance of the creature within an always-greater dissimilitude. Liturgical celebration thus presupposes the metaphysics of being, and the Christian is here the guardian of being.

● The entire world was created for man in view of the end for which he was made, that is to say, the praise, adoration, and service of God. The liturgy, then, is neither the sign of man's transcendence of the world nor the means of realizing it but a sign and a means of the celebration of God by man. Similarly, it is sacramentally structured, and this sacramental structure became effective thanks to the accomplishment, by the Son-made-man, of the loving plan of his Father. The liturgy does more consequently than save the environment; it causes the created world to participate in the glorification of God. That supposes two things: First, a cosmology which would not be exclusively scientific but also theological and therefore also philosophical; and second, a cosmic liturgy, that is to say, a liturgy that would cause man to enter into a time and space received from God in the interior of the Church which transfigures the rites.

● The creature loved for itself is man and woman. Being-as-gift and ontological difference are felt and experienced by man and woman in their sexual difference. And this difference finds its meaning and truth only in the spousal relation between Christ and the Church. Once Christ rose from the dead, it is impossible to think of the difference between man and woman other than in terms of that relationship of Christ and the Church—unless one were to return to myth and, in a post-Christian world which does not acknowledge the Creator and the finitude of the creature, one were to annul the difference between man and woman. In such a world, the one would *be* the other and liturgical celebration would be nonsense. Celebration thus causes man and woman to play out their responsibility as redeemed creatures according to their proper differences.

This is manifested particularly in the eucharistic celebration. Christ-the-Husband there offers himself up to his Father for the salvation of the world and unites himself with his Church, which, as wife, is feminine. The minister who offers the Eucharist represents the Christ who has the absolute initiative of the offering as man as man (and this is why Christ is himself a man). United to her spouse, the Church offers herself in the offering. This assertion (which the majority of Protestants reject) expresses the feminine capacity of the Church which, on the basis of the created difference between man and woman, gives an infinite fecundity to the Church of Christ through the power of the Spirit. In the years to come, the test of a true eucharistic celebration in the Catholic Church will be the dialogue between the masculine priest, representing Christ-the-Husband, and the assembly of the faithful, representing the Church-as-wife. When such a dialogue ceases, the eucharistic celebration ceases; and the difference between man and woman being no longer celebrated, humanity would no longer have grounds for recognizing God as Creator.

— Translated by John Lyon

The Meaning of Christian Culture: A Historical View

Glenn W. Olsen, University of Utah

In his *Attack Upon "Christendom,"* Søren Kierkegaard claimed that there could not be a Christian culture, only Christians. As he wrote elsewhere about the time the *Attack* was published: "A Christian world is nonsense."[1] Only the individual could receive grace and be justified by faith: there was no meaning in speaking of a culture as living by faith, or making some kind of collective assent to Christian revelation.[2] In such a claim Kierkegaard, if nothing else, understood a certain internal logic of especially Lutheran Protestantism, and of an ecclesiology which refuses to identify the Church with any visible expression, let alone to see it as intended to embrace all mankind in the course of history.[3] In a radical way, for him Christianity was about the individual standing before God. His thought was very far from, and in fact was an attack on, the historical tendency of Catholic Christianity at least partially to merge the Church with the world, so that ecclesiology itself, at one level, becomes virtually the same as consideration of man's social nature, of both Christendom and of the earthly City, insofar as these are seen as the place of the birth of the *eschaton.*

Today in enlightened circles we are all, seemingly, Protestants, and Kierkegaard seems prophetic. On every side we see the disintegration of almost all the intentionally culture-building forms of Christianity in Europe and America, and I suspect that there is a deep prejudice at work that holds that wherever Christianity apparently still flourishes in some form of public expression, perhaps in the new fundamentalism wherever it is found or in the growing churches of the Third World, this is only possible because these peoples are simple and unenlightened.[4] When they "grow up" and are capable of a mature Christianity, this prejudice assumes, they will desire to live in a neutral or secular culture, where all points of view can happily coexist because no religion is culturally formative. That is, they will have become Americans, and understand the wisdom of the separation of Church and state, and the healthiness of religious competition and pluralism at the cultural level. No one will dream of "capturing a culture," and religion, as the mainline Protestant churches and progressive Catholicism have already found, will play its proper societal role of defending the defenseless in society and urging those forms of altruism, law, and personal behavior which advance the natural goods of society on which all men of good will, irrespective of religion or the lack thereof, can agree. That is, Christianity will be reduced to a kind of Augustinian God, and the soul and Christian culture will indeed have no meaning. Kierkegaard will have been proven right, and only the individual will be seen as worthy of the name Christian.

Such views, in spite of their popularity, present great problems for historical understanding. These have in recent years sometimes centered on the question of secularization, on whether we live, as I have already suggested, in a culture in which religion is being marginalized, or whether we are rather experiencing one of those continuing permutations in which traditional forms of religion find new modes of expression in a changing culture. Even conservative writers like Richard John Neuhaus have suggested that our culture is not becoming less religious, but by any statistical measure remains religious. Hence he can point to the increasing, rather than decreasing, role of Catholicism in American life, of the influence, for instance, of the American bishops on a wide range of issues from peace to the economy. As the title of his latest book witnesses, he can even suggest that this may be the Catholic moment.[5] Here the issues are rooted in definition, and often center around how meaningful it is to measure religiosity by old-fashioned standards such as Mass attendance and adherence to doctrinal and moral positions, in comparison — the Gallup-Castelli report is an example here[6] — with accepting new self-definitions of Christianity in which the researcher is sensitive to respondents' views of themselves and of their relation to Christianity. If the researcher is willing to accept as Catholic modes of practice and belief that in an earlier generation would have been considered marginally or incompletely Catholic, then it would seem to me that those who insist that deep secularization is not taking place have really altered what is being measured and, as they say, win this argument by definition.

The question of secularization is simply the question of Christian culture in one of its most contemporary forms, and thus, to be understood adequately, must be placed in long historical perspective. Because the very term "Christian culture" implies a relation between grace and nature, I will attempt an overview at once historical and theological. My argument is that in fact it would be difficult to come up with a rendition of the problem less faithful to Christianity than that of Kierkegaard. I say this in spite of my sympathy for the reasons behind his attack on Christendom as he understood and experienced it. My argument is implicitly an attack on much else, on the very way that the place of Christianity in American society has been conceived in most enlightened thought. I am going to take a radical position, which will underline the imperfection of such documents as the First Amendment, and which will take very seriously the implications for the study of Christian culture of Cardinal Jean Daniélou's insistence that religion in the first instance belongs to the order of nature, and of Cardinal Henri de Lubac's and — by analogy to the doctrine of baptism by intention, I will call him Cardinal — Hans Urs von Balthasar's rethinking in the middle of the present century of the relation of nature to grace.[7]

The towering problem that confronts the historian, if we abandon the notion of Christian culture, is what to make of most of the history of the world. To me it is clear that, at least until the past few centuries, and even here only in the degree that enlightenment ideas have spread through the world from the West, almost all the cultures of the world may be seen as embodied religions. We do not have to focus on the "beginnings," on the way in which in Mesopotamia land ownership was determined by the idea that God through temple and priesthood was the ultimate owner of property, or on the way that in Egypt the concept of *maat* (truth, justice, rightness) gave to each a strong sense of where they belonged in the order of being. We may turn to the civic ritual of Renaissance Florence or Venice, in which the liturgical cycle of the Church still had a large role in the rhythms of life, or to the attempt to maintain Islamic banking in our own day. Robert Darnton concluded a meditation on the French Revolution: "It may not have succeeded any better than Christianity christianized, but it remodeled enough of the social landscape to alter the course of history."[8] There are no definitive and irreversible victories in history, no permanent "christianizations," but there are relative and momentary partial successes, "remodelings of the social landscape," and this is truer for Christianity than it is for mirror reflections or alter egos like the secularized passion for equality of the Revolution. Only on a large scale in the West and the West's imitators, do we seem to find, in the past few centuries, a concerted attempt to diminish or remove religion from

100

the center of life — again the French Revolution is an example of an attack on religion, an attempt to drive it from the center, which was arguably itself simultaneously a new "irreligious" religion which drained most of the transcendent from traditional religion while retaining the notion of virtue. In this perspective it is the recent West that has embarked on the perilous attempt to discover whether culture can be coherent without a formative religion. The enlargement of the sphere of the private in the past few centuries against common belief and ways of life, an enlargement so valued in a culture as our own under the heading of freedom but often not expressing the retreat of the state itself so much as the retreat of intermediary institutions between the state and the individual, carries on the obverse of its coin the disintegration of the ties that bind. Such disintegration provokes its own reactions, perhaps the attempt to shore up the family or the neighborhood or to find some public philosophy, at least a least common denominator, but doubt as to whether such will succeed is reasonable.[9]

Let me review, for the Christian West, how we have come to this pass. As Robin Lane Fox has again shown us, it was not inevitable that Christanity should become the official religion of the Roman Empire, but given the importance of religion in ancient life, it was not at all surprising that following the conversion of Constantine the public cult should have been replaced with the new public cult of the Christians.[10] Emperors who felt themselves responsible before God that their subjects believe and live by what truth was available, were at most intensifying the classical conception of the state as found already in writers as different as Plato and Aristotle, namely that the end of civic life was to make people as good as they reasonably could be made. All life was educative, and in this education law had a role to play. Because the truth was one, all men reasonably could be asked to follow what seemed the fullest forms of truth, and *ipso facto* the truest religion. Although those who knew the Roman law or had read *Antigone* or Cicero's *De republica* knew that the individual had rights against the state, little thought had been given to the exact nature of what, more than a millennium and a half later, John Paul II would see as the inviolable center of the person, this for the obvious reason that the individual was almost always defined in a social context, so that the very notion of a distinct personhood was still vague.[11] Until past the time of Leo XIII, the central question in Catholic thought was the rights of the truth, rather than the rights of the individual. Moreover, because there was no clear line between the life of the individual and the life of society, it was assumed that anything that was true would permeate all life and express itself in social cultural forms. Any religion which carried with it the claim to be true would inevitably embody itself in the lives of its adherents, even the indifferent and morally mediocre among them, who in manifold ways would wish to share what seemed true in their public lives also, and in the institutions of their culture.

Such an instinct could only be reinforced by the inability clearly to distinguish between grace and nature, as the high Scholastic terminology later would have it. Although the first two chapters of Romans show Paul's familiarity with the Stoic conception of nature, of a natural moral and physical order which can be understood by reason, he with Christians for more than a thousand years habitually spoke as a Christian man, that is, from the perspective of grace and revelation. Although no more unaware of a natural level of secondary causation with its own cause-effect relationships than Augustine, and heir to the distinction already found in Thucydides and Hippocrates between a natural order of human life with its own laws and a higher order directly subject to the divinity and impenetrable by human beings, Paul could not clearly put the question, the Scholastic question, of what man could know for sure without revelation, without a message from the realm of primary causation.[12] Therefore consciences could only sporadically be troubled by one of our questions, namely what place to find in a religious empire for those who followed another religion, or none at all. The need to bring as many to the truth as possible, the sense that one would eventually have to answer to God for all those who did not find their way, already very strong in Constantine, overrode such considerations, or rather made it difficult to appreciate them.

Yet, from the first, Christians were probing here. Athanasius, writing in the years immediately preceding the declaration of Christianity as the official religion of the Empire and standing in the tradition of the early Greek Fathers, with their strong emphasis on free will and their confidence that "the truth is not preached with swords or with darts, nor by means of soldiers; but by persuasion and counsel," does not yet have the position of Ambrose or Augustine.[13] Thus in the same *History of the Arians* from which I have yet quoted, he could reject the use of force in matters of religion: ". . . what persuasion is there where fear of the Emperor prevails? or what counsel is there, when he who withstands them

— the reference of course is to Athanasius himself *contra mundum* — receives at last banishment and death?"[14] Even in the fourth century, it was easier to see the problem of the unconvinced individual in a society tending to one point of view if one was among the dissenters than if one agreed with the public orthodoxy, in this case Arianism. Thus Athanasius could cast about for a boundary between Church and state, anticipating Gelasius a long century later by warning the emperor "against infringing ecclesiastical order, and mingling Roman sovereignty with the constitution of the Church."[15] There had to be "rights from the bottom," both of the individual and of institutions like the Church: Athanasius continues by recording Bishop Hosius' letter to Emperor Constantius, "Neither therefore is it permitted unto us to exercise an earthly rule, nor have you, Sire, any authority to burn incense."[16] Thus was laid down a boundary to be the subject of struggle and contention for the rest of Christian history.

After the declaration of Christianity as the official religion of the Roman Empire, a new situation presented itself with new problems, and this is clearly evident in the writings of Ambrose and Augustine. Ambrose, who had become bishop six years before the fateful edict of February 28, 380, which declared that all the subjects of Gratian and Theodosius were to practice "that religion which the divine Peter the Apostle transmitted to the Romans," was a man by nature Roman and by grace Christian, and indeed was one of the first to attempt the explication of the difference between these two inheritances.[17] An acute criticism of Christianity had been made two centuries earlier by the pagan critic Celsus, who, having met Christians who refused to serve in the army, leveled against Christianity the charge, to be repeated in various forms by Machiavelli, Gibbon, and Nietzsche, that Christians made poor citizens. The command to turn the other cheek was hardly the instruction soldiers needed, and the logic of Christianity was that to the extent it spread and was seriously practiced it undermined what a later age would call the order of nature, in this case the right of the state to defend itself. Origen, himself a pacifist, was hardly the man convincingly to answer such criticism, and when in his famous *Against Celsus* (A.D. 249) he came to this question he could only lamely respond that if all the Romans became Christians, that is, would no longer fight, then God would fight for them.[18] This certainly was no adequate response to Celsus' criticism, which, if I may use words he could not have, showed that by asking of man behavior that went beyond reason, Christianity tended to undermine nature. Again, to use the vocabulary of a later time, Celsus was asking by what right a counsel of grace, coming from revelation, could violate the order of nature, in this case prohibiting the right to self-defense which, as the Stoics had shown, is discoverable by unaided reason. I still half-remember the request put by Hans Jonas when, at another colloquium sponsored by *Communio* that has turned out to be one of the two times Hans Urs von Balthasar visited the United States, Jonas asked that Christian thinkers remember justice and its rights: that is, Jonas perceived a persistent tendency in Christian thought, I suppose in Balthasar's thought, when it was taken seriously, so to stress grace and revelation that the rights of nature were overturned. In an era when even Catholic thinkers are inclined to say that general pacifism is a moral tradition as respectable as the just-war tradition, Celsus' criticism and Jonas's request retain their point.

So far as I know, the first Christian with the intellectual resources to deal with the problem Celsus had raised was Ambrose, and for this he had been prepared by the synthesis in his own life of a Roman upbringing and patriotism with the duties of a Christian bishop. Seizing on the Stoic distinction between *officium medium* and *officium perfectum*, Ambrose forged an early form of the medieval and Tridentine distinction between an order of justice, which all must follow, and an order of perfection, which those who wish to go beyond what is required to what most closely imitates God, must follow.[19] As many writers, Heinz Schürmann among them, have shown, such a distinction is arguably present in the New Testament text, most apparently in the words of Jesus to the Rich Young Man in Matthew 19:21, "If you would be perfect. . . ."[20] For Ambrose and many others after him, the distinction implicitly was between one order of knowledge, open to unaided reason, in which, for instance, the relative right to property could be justified, and another order, given as part of the Christian revelation, in which Christians were asked or counseled to go beyond the obligations laid on them by reason to the more perfect things, centering in charity, which asked of them more than justice, for instance, the call to the abandonment of all property.[21] In later writers like John Cassian, such a distinction could be used to divide the laity from the monks: the former, with all men, were obliged to all the teachings of reason — the Stoic natural law or the Ten Commandments — while the monks were those determined to respond with a more perfect charity which, while not violating justice, gave more than to which in strict justice they were obliged.[22]

The point here, as perfected by Thomas Aquinas and others, was that no one could follow the order of charity, grace, faith, or revelation in such a way as to destroy the lower order of justice, nature, and reason.[23] Applied to Celsus' objection, this meant that something perceived as following from Christ's commands, such as the abandonment of all arms, is *prima facie* a misreading of Christianity, because it makes impossible one of the rights open to all men in the order of nature, namely the right of self-defense. The order of charity or grace can only be followed in such a way that one's own rights are sacrificed, not those of others, for no man can sacrifice the rights of another. This is for the simple reason that the order of nature, as an order discoverable by reason, must be followed by all, while the order of grace, as something dependent on faith and revelation, is by definition only given to those living the life of grace in faith. Because both orders find their source in God, it is not possible that the higher order can be followed in a way that destroys or harms the latter.

Implicit in such a distinction was a way of relating grace, nature, and culture, but here culture was revealed in its complexity as sometimes an embodiment of natural religion, sometimes of revealed religion, and sometimes of both, or indeed of religions which possessed natural and supernatural aspects.[24] The question posed by the conversion of the Roman Empire to Christianity was whether and in what manner culture could be shaped by both forms of religion. Ambrose himself had few reservations about asking his own congregation to adopt a form of life which we might call countercultural, for he persistently intervened in Milanese life in such a way as to separate Christians from common habits of life.[25] In a well-known confrontation, he enforced the teachings of nature by excommunicating Theodosius for an action not just offensive to Christians, but in violation of the dictates of reason, against justice.[26] His expectations of the Church, however, went far beyond enforcing the teachings of justice among active Christians, for, with a line of thinkers running back to Justin Martyr and Clement of Alexandria, and represented in his own age by the Cappadocian Fathers, he dreamt of a coming together of the mission of Christianity with the mission of Rome, that is, he dreamt of a Christian Roman culture. He of course never quite said this, but this enterprise seems rooted in the assumption that now that all are (nominally) Christian, there is no grave violence done to conscience

105

in ordering public life by Christian principles, that is, in intruding into social life practices sanctioned by grace rather than nature. The Sabbath can be kept by all.[27]

Yet whereas, in the case of Theodosius, the act to be condemned was clearly one that all men, Christian or not, should condemn, Ambrose recognized that, whatever the officially promulgated law, not all in fact were Christian, nor had given their consent to some Christian culture. Thus, in his famous response to Symmachus — the still-pagan prefect of Rome who in 384 asked of the emperors and Christians that those who still believed in the old gods be allowed the public practice and symbols of their religion, specifically the restoration of the Altar of Victory in the Roman Senate house — Ambrose, if I may put it in this manner, moved halfway from Athanasius to the views of the elder Augustine. Ambrose saw his great opponent as both noble in his opposition to the new Christian order, and as the spokesman for truths that had already been known in the "natural" religion of the Romans. Ambrose could take the "Athanasian" position that against such an opponent argument, not force, was appropriate.[28] But he anticipated Augustine in seeing that Symmachus's argument for toleration — that is, for the pagans being allowed to keep the old ways within the new Christian order — was not completely persuasive. Symmachus had said that since the sky is common to all, all "learned theory," that is, opinion about the gods, should be tolerated as a "matter of discussion for men of leisure."[29]

Here we have the most difficult questions of Christian culture posed. Ambrose asked why, if Christianity contains more truth than paganism, Symmachus and his fellows should be ashamed, in the old age of paganism, to pass to something fuller. He acknowledged that the pagans had seen many things truly, and wished them to complete the insights they already had. Should they not, this became a problem of conscience for Ambrose, who as a Christian bishop was responsible for his own people's finding the kingdom of God, and it seemed clear to Ambrose, who was not above the fourth-century equivalent of picketing pornography, that it was more likely that his congregation would find the kingdom if it lived in a cultural context that represented and reinforced Christian teaching than if it did not. To allow the public practice of paganism was to endanger souls. Thus we have various rights of conscience pitted against one another. On the one hand — and Ambrose did finally decide for argument in such matters — it seemed meaningless to force convinced pagans not to practice their paganism. But this did not mean that truth had no rights, and that at the cultural level everything should not be done to make what the Jesuits would later call the Christianity of the average mediocre man easy by situating him in a culture that fostered rather than attacked his Christianity.

In some ways Ambrose's solution — not unlike the much later Spanish solution after Spain's failure to achieve religious unity by the radical measure of exclusion of unbelievers — was a compromise. The Altar of Victory, the symbol of public commitment to paganism, would have to go, but the pagans could stay. May we say that this was an attempt to have a Christian culture — that is, to live out the Christian faith in every area of life—while respecting the consciences of those who lacked faith? Yes and no. Both sides failed to get something essential. Ambrose obtained a substantial public expression of Christianity, and some acknowledgment of the implicit higher importance of the right to live the truth, natural and revealed, out in one's total life at the expense of those who in good conscience could not see this truth as higher. I suppose he would have to say that he respected the rights of the insufficiently formed conscience and of unbelief enough not to use force against them, but was not against a more psychological form of force or disability in which the pagans, while tolerated in the most obvious sense of that word, had lost their public control over society. The pagans, on their side, could continue their existence indefinitely, but in a form analogous to the place of minorities in a later period, who could practice their religion but not prosyletize or undermine established religion. They no longer could fulfill one of man's most natural instincts, to express the truth as it is seen at every level of social life.

Probably for much modern taste Ambrose goes too far. I want to underline two points here. The first is something obvious but continually forgotten, namely that every historical resolution of such questions is both unsatisfactory and impermanent. Grace is too mysterious and life too messy for there ever to be anything like Plato's *Republic*. The error of every form of integralism, noble as the desire for an integrated earthly life is, is the belief that time can be stopped. My second point is that we have a real either/or situation here, not unlike the competition between the desires for liberty and equality in societies like our own. All the democratic rhetoric starting with Pericles's funeral oration taken into consideration, logic suggests that equality and liberty always proceed in history to each other's disadvantage. In a similar manner, at the cultural level there always is a conflict between the rights of those who have and those who have not accepted either the teachings of the moral law or of the Church. A full Christian life is one lived out in one's art, one's politics, the form one's city takes, and any check placed on public expression of one's Christianity is an attack on the possibility of living an integrated life, an attempt to disallow Christian maturation. On the other hand, an individual conscience which cannot make the assent of faith or perhaps even see the goods of natural reason, if forced by social context to be at least partially quiet about what is most dear, similarly receives a check on the inviolable center of the person. So far as I can see, in history these public and private claims always are in tension with one another, and no better than an integralism which stands on the rights of the public order is a pluralism which makes impossible full Christian maturity and expression by taking away some of the stage on which man was meant to live. Indeed, for those who can see by taking off their American and modern blinders, pluralism, in the form we find it in a society like our own, makes it unlikely that the average person will hear or experience anything like the fullness of truth once in a lifetime. Although all our sensibilities are now on the side of the individual and moral and religious pluralism, to take this side, either on the issues of nature or grace, against the claims of a culturally formative truth is as incomplete a response to the question of human dignity as an earlier integralism. In laying stress on either the culturally formative mission of Christianity, its incarnationalism, or on the integrity of the individual, something is going to be sacrificed, just as surely as insisting, against all observation, that people are by nature equal is going, in the name of equality, to do violence, to be unjust, to all the distinctions between people found already in the order of nature.

It would be nice here to pass over Augustine, for if Ambrose already makes most of us uneasy, what are we to say of the bishop of Hippo, who on the basis of a less optimistic reading of human nature than Ambrose, ultimately came to justify not just psychological pressure against the mis- or underinformed, but force? It would be easy to dismiss him, as is often done, as an aberration, as someone who, at least on this point, did not understand Christian charity and the rights of conscience, but if we dismiss him we are refusing fully to look at the problem of Christian culture. In the interest of brevity, let me restrict myself to *Letter 185*, "On the Treatment of Donatists," written in 418 to Boniface, Count of Africa, the governor and general in charge of dealing with the Donatist problem in Africa and a devout Christian.[30] The Donatists had a view of free will which Augustine associated with that of the Pelagians, and which sounds very much like a common view of our own day. In an ironical way, Augustine was right to associate the Donatists and the Pelagians, for on free will he was the innovator. That is, the views of the early Greek Fathers, of Athanasius, and of the Pelagians and Donatists were close to one another, traditional in comparison to the views of Augustine the innovator, from whose perspective all these other positions came to appear primitive, simplistic, naïve, and unjustifiedly optimistic in their idea of what is involved in the problem of human freedom. The reason why an Athanasius appears so attractive to so many of us is that we have lost a sense of the complexity of the problem of human freedom, and have an unexamined, overly rational, and optimistic view of human nature like that of the early Greek Fathers.[31]

In the view of the Donatists, because men are free to choose, "a policy which forced this choice was plainly irreligious."[32] For Augustine, like Newman in the *Grammar of Assent* after him, such a view was one of those terrible simplifications—the kind which John Stuart Mill could hardly write a sentence without committing — which befuddle human discourse. In Peter Brown's description: "The final, individual act of choice must be spontaneous; but this act of choice could be prepared by a long process, which men did not necessarily choose for themselves, but which was often imposed on them, against their will, by God."[33] Augustine had a growing sense that man does not stand undetermined in his choices: environment has a great role to play. Without denying that man does have a free will, Augustine wished to underline the myriad ways in which what we choose is determined by factors outside us, in his case— and that of Newman — for instance, his mother. We are predisposed to the choices we make by many factors, some of which we are conscious of and some of which we are not, but in no case do we make an "absolutely free" choice, if by that we mean a choice that can be freed from our own history and context. One of the great difficulties a modern has in appreciating Augustine here is that so many of us habitually think of freedom as absolute.

Beginning with an idea of freedom not very different from earlier writers, Augustine came to appreciate the way in which Judaism already had dealt with the problem of "Jewish culture." The Law of Moses had never been followed by more than a minority, who had imposed the Law on the majority by force, thus more or less saving the majority from their own worst inclinations, polytheism for instance. While earlier Augustine had been inclined to see Christianity as a "spiritual" religion which did not need physical sanctions, a view that neatly flowed from a Neoplatonism which saw man as essentially the soul, as in a hundred ways in his maturity he came to reassess the place of *corpus*, matter, and time in human life, and haltingly to see that man is a soul united to a body, he also came to doubt that religion was essentially spiritual.[34] Man becomes what he becomes not just through argument, but through his bodily experience, and any religion which could not see this was not really speaking to man but to souls.

It seems clear to me that we are again living in a profoundly Platonic age: the devastation of the liturgy and the material in religion in the past twenty years, of those things which try to make the holy palpable, and the attack by moral theologians on traditional notions of what sexually one does with one's body, should be viewed in the setting of a re-Platonizing age in which man is conceived as essentially soul, rather than as soul expressed in body. John Paul II's lifework almost might be seen as an attack on this tendency in the name of an embodied Christianity.[35] Augustine for his part never fully relinquished his notion of spiritual religion, but he came more and more to believe that the spiritual few had responsibility for the indifferent many, and that there were cases in which the boundaries for all had to be drawn by force. Implicit in such an idea was the conviction that Origen's earlier suggestion that man might advance indefinitely by reason was wrong: history was likely to remain forever not a place of continuing progress, but of education and testing in which the ground base of a universally shared sin set a limit on how far man in society could advance. Likely the intellectually and morally indifferent would always dominate numerically, and law and force would be needed both to set tolerable limits and to encourage the many in the personal progress of which they were capable.

Such a view of what man is goes against most of our deepest instincts, but does have the merit of being honest. Augustine's argument in *Letter 185* is that the conversion of the emperor and then of the state to Christianity presented a new situation in which a Christian emperor now enacted laws against "wicked deeds" and "irreligion."[36] Most of us, while granting the right of the state and of law to work against the first form of impiety, would not want to allow the state to legislate on matters which are only seen as impious by the light of revelation, but Augustine could not see it this way because he — in spite of the vague location by Roman law of sovereignty in "the people" — had no democratic notion that political authority derives "from below."

Here we come to a most difficult, perhaps inexplicable, problem. Augustine, like a good Roman, saw social life, the public and the private, as one, and assumed that the emperor had the right to legislate on all matters regarding truth and justice, whether the principles used derived from what we would call grace or nature. Because most of us assume that authority derives from the people, we tend to assume that what at least the majority of the people cannot see as true ought not be legislated for all. The perspective of faith ought not be imposed on those lacking faith. Both views about the sources of authority, that of the Romans and that of the democrats, seem to me mythological, and I take it that this is one of the reasons why a long line of popes from Leo XIII to at least Pius XII refused, whatever their personal views, to place the Church on any side in the classic debate over the best form of government.[37] Some, arguably themselves sympathetic to monarchy, like Leo XIII himself, while pointing out that democratic theory was clearly flawed in deriving political authority from the people rather than God, nevertheless were content — rightly I think — to say that the Church and Christians could live and work within any system, as long as that system did not make freedom to do the will of God impossible for those who believed. But the question of mythology remained. While personally I think the classical arguments for monarchy — prudential judgments of time and place aside for the moment — are decisive, the proposal of romantic Catholicism that the most natural kind of authority is that which was already there when the royal family emerged out of the prehistorical mist, does not seem convincing.[38]

To say that the only legitimate authority is that which God ordains does not speak to the question of how, from a human point of view, this authority first became an authority. As Hans Blumenberg has insisted, what is prehistory for us was the seventeenth or forty-seventh generation for the people in prehistory, and there is no good reason to refer to, say, the myths of the Greeks as early myths, in the sense that they lie close to the beginnings of human history, when they are only myths earlier than our own.[39] On the other hand, the notion of a writer like John Rawls that

111

human authority should rest on the rights of the individual seems as mythical as the monarchists' story of the origins, or rather lack of origins, of monarchy. Rawls merely gives us a late and especially sophisticated view of human society resting — not to go back to Plato here — on the Lockean and Kantian hypothetical state of nature whch begins with the first state of man in which equality and individualism defined human relations and government appeared through a social contract. From this historian's point of view, both monarchy and democracy rest on an act of faith in one of these myths about origins, myths, especially the democratic one, at odds with what *is* known of human history, and strangely unaware of their genesis as responses to specific historical situations, in the case of the second, the need for a nonreligious source for authority after the wars of religion.[40] I cannot linger here, but I do not see that much more can be said than that every form of political life in part rests on assent from those governed, and in part on force imposed from the top.

This said, one can be more sympathetic toward Augustine's acceptance of an emperor who did acknowledge that his authority came from God. Although of course with time sophistication grew, I do not see that his situation was essentially different from those in much later states of Christian culture. His position does speak to the problem of whether, for any reason, the state may impose a point of view at least partly derived from revelaton, for he sees that the notion of legitimate authority is always in part going to be what a society defines it as. Because the first obligation of a state cannot be the enhancement of an absolute notion of the freedom of the individual — a definition of freedom in such a way is itself mythical, as we have seen — but is rather the guiding of its people to as much of the truth, from whatever source this truth derives, as it reasonably is capable of, there is no more against a public order founded on the truths of reason and revelation than one founded purely on the natural. As the medieval historian R. W. Southern notes in an extraordinarily perceptive discussion on the rights of the medieval state to foster Christianity, any constitutional order has a boundary beyond which it refuses to tolerate action, and an enshrined truth.[41]

Such a view, even if it can maintain itself against the more optimistic anthropology underlying Aquinas's fragmented political views, is certainly headed for deep resistance as we approach the American experience, where a writer like John Courtney Murray can be lionized by

Left and even sometimes Right together for the touching view that civic life is analogous to that of a great debating society.[42] In America, a country in which already in the seventeenth century a minuscule Catholic population prided itself in its ability to reverse traditional understandings of the relation of the state to individual conscience, what chance is there for an honesty that asks how long we will have to wait for the truth to emerge by free debate, and notices that the freer the debate the less anyone agrees on anything, that in fact the very existence of truth itself falls under question?[43] What hope is there for intelligent discussion of the problem of Christian culture in a country where virtually all right-thinking Catholics support some reading of the First Amendment, not, as I do, as a matter of prudence, but as genuinely an improvement over earlier attempts to find the proper place for revealed religion in society?

Let me elaborate on this last point as a way of sketching in conclusion a theory of the relation of nature, grace, and culture. My position flows from de Lubac's reconsideration of the relation of nature to grace. He, in attacking the manual tradition on this question, showed that Aquinas, "whenever he speaks of the nature of created spirit, never ascribes to it any other finality than a supernatural one."[44] We were made for God. Jean Daniélou made cultural application of this idea by arguing that man is already *by nature* religious.[45] If we had not become such secularized Calvinists — that, after all, is what a great slice of American history is all about — we could see that, without revelation at all, man is already by nature a creature who prays, worships, and acknowledges his dependence on some Other. In the order of nature therefore a good government has the responsibility not to remain indifferent on the question of religion but to foster this along with man's other natural orientations, to knowledge, beauty, and virtue, above all. It is as much — more — an obligation of a good state, all questions of revelation aside, to foster religion as it is to educate its people. We stand late in a process in which the function of the state has been largely reconceived as the pursuit of freedom rather than the pursuit of good — this of course was inevitable when we no longer could agree on the good — and thus we can hardly psychologically take seriously such a view. Pluralism in this sense makes the fullness of human life impossible, and none of us, myself included, can see this condition of life as likely to disappear. I stress that I speak here not necessarily of Raimundo Panikkar's or David Tracy's "pluralism," which while insisting that the point of view of all religions

113

is particular, partial, and in some degree incommensurate, does not deny a larger reality to which each religion stands as a hermeneutic moment, but "deep" pluralism in which, as I have just stated, imcompatible claims, for instance about the good, are made.[46]

Perhaps, to anticipate objections, a few words are in order about *Dignitatis Humanae*, the "Declaration on Religious Freedom" of Vatican II. It is clear, whatever those like Archbishop Lefebvre have said about this document's teaching new and erroneous things, that its explicit intention is to bring "forth new things that are in harmony with the things that are old (1)."[47] The primary new thing is "that in the course of time men have come more widely to recognize their dignity as persons, and the conviction has grown stronger that the person in society is to be kept free from all manner of coercion in matters religious (12)." Yet the document insists on balancing a number of competing interests, above all the freedom of the Church, the religious freedom of the individual, and the need of civil society for order and civility.[48] I think it fair to say that none of these rights are understood as absolute: each must be pursued in a manner that does not undermine the others. The qualifying phrase is common: "No one is to be forced to act in a manner contrary to his own beliefs, whether privately or publicly, whether alone or in association with others, within due limits (2)." Again: "Injury . . . is done to the human person . . . if the free exercise of religion is denied when the just requirements of public order do not so require (3)." Because of this — that is, because the articulation of religious freedom involves prudential judgments about the relation between various kinds of right — *Dignitatis Humanae* is necessarily vague about most matters going beyond questions of principle. Nevertheless, at several points it articulates certain limiting ideas, and I would argue that everything proposed in the present essay is both within the boundaries thus set down, and an expression of the document's major thrust.

First, from the beginning the document declares "that this one true religion subsists in the Catholic and Apostolic Church, to which the Lord Jesus committed the duty of spreading it abroad among all men (1)," and frequently *Dignitatis Humanae* returns to the obligation of Christians to the missionary enterprise, while insisting that this must not be a coercive process. Lest anyone doubt, the document declares that "it leaves untouched traditional Catholic doctrine on the moral duty of men and societies toward the true religion and toward the one Church of Christ

(1)." More directly related to the question of Christian culture are declarations such as that men "are bound to adhere to the truth, once it is known, and to order their whole lives in accord with the demands of truth (2)." Since the document repeatedly insists on the social nature of man, it seems fair to conclude that a public ordering of the believers' lives is intended: "The social nature of man . . . requires that he should give external expression to his internal acts of religion: that he should share with others in matters religious; that he should profess his religion in community (3)." Undoubtedly what is primarily intended here is the right to public worship and practice of one's religion, but, and I would stress this, the document is explicitly opposed to the neutrality of government in religious matters. "Government therefore ought . . . to take account of the religious life of the citizenry and show it favor, since the function of government is to make provision for the common welfare (3)." Even more explicitly: "Government is . . . to help create conditions favorable to the fostering of religious life. . . (6)."

Finally, and I need for my purposes go no further than this: "If in view of peculiar circumstances obtaining among peoples, special civil recognition is given to one religious community in the constitutional order of society, it is at the same time imperative that the right of all citizens and religious communities to religious freedom should be recognized. . . (6)." That is, contrary to the claims of many American interpreters of this document, it not only is against a religiously neutral government, it allows the possibility of a confessional state. Because my hopes for the present age are generally much more modest than the latter, by definition everything I have proposed is not only within the bounds of what *Dignitatis Humanae* understands as possible constitutional arrangements under which an acceptable religious freedom may be found, but more importantly are in the spirit of the positive relation between government and religion envisioned by that document.

My point, to return to the larger argument, is that it is one thing to accept the seeming inevitability of the disappearance of Christendom, to understand the compelling reasons why the First Amendment was necessary, to see what some have called "civil religion" as the political bottom line to which religion in America must adjust, and to note the continuing privatization of religion and secularization of life; it is quite another thing to see this as a progress, and to become apologists for the process. Here one must admire a kind of half-seeing immigrant stance that at once used

115

the First Amendment for self-protection, yet understood that the status of Other was inevitable as long as Catholics retained a more integrated and public form of Christianity than they found in this Protestant land. By resisting the political bottom line of the First Amendment, that in America all in religion that is incompatible with a shared political life must be jettisoned or privatized, a kind of Catholic subculture was maintained. John F. Kennedy is as good a symbol as any of the abandonment of this attempt to maintain a tail-end Catholic subculture.[49]

I have no illusion that any of these processes can be reversed, and know that we must go forward from the present moment, to capture what good we can in what is to come. Yet there is some merit to—as they say—having our heads on straight, to seeing genuine evils as evil. It is perhaps unfair and callous for me, an adult convert, to dwell on the disaster of the Americanization of the Catholic ethnic groups, and of course this is a story by no means unique to our century or country. I do not see how it could have been avoided, this selling of one's inheritance for a mess of pottage. But is it not quite another matter so to assimilate as to embrace opinions which make an embodied faith impossible? It seems to me that, as much as for any earlier generation, the realization of our full humanity lies in the embodiment of our beliefs in cultural forms, not of course as the end of Catholic life, but as one of its expressions. America is no more a democracy than a monarchy. It is a potpourri that cannot be characterized by any classical label. Plutarch said that Rome had a mixed form of government; this is no less true of us. While we can see that we are not a monarchy, we have trouble seeing that we are also not a democracy. The word, rather, operates for us in a normative way, not describing what we are but the ideals to which we commit ourselves. My suggestion is that the notion of an embodied Christianity should play for Catholics the role that "democracy" has come to mean for most Americans.[50] That is, as most Americans in their sober moments recognize that we are not democratically governed, yet continue to make concrete decisions they believe will make them "more democratic"; I would like Catholics to see that the First Amendment is at once, granted the fateful decision that a shared political experience is more important than a shared religion, historically necessary, protective of minorities, and humanly damaging. I would like to see them gain some critical distance from those Americanist ideals after which they have so longed, with the longing of the poor immigrant to be accepted, so that they can

116

see the First Amendment not as religiously neutral, but as the establishment of a Protestant notion of society, that is, of a society in which religion is privatized. I would like them to see that the First Amendment is antireligious and anti-Catholic, that it wounds any person who wishes to live a full life in which the private and public are integrated. Tocqueville was for the short run correct in believing that a disestablished religion could flourish at the level of society, but for the long run he could not see the fate of religion in a pluralistic society.[51] It has been left to us to live in a society in which the two things people are not supposed to discuss at parties — religion and politics — are the two things most worthy of discussion. I have no expectation of reviving anything like a traditional, vaguely unitary Catholic culture, but what of the venerable categories of Exile and Pilgrimage? Should we not see ourselves as ill at ease in this culture that toleration has made necessary? Can we not capitalize on the emphasis of Vatican II on the People of God—Wolfhart Pannenberg develops a similar emphasis for reasons partly parallel to my own—always on the one hand hoping for some publicly shared life and some influence on the larger society, but also knowing that all cultural arrangements are temporary, and that our first obligation is to embody the truth as best we can, in ourselves and in social groupings less than the whole? It would be a real advance to see America not as the Promised Land, except insofar as it was and is a haven for the oppressed elsewhere; not as the achievement of the finest political arrangement that man has discovered; but as a culture like all others understandable in and in great measure dictated by historical context. In this time and place we must continue the one thing necessary to embody Christ in our own lives. The culture of one life is already a culture, the culture of one Catholic family is a more public culture, the culture of a committed group of Christians, perhaps *Communione e Liberazione*, is again more public, and who can know where it will end? As Augustine said, "We are the times: such as we are, such are the times."[52]

Notes

1. Søren Kierkegaard, "Christianity a Fortress," in Walter Lowrie, *Kierkegaard*, Vol. 2 (New York, 1962), p. 536. The sentence quoted was preceded by a comment to the effect that Christianity has had no

effect on the world: "The world in fact is the same old world; it has not been changed. . . ." Although he does not condemn those forms of Christian culture which emerge when the Church impresses "on the world the otherworldly distinctness of a transcendent faith (p. 31)," a similar point of view informs Karl Löwith, *Meaning in History* (Chicago, 1949), pp. v, 190 ("Jesus . . . never intended to make Rome and its empire Christian. Why, then, should a follower of Christ expect that any other empire should become Christianized? A 'Holy Roman Empire' is a contradiction in terms . . . . [This] implies in principle also the theological impossibility of a 'Christian democracy' and of a Christian civilization. . ."). An innocuous meaning could be attributed to such comments, namely that "human nature" has not changed, or that despite Christianity man's situation in the world has not substantially altered, but Kierkegaard clearly intends to deny the label "Christian" to all but the subjective individual. As H. Richard Niebuhr, *Christ and Culture* (New York, 1956), pp. 181-182 at 181, wrote of him, ". . . cultural societies do not concern Kierkegaard. In state, family, and church he sees only the defections from Christ." Pages 243-245 criticize this point of view. Stanley Hauerwas's contribution to Charles H. Reynolds and Ralph V. Norman, eds., *Community in America: The Challenge of Habits of the Heart* (Berkeley, 1988), pp. 250-265, is a current form of "Kierkegaardism."

2. The position is reasonably well described and usefully criticized in Niebuhr, *Christ and Culture*, pp. 179ff., 241ff.

3. Again Löwith, *Meaning*, p. 190, draws attention to this logic of Protestantism. Jeffrey Stout, *The Flight from Authority: Religion, Morality, and the Quest for Autonomy* (Notre Dame, Ind., 1981), pp. 140-147, develops the alternatives facing Kierkegaard.

4. On the current stance of the progressive forms of Christianity in America, see Richard John Neuhaus, *The Catholic Moment: The Paradox of the Church in the Postmodern World* (San Francisco, 1987), with my critical response, "The Catholic Moment?" *Communio* 15 (Winter, 1988), 474-487. For introduction to recent discussion, see Leroy S. Rouner, ed., *Religious Pluralism* (Notre Dame, Ind., 1984). Context will hopefully make the senses in which I speak of "Protestant" clear in what follows, but the "new fundamentalism" in its Christian culture building aspect is clearly a descendant of much of nineteenth-century American Protestantism, while mainline twen-

tieth-century Protestantism has, at least overly, largely abandoned the idea of "Christian culture."

5. All these points are considered in the bibliography of the previous note. One of the more impressive students here is David Martin, *A General Theory of Secularization* (New York, 1978). Cf. Seyyed Hossein Nasr, *Knowledge and the Sacred* (New York, 1981); William Clebsch, *From Sacred to Profane America: The Role of Religion in American History* (New York, 1968), written in approval of the profanation of religion understood as not much more than ethical culture (see n. 50 below), but with real and valuable worldly results; Heinz-Horst Schrey, ed., *Säkularisierung* (Darmstadt, 1981), for a wide range of opinion; and Robert Wuthnow, *Meaning and Moral Order: Explorations in Cultural Analysis* (Berkeley and Los Angeles, 1987). Roland Jaccard, *L'exil intérieur, schizoïdie et civilisation* (Paris, 1975), esp. pp. 111-115, is a more radical analysis of the loss of religion by society. On such related questions as the secularization of discourse, see Stout, *Flight*. Georges Chantraine, *Les laïcs, chrétiens dans le monde* (Paris, 1987), pp. 33ff., 233ff., gives interesting analyses of secularity and proper response to it. One might speak of a proper secularization as one which deprives an institution or body of thought of unjustified religious sanctions. Thus Augustine, by reducing Roman "civil" to "fabulous" theology in the *City of God* (see esp. VI, 9), "secularized" the Roman Empire (see R. A. Markus, *Saeculum: History and Society in the Theology of St. Augustine* [Cambridge, 1970], esp. Chs. 2-3); Gregory VII secularized German theocratic monarchy; Thomas Aquinas secularized Augustine; and the present essay is an attempt to secularize or demythologize the "civil religion" of the American experience (see nn. 9, 37-40, 49-51 below). The argument of Rodney Stark and William Sims Bainbridge, *The Future of Religion: Secularization, Revival, and Cult Formation* (Berkeley, 1985), is that secularization, p. 2, "is always going on in all societies," along with religious reaction to secularization. Mona Ozouf, *Festivals and the French Revolution*, tr. Alan Sheridan (Cambridge, Mass., 1988), traces the attempt to sacralize a secularized society. For an earlier period, see Stephen A. McKnight, *Sacralizing the Secular: The Renaissance Origins of Modernity* (Baton Rouge, La., 1989).

6. George Gallup, Jr., and Jim Castelli, *The American Catholic People:*

Their Beliefs, Practices, and Values (Garden City, N.Y., 1987), which uses old and new standards of measurement, but, p. viii, makes clear that this study is based on "self-defined Catholics," twenty percent of whom "are not church members." Obviously self-definition allows great latitude. Of interest here is the discussion, p. 162, of the replacement of the term "lapsed Catholics" with "alienated Catholics," which latter suggests the Church is at fault. Not surprisingly, following this study's approach to definition, " 'Alienated' . . . Catholics in many ways do not look much different from active, church-going Catholics." See also pp. 178-179, for the argument that American Catholics (p. 178) "have forced the American bishops to accept their new definition of Catholicism." Gallup and Castelli are optimistic about the future of American Catholicism (p. 179), but one wonders if the Dutch experience is not relevant here: Jan Bots, "Dutch Catholicism in historical perspective, 1919-1977," *Communio* 6 (Fall, 1979), 295-320, at 319: "The Dutch do not notice that they have become more and more isolated from the universal Catholic church." Perhaps in both cases it is not so much "not noticing" as not taking the implications seriously. Cf. Francis Canavan, "The problem of belief in America," *Communio* 2 (Winter, 1975), 380-392. From p. 1, the Gallup-Castelli book is full of value judgments rendered by its authors. With the election of J. F. Kennedy, "American Catholics came of age politically," and with Vatican II, "American Catholicism came of age religiously." This begs the question of whether "coming of age," a phrase normally associated with maturation, involves something more than acceptability to, that is, becoming like, the larger culture: see the articles by George Weigel and Priscilla Hart in "Only Yesterday: John F. Kennedy," *30 Days*, No. 7 (Nov., 1988), 74-78. Not untypical of the incomprehension of religion built into many of the questions in the Gallup-Castelli study is (p. 12) the antithesis. "Do you believe that religion can answer all or most of today's problems, or that religion is largely old-fashioned and out of date?" On the silliness of such "social science," see Glenn W. Olsen, "Transcendental Truth and Cultural Relativism: An Historian's View," *Historicism and Faith*, ed. Paul L. Williams (Scranton, Pa., 1980), pp. 49-61.

7. Jean Daniélou, *Prayer as a Political Problem*, ed. and tr. J. R. Kirwan (New York, 1967), with my " 'You can't Legislate Morality': Reflec-

tions on a Bromide," *Communio* 2 (Summer, 1975), 148-162; Henri de Lubac, *The Mystery of the Supernatural*, tr. Rosemary Sheed (New York, 1967); Hans Urs von Balthasar's lifework is in many ways an embodiment of his ideas on grace, but see especially *The Theology of Karl Barth*, tr. John Drury (New York, 1971), esp. Pt. 4, and "The Achievement of Henri de Lubac," *Thought* 51 (1976) 7-50, esp. 24-29. For problems with the notion of "beginnings," see the text at n. 39 below.

8. Robert Darnton, "What was Revolutionary about the French Revolution?" *The New York Review of Books* 35, 21, and 22 (Jan. 19, 1989) 1-10, on this and the following, at 10.

9. On Mesopotamia and Egypt, see Henri Frankfort, *The Birth of Civilization in the Near East* (Garden City, N.Y., 1956). On Renaissance Italy see Richard C. Trexler, "The Magi Enter Florence," in *Studies in Medieval and Renaissance History*, ed. J.A.S. Evans and R. W. Unger, Vol. 1 (Old Series, Vol. 11: Vancouver, B.C., 1978), pp. 129-218, and Edward Muir, *Civic Ritual in Renaissance Venice* (Princeton, 1981). The reference to "public philosophy" is a reference to John Dewey, *The Public and its Problems* (Chicago, 1927), and Walter Lippmann, *Essays in the Public Philosophy* (New York, 1955), critiqued in my "You Can't Legislate Morality." Cf. William M. Sullivan, *Reconstructing Public Philosophy* (Berkeley, 1982), a critique of philosophic liberalism and plea for renewal of the tradition of civil republicanism (see nn. 40, 49-51 below). For orientation to more recent discussion see Thomas Bender, *Community and Social Change in America* (New Brunswick, N.J., 1978), Robert Bellah et al., *Habits of the Heart: individualism and commitment in American life* (Berkeley, 1985), and Reynolds and Norman, eds., *Community*. Jean H. Baker, *Affairs of Party: The Political Culture of Northern Democrats in the mid-nineteenth century* (Ithaca, N.Y., 1983), pp. 269-274, gives additional bibliography in tracing the convergence between religion and politics in the nineteenth century, and see n. 50 below. My colleagues W. Lindsay Adams and Ray Gunn have given me useful criticism and (here Prof. Gunn) have drawn this and a number of other studies to my attention.

10. Robin Lane Fox, *Pagans and Christians* (New York, 1987).

11. See Glenn W. Olsen, "St. Augustine and the Problem of the Medieval Discovery of the Individual," *Word and Spirit: A Monastic Review* 9 (1987), 129-156, and n. 35 below.

12. Although in my opinion among his least satisfactory books, see Etienne Gilson, *Reason and Revelation in the Middle Ages* (New York, 1938).

13. Athanasius, *History of the Arians*, 33, tr. *A Select Library of Nicene and Post-Nicene Fathers of the Christian Church*, Second Series, Vol. 4 (Grand Rapids, Mich., 1982), p. 281. Elaine Pagels, *Adam, Eve, and the Serpent* (New York, 1988), is of some use for tracing the ideas of freedom and free will, but might be read in conjunction with my "St. Augustine and the Problem." I share all of the reservations about Pagels's book expressed in the review by Robert J. O'Connell in *Theological Studies* 50 (1989), 201-202. Unfortunately, Pagels does not use Etienne Gilson, *The Christian Philosophy of Saint Augustine*, tr. L.E.M. Lynch (New York, 1960), which is much to be preferred to Pagels's reading of Augustine's views on free will from the perspective of the Reformation, or Emile Schmitt, *Le mariage dans l'oeuvre de Saint Augustin: Une théologie baptismale de la vie conjugale* (Paris, 1983), which is much to be preferred on any question touching Augustine's views of sexuality and marriage, and is also a good corrective to the surprisingly unfortunate portrayal of Augustine in Peter Brown, *The Body and Society: Men, women, and sexual renunciation in early Christianity* (New York, 1988), on which see the review by Henry Chadwick in the *Times Literary Supplement*, Dec. 23-29, 1988, 1411-1412. Pagels could not have used the very well-informed Giovanni Cappelli, *Autoerotismo. Un Problema Morale nei Primi Secoli Cristiani?* (Bologna, 1986), which in tracing its chosen subject summarizes very well the views, important for such subjects as free will, of pre- and post-lapsarian sexuality in the various Fathers.

14. C. 33, tr. p. 281.

15. C. 34, tr. p. 281.

16. C. 44, tr. p. 286.

17. *Codex Theodosianus*, 16.1.2, tr. Clyde Pharr, *The Theodosian Code and Novels and the Sirmondian Constitutions* (Princeton, 1980), p. 44.

18. *Contra Celsum*, tr. Henry Chadwick (Cambridge, 1965), pp. 505-506, 509-510. The mistaken notion that the early Christians were pacifists — broadcast for instance through the writings of Adolf von Harnack

and still widely found in serious scholars like Gerald E. Caspary, *Politics and Exegesis: Origen and the Two Swords* (Berkeley, 1979), and popular writers like John Cort in the *New Oxford Review* — is corrected in the work of John Helgeland, Robert J. Daly, and J. Patout Burns, *Christians and the Military: The Early Experience* (Philadelphia, 1985). A century after Origen, Athanasius could see that in spite of what he took as a prohibition of killing, war was lawful, but he could give no good argument for this: *Letter 48*, in *Select Library*, Second Series, Vol. 4, p. 557. For my following comments, see David Hollenbach, *Justice, Peace and Human Rights: American Catholic Social Ethics in a Pluralistic World* (New York, 1988), on the American bishops' stance on pacifism (also on pluralism), with the review by Ernest L. Fortin in *Crisis* 7, 2 (Feb., 1989), 48-51.

19. Charles Norris Cochrane, *Christianity and Classical Culture* (New York, 1957), pp. 374-375; Paul Christophe, *L'usage chrétien du droit du propriété dans l'Ecriture et la tradition patristique* (Paris, 1964), p. 167; Luciano Orabona, *Cristianesimo e proprietà. Saggio sulle fonti antiche* (Rome, 1964), p. 134.

20. Heinz Schürmann, "Der Jüngerkreis Jesu als Zeichen für Israel (und als Urbild des kirchlichen Rätestandes)," *Geist und Leben* 36 (1963), 21-35. Lane Fox, *Pagans*, as at pp. 336ff., while not sympathetic to those he calls the "overachievers," is often up to date in his knowledge of early Christian perfectionism.

21. Orabona, *Cristianesimo*, pp. 126-151.

22. Paul Cristophe, *Cassien et Césaire: prédicateurs de la morale monastique* (Gembloux, 1969). Philip Rousseau, *Ascetics, Authority, and the Church in the Age of Jerome and Cassian* (Oxford, 1978), while a good book, seems sometimes inadvisably to follow too far the work of Peter Brown, making the monks more holy men mediating within lay society than Cassian had envisaged them.

23. The best chapter in Gilson, *Reason and Revelation*, is that on Albert the Great and Aquinas.

24. I retain the old-fashioned and unpopular distinction between natural and revealed religion because it accurately describes how many of the Church Fathers looked at the matter, and because some such claim is involved in any claim that by faith man can see more than by unaided reason and his natural dispositions toward piety, awe, and wonder.

25. Examples are given in Cochrane, *Christianity*, index under "Ambrose of Milan."

26. Cochrane, *Christianity*, pp. 348-350, describes the incident.

27. Cochrane, *Christianity*, while not always reliable, gives the sweep of the history of these developments. Guido Horst, "And on the Seventh Day . . . Everyone to Work," *30 Days*, No. 8 (Dec., 1988), 24-25, is a useful discussion of contemporary debate in West Germany over retaining Sunday as a day of rest.

28. Edward K. Rand, *Founders of the Middle Ages* (New York, 1928, pp. 15-21), retains its usefulness. See Richard Klein, ed., *Die Streit um den Victoriaaltar* (Darmstadt, 1972), Jelle Wytzes, *Der letzte Kampf des Heidentum in Rom* (Leiden, 1977), and Richard Klein, *Symmachus. Eine tragische Gestalt des ausgehenden Heidentums*, 2nd ed. (Darmstadt, 1986).

29. The phrases quoted are taken from Rand, *Founders*, p. 16.

30. Peter Brown, *Augustine of Hippo. A Biography* (Berkeley and Los Angeles, 1969), pp. 421-423, 425, with Ch. 21. The translation of Wilfrid Parsons, *Saint Augustine. Letters*, Vol. 4 (The Fathers of the Church; New York, 1955), pp. 141-190, dates the letter to 417.

31. While rejecting her sympathies, I am accepting one thesis of Pagels's, *Adam*. Stout, *Flight*, as at pp. 2-5, in portraying the quest for autonomy from tradition since Descartes, shows how this quest, which is also a quest for an absolute freedom, can only fail.

32. Brown, *Augustine*, p. 236.

33. Ibid.

34. For Augustine's views on discipline, I am following Brown, *Augustine*, pp. 237-238, who personally is alarmed by Augustine's views. I am working on several studies which touch both Augustine's changing ideas of what man is, and of the place of the body in Christian thought, but for now see n. 11 above and "From Bede to the Anglo-Saxon Presence in the Carolingian Empire," in *Angli e Sassone al di qua e al di là del Mare*, 2 vols. (Settimane di studio del Centro italiano di studi sull'alto medioevo, 32; Spoleto, 1986), I, pp. 305-382.

35. I refer in the first instance to the theology of the body developed in John Paul II's Wednesday audience talks beginning in 1979, on which one reflection is Mary G. Durkin, *Feast of Love: Pope John Paul II on Human Intimacy* (Chicago, 1983), and in the second, social or cultural, instance, to the policy of so-called Catholic

Restoration (a poor label, if taken to imply that an earlier historical situation can be reobtained) which, although aimed primarily at the reinvigoration of the Church, also aims at a more sensitive embodiment of Christianity, through a missionary enterprise, in the diverse culture of the world. One may begin with the popular essay of Paul Johnson, *Pope John Paul II and the Catholic Restoration* (London, 1982). For introduction to both John Paul II's understanding of sexuality and of Christian culture, see Andrew N. Woznicki, *The Dignity of Man as a Person: Essays on the Christian Humanism of His Holiness John Paul II* (San Francisco, 1987). Woznicki's lucid discussion of the relation of freedom to truth in John Paul's thought is relevant to what is said in n. 11 above. On the idea of the "holy palpable," see also James Hitchcock, *The Recovery of the Sacred* (New York, 1974).

36. *Letter 185*, 19, tr. Parsons, pp. 159-160.

37. Leo XIII, "On Christian Citizenship," 28, ed. Etienne Gilson, *The Church Speaks to the Modern World: The Social Teachings of Leo XIII* (Garden City, N.Y., 1954), p. 262. Edmund S. Morgan, *Inventing the People: The Rise of Popular Sovereignty in England and America* (New York, 1988), is very instructive. See also Jacques Ellul, *The Political Illusion* (New York, 1967), p. 187, with Baker, *Affairs of Party*, p. 274, on the "mythologization of the people," and of sovereignty, and n. 50 below. Martin, *Secularization*, p. 29, argues "that [American] civil religion also illustrates a basic Protestant tendency, which is the cumulative character of legitimation whatever the logical contradictions of the component parts."

38. How different from the vagueness of this romantic view is the account of the economic forces generating changes in early forms of leadership given by Barry Cunliffe, *Greeks, Romans and Barbarians: Spheres of Interaction* (New York, 1988).

39. Hans Blumenberg, *Work on Myth*, tr. Robert M. Wallace (Cambridge, Mass., 1985).

40. John Rawls, *A Theory of Justice* (Cambridge, Mass., 1971), lamentably of some influence on the American Bishops' 1986 pastoral letter, *Economic Justice For All*, but see the critique of David Hollenbach in Reynolds and Norman, eds., *Community*, pp. 217-229. Dan McMurry, "Down and Out in America," *Crisis* 7, 2 (Feb., 1989), 27-31, in criticizing the U.S. Catholic Conference's Committee on Social

Development and World Peace statement "Homelessness and Housing: A Human Tragedy, a Moral Challenge," raises considerations that apply to the earlier pastoral. See the excellent criticisms of Rawls by Stout, *Flight*, pp. 218-223, 226, 232-241, who concludes of this tradition (p. 242): "By conflating the moral imperative to contain the effects of religious disagreement with the myth of the completely autonomous man, they made what was in fact a form of self-deception seem the height of virtue." What is said of Locke seems to survive the revisionism of writers like John Dunn, *Locke* (Oxford, 1984), and what is said of the social contract does not of course deny the presence of other influential strands of thought, such as the ideas of popular sovereignty following Montesquieu and Rousseau: on all this see James T. Kloppenberg, "The Virtues of Liberalism: Christianity, Republicanism, and Ethics in Early American Political Discourse," *The Journal of American History* 74 (1987), 9-33. On the Lockean myth see the essay of William F. May in Reynolds and Norman, eds., *Community*, pp. 185-201.

41. R. W. Southern, *Western Society and the Church in the Middle Ages* (Harmondsworth, 1970), pp. 16-23: "The church was a compulsory society in precisely the same way as a modern state is a compulsory society (p. 17)."

42. I have criticized the recent espousal of Murray's ideas by a number of conservative writers in the study listed in n. 4 above, and see the quotations in n. 50 below.

43. Thomas O'Brien Hanley, *Their Rights and Liberties: The beginnings of religion and political freedom in Maryland* (Chicago, 1984), analyzes the revolution forged by the Maryland colonists from 1634 to 1649. See n. 7 above for my criticisms. One of the best presentations of American Catholic history is Philip Gleason, *Keeping the Faith: American Catholicism, Past and Present* (Notre Dame, Ind., 1987). Martin, *Secularization*, p. 19, notes that "Catholics in Protestant societies have allied themselves to the political left [even if militantly secularist, for protecting oneself as a minority is of the first importance], except of course that Protestant societies do not breed militant secularism, or indeed a militant left. It is monopoly, above all Catholic monopoly, which ensures abrasive division and militant secularism." In making such useful observations, Martin may undervalue the seriousness with which ideas are taken in a religion — an evidence

126

which will be the attempt to implement them in society—as a decisive factor in whether it generates a secularizing opposition (or a left).

44. Balthasar, "Achievement of Henri de Lubac," p. 25.

45. See the studies by Daniélou and myself in n. 7 above. Joseph Gremillion, ed., *The Church and Culture Since Vatican II: The Experiences of North and Latin America* (Notre Dame, Ind., 1985), gives some idea of the range of recent approaches, and in Pt. II recent "Documents of the Church on Culture." For the idea of "evangelizing culture" developed at the Third General Conference of the Latin American Episcopate at Puebla in 1979, see the articles in *30 Days* (Jan., 1989), esp. Alver Metalli, "And Meanwhile the Cities are Becoming Pagan," 48-51, with the responses the following month, esp. Horacio Vignolo, "For Us 'Evangelizing Culture' is not a Slogan," 51-52, Alberto Methol Ferré, "Secularism and the Poor," 54-55, and Bonaventura Kloppenburg, "Secularism is Increasing, but not in Latin America," 57. Cf. Glenn Tinder, *The Political Meaning of Christianity: An Interpretation* (Baton Rouge, La., 1989).

46. I say "not necessarily" because the views of especially Panikkar contain considerable ambiguity. See Rouner, ed., *Religious Pluralism*, pp. 7-8, 97-129, and Thomas A. Russman, "Foundations for unity amid pluralism," *Communio* 7 (Winter, 1980), 320-331, on the limits of theological pluralism. One aspect of the argument of this paper is that the Madisonian-pluralist answer (yes) to the question of whether it was possible to construct a political community on republican principles over a great diversity of interests has not been the clear-cut success it is often taken to be. Cf. David Hollenbach, "The Common Good Revisited," *Theological Studies* 50 (1989), 70-94.

47. All quotations are from *Dignitatis Humanae*, here 1, N.C. Translation, comp. J. L. Gonzalez and the Daughters of St. Paul, *The Sixteen Documents of Vatican II* (Boston, n.d.). See my "The Catholic Moment," pp. 476-477, and n. 7 above.

48. See for instance *Dignitatis Humanae*, 7 ("Men are to deal with their fellows in justice and civility." "These [juridical norms which are in conformity with the objective moral order] arise out of the need for the effective safeguard of the rights of all citizens and for the peaceful settlement of conflicts or rights, also out of the need for an adequate care of genuine public peace, which comes about when men live together in good order and in true justice, and finally out of the need

for a proper guardianship of public morality."),13 ("Therefore, a harmony exists between the freedom of the Church and the religious freedom which is to be recognized as the right of all men and communities and sanctioned by constitutional law.").

49. See n. 6 above (*30 Days*). *Communio* 3 (Summer, 1976) is devoted to the question of Catholicism in American culture. On the First Amendment itself, see Leonard Levy, *The Establishment Clause: Religion and the First Amendment* (New York, 1986). For civil religion see Robert N. Bellah, *The Broken Covenant: American civil religion in a time of trial* (New York, 1975); and, with Phillip E. Hammond, ed., *Varieties of Civil Religion* (San Francisco, 1980). Martin, *Secularization*, pp. 16-18, draws instructive comparisons between duopolistic countries like Holland, where allies shift according to issue, and countries in which Catholicism dominates, where irreconcilable parties are permanently hostile, separated by the question of irreligion. Cf. Clebsch, *Sacred to Profane*, pp. 16-17, 19, 207-218, for the description of the U.S. as "Polypolitan," benignly viewed.

50. For origins see Forrest McDonald, *Novus Ordo Seclorum: The Intellectual Origins of the Constitution* (Lawrence, Kans., 1985). Michael Lienesch, *New Order of the Ages: Time, the Constitution, and the Making of Modern American Political Thought* (Princeton, 1988), in addressing the much controverted question of whether the Founding Fathers were republicans or liberals, rightly stresses the inconsistency of the ideas enshrined in the American Constitution, and thus of American politics ever after. Steven Watts, *The Republic Reborn: War and the Making of Liberal America, 1790-1820* (Baltimore, 1987), traces the relative displacement of republicanism, and see Kloppenberg, "Virtues of Liberalism," a perceptive essay, good on the varieties of liberalism, although conceiving religion in a very American way: "Virtue in various forms lay at the heart of Christian doctrine" (p. 12). Bernard Bailyn, *The Origins of American Politics* (New York, 1968), esp. Ch. 1, and Gordon S. Wood, *The Creation of the American Republic, 1776-1787* (New York, 1969) (see index under "Mixed government" on the meaning of this term specific to the eighteenth century), are seminal works here. Joyce Appleby, *Capitalism and a New Social Order: The Republican Vision of the 1790's* (New York, 1984), is useful on the idea of equality as a premise followed in much later American thought. What Stuart Hampshire,

"Engaged Philosopher," *The New York Review of Books* 36, 1 (Feb. 2, 1989), 7-9, at 9, says of democracy and war could be given more general application: "There is an ideology of democracy that is as deceiving as the ideologies of capitalism and of communism. This ideology suggests that, given democratic institutions, the people as a whole, through their representatives in the Congress, and perhaps also through public opinion polls, are able to make their wishes known on the acceptability of any specific risk of war when it arises." Further, in regard to why serious questions cannot be discussed in U.S. presidential campaigns: "Most voters recognize constraints such as this [no one can be seen as 'soft on defense'] in a spirit of controlled contempt for such democratic elections."

51. See my article in n. 7 above. Stout, *Flight*, p. 294, n. 21, gives a very sober account of the alternatives facing anyone who would reintroduce theology into public life. His point is not only that history cannot be reversed, but that the secularized discourse of the modern period itself limits any "translation" of religion into contemporary categories. As indicated in n. 4 above, "privatization" has its stages, and much nineteenth-century Protestantism wished Christianity to have a public impact at the "social," if not the "governmental," level. Often brilliant in its insights is James Turner, *Without God, Without Creed: The Origins of Unbelief in America* (Baltimore, 1985). I have consciously avoided the problem of providence in the present study. Tocqueville's insistence that even something as filled with foreboding as the spread of democracy must have a providentially determined role certainly deserves reflection and response, as does Stout's observation of the irreversible secularization of discourse, but I am here again inclined to an Augustinian perspective which insists both on providence and on man's inability to read providence (on this latter, Karl F. Morrison, *The Mimetic Tradition of Reform in the West* [Princeton, 1982], pp. 54ff., is useful). I am not inclined to take great historical events, say the Enlightenment or French and American Revolutions, as irreversible goods which must be permanently incorporated into some sense of human advance, but as very mixed blessings, giving us on the one hand the tools of critical scholarship, clearly an advance in the human capacity to know, but also the most contradictory and incompatible assertions as to what man's life in society is to be. David Tracy, *Blessed Rage for Order* (New York, 1975), seems to

me insufficiently critical of the achievements of the Enlightenment; Darnton (n. 8 above) too uncritical of the French Revolution. Many of Joseph Ratzinger's and Andrew Louth's books seem to me quite successfully to sift what is permanently valuable in the extension of human rationality since, say, the seventeenth century, from what should have no claims on us. Many of Romano Guardini's books articulate what seems to me a wise stance in dealing with our own times, uniting as they do great sobriety and skepticism about any "advances" made in the twentieth century, with the commitment to discover the forms that good may be given under present conditions. Although I would go a long way in agreement with Karl Rahner's analysis of the decline of Christian culture, I would not compact the imperative always to embody Christianity anew, to build what forms of culture we can, into his idea of the servant Church: Eugene B. Borowitz, "On the Jewish Obsession with History," in Rouner, ed., *Religious Pluralism*, pp. 17-37, esp. 28ff. It seems that only recently have we even been able to see the fate of education in a highly pluralistic society, if that pluralism destroys common knowledge in the curriculum: E. D. Hirsch, Jr., "The Primal Scene of Education," *The New York Review of Books* 36, 3 (March 2, 1989) 29-35, is instructive. According to "Vatican official assails U.S. Catholic Church for giving 'easy' divorces," *Deseret News*, March 11, 1989, in the March, 1989, meeting of a thirty-five-member U.S. delegation of Church leaders with top Vatican officials concerning U.S. Catholic practices, Archbishop John R. Quinn of San Francisco neatly described the impact of the tradition of the separation of Church and state in other areas of life: "The media's commitment to 'religious neutrality' has all too often led to a purely secular view of the world which, consequently, ignores the sacred dimensions of marriage, family and social life."

52. *Sermon 80*, quoted in Markus, *Saeculum*, pp. 40-41. For Pannenberg see n. 51 above (Borowitz). Cf. Everett J. Morgan, ed., *Christian Witness in the Secular City* (Chicago, 1970); Inos Biffi, *Cultura cristiana: distinguere nell' unito* (Milan, 1983); Hans Urs von Balthasar, "Is There a Christian Culture?" in *Test Everything: Hold Fast to What is Good*, an interview with Hans Urs von Balthasar by Angelo Scola, tr. Maria Shrady (San Francisco, 1989), esp. pp. 50-51.

Response to Glenn W. Olsen

by Michael Waldstein,
University of Notre Dame

Professor Glenn Olsen's central thesis is that a full and mature Christian life is one that embodies itself and expresses itself in the full breadth of human life. It cannot be limited to the inwardness of the heart and conscience before God. "A full Christian life is one lived out in one's art, one's politics, the form one's city takes, and any check placed on public expression of one's Christianity is an attack on the possibility of living an integrated life, an attempt to disallow Christian maturation."

This central claim flows directly from the Christian understanding of the world outlined by Professor Walter Kasper in his opening address. "Unmixed and undivided," he argued, can function as a kind of world-formula. All created reality remains, as a creature, undivided from the Creator, who, as Augustine puts it, is more interior to it than its innermost; yet, precisely in this undividedness, the creature is released into its own and achieves its integrity and legitimate autonomy, unmixed with the Creator, yet destined for communion with the Creator. This general structure, which is found in all created reality as such, Professor Kasper argued, is concretized in Jesus Christ, through whom the human race, and the whole cosmos, is drawn into a freely given communion with the Trinity of Father, Son, and Holy Spirit. And this gift is sacramentally mediated by the Church as the body of Christ.

According to this principle of "unmixed and undivided," all of reality, and specifically all human reality, is inseparable from an interior relation to the mystery of God as mediated by Christ through the Church, regardless of whether the relation is explicitly acknowledged and willed or not.

One cannot exempt the political sphere from this principle, as if only the first half of "unmixed and undivided" applied to it. "Unmixed and undivided" contradicts any view that would privatize religion as a matter of principle, any view that would affirm the religious neutrality of the political sphere as a matter of principle. The stringent separationism

131

between Church and state that has been developed by some interpreters of the First Amendment can therefore only be seen as opposed to Catholic Christianity. From this perspective I find it difficult to disagree with Professor Olsen when he raises strongly critical questions about the First Amendment.

Yet the concrete problems of a Catholic experience and a Catholic culture in our American setting don't yet emerge in this general and abstract look at the issue. The City of God has not yet reached its goal; it is on a pilgrimage together with persons and cities who are indifferent or even opposed to it. This situation requires compromise and it is impossible to reach a completely satisfactory and permanent solution in which all contrary interests are completely reconciled.

It seems to me that by clarifying this point Professor Olsen does much to set the debate about the American experience, including the First Amendment, on the right track. The real question is a question of prudence in weighing necessarily conflicting interests. Is the particular contingent compromise worked out in America flowing in the right direction?

This is where I find Professor Olsen's historical anaylsis particularly helpful. The development he traces from Athanasius through Ambrose to Augustine can be understood as a true development propelled by a more practical and multifaceted understanding of the human condition in Ambrose and, even more so, in Augustine. It is in many ways the opposite of the development of our political system in America. For this reason it can be helpful as a corrective against a naïve and unreflected acceptance of every aspect of the American experience.

All of that being said, I trust I will be continuing in Professor Olsen's spirit, if I raise some differentiating historical questions about his critique of the First Amendment. His wishes for Catholics in America are spelled out quite forcefully: "I would like to see them gain some critical distance from those Americanist ideals after which they have so longed, with the longing of the poor immigrant to be accepted, so that they can see the First Amendment not as religiously neutral, but as the establishment of a Protestant notion of society, that is of a society in which religion is privatized. I would like them to see that the First Amendment is anti-religious and anti-Catholic."

I am not a historian of the Constitution, but a biblical scholar, and so I hesitate to enter a detailed discussion of the First Amendment. Still, I want to raise some differentiating questions. One should perhaps distinguish what the First Amendment originally meant and what it has come to mean for American judges in the twentieth century, especially for the stringent separationists among them. When it was originally promulgated, the First Amendment was intended as a restriction on the *national* government alone. Several state governments had a formally established religion in the precise sense in which the First Amendment prohibits Congress from establishing one. The immediate purpose of the amendment was to acknowledge and protect the *de facto* multiplicity of religiously formed political structures in the individual states. Only through twentieth-century interpretations of the Fourteenth Amendment was the First Amendment taken as rigorously applicable to all governments in America and to American society as a whole.

In addition, the constitutional scholar Walter Berns shows that in the mainsteam of American tradition the First Amendment was always open to "public support of religion, albeit on a non-discriminatory basis" (Berns, *The First Amendment and the Future of American Democracy*, 60). If he is correct, stringent separationism is not truly representative of the best American tradition. From this perspective it is difficult to agree with Professor Olsen's charge that the First Amendment is antireligious.

Of course, the increasing unification and homogenization of the United States was an unavoidable process and, in the long run, local autonomy of religious politics could not stand up against it. In this way the First Amendment, against its original intention, favored the privatizing of religion characteristic of many currents of Protestant theology.

There is a more fundamental problem. The neutral posture assumed by the national government can probably not be understood without an Enlightenment context: human reason rises above confessional strife to a unity that abstracts from divisive religious differences. And here one can observe the dialectic of the Enlightenment of which Professor Kasper spoke: the strategy of the founders is inherently unstable. They surely assumed that the American commonwealth would develop in some religious framework, however abstract and unspecified, indebted to the Judeo-Christian tradition. That is quite clear, even in the writings of Jefferson. Yet the First Amendment offers no recourse against an increasing elimination of religious life from the public forum. Its authors may have assumed that public discourse in America would remain within the perimeter of enlightened religiosity. This mistaken assumption puts the opponents of religiously formed public life in a decided advantage because they can preempt the First Amendment for their own a-religious vision of public life. From this perspective, it is difficult to escape Professor Olsen's conclusion that it is not religiously neutral, but, against its own intention, antireligious.

Professor Olsen shows, I think convincingly, that the Vatican II document on religious liberty does not support the view of stringent separationists. "Government therefore ought . . . to take account of the religious life of the citizenry and show it favor, since the function of government is to make provision for the common welfare." "Government is to help create conditions favorable to the fostering of religious life."

Still if one compares the document with earlier pronouncements of the magisterium — for example, Pius IX's encyclical *Quanta Cura* or Leo XIII's *Immortale Dei* — one can observe a certain convergence of official Catholic teaching with the American experience. For example, Leo XIII writes: "Although the Church does not consider it licit that various forms of worship of God should have the same rights as the true religion, yet she does not thereby condemn the authorities of the nations who, for the sake of attaining a great good or of avoiding to cause evil, tolerate in practice and by custom that they all have the same place in the city" (Neuner-Dupuis 1014; DS 3176).

Dignitatis Humanae does not say anything that would contradict Leo XIII, but in the prudential balancing of conflicting interests it is considerably warmer toward the interests of freedom. Now, I think it would be a mistake to interpret this warming as a simple and undifferentiated acceptance of the ideal of freedom in liberal democracy. Freedom in the sense of liberal democracy means absence of any coercion. It involves a negative definition of autonomy as the absence of bonds. Freedom in the Christian sense indicated by "unmixed and undivided," on the other hand, means entering into relation and being bound by love. It involves a positive definition of autonomy, autonomy as directly proportional with being bound into relation.

This distinction suggests that Catholics should not simply jump on the bandwagon of liberal democracy, although such a move may be politically useful. Still, they can seize the ideal of freedom that runs through our liberal political system and use the space granted by this idea to construct a truly public and embodied Christianity. In doing so they should not think they are being un-American. Quite on the contrary, they are actualizing a right spelled out in the First Amendment.

Professor Olsen proposes that in actualizing this right, Catholics should be guided by the ideal of "embodied Christianity" as Americans in general are guided by the ideal of "democracy." A crucial question, it seems to me, is how such an ideal can become operative. As a mere idea it has little chance, it seems to me, against the overwhelming power of our culture.

The Vatican II understanding of the Church as a sacrament of communion with God and of all human beings among one another can perhaps be taken as an answer. The Church is, at root, *already* embodied Christianity. It is already the body of Christ. It already continues the event of Christ, as Father Sheets puts it in his response. Encountering the Church as this sacramental event and actualizing it in one's own existence, together with others — this, it seems to me, is what the Vatican II consciousness of the Church requires. Such an encounter and such actualizing is a responsibility that must be taken seriously by lay people as members of the one People of God. Here, it seems to me, lies the exemplary significance of lay movements and communities that have sprung up without ecclesiastical planning.

Priority of Community, Priority of Person

Michael Novak,
American Enterprise Institute

One of the fundamental principles of the Catholic Whig tradition is ordered liberty. Another is the co-definition of community and person. A true community respects free persons; an inadequate or false community does not. Correlatively, a fully developed person is capable of knowing and loving; but these are exactly the two human capacities that are inherently communitarian. Note again the co-definition: To be a free person is to know and to love others in community — and a community is true when, in the ordinary circumstances of daily life, its institutions and practices enable persons to multiply the frequency of their acts of knowing and loving. False community represses capacities for reflection and choice. True community enlarges them. These are the lessons that guided the new human experiment in the Americas, in the city aptly named for the love of brothers, Philadelphia.

1. Community: The Primal Experience of the Americas

The primal experience of our two continents in this hemisphere, the two continents of the Americas, has been the struggle to build new communities. When the first pilgrims departed from Leyden, Holland, to set sail across the great Atlantic for what they would call New England, they knew what they would *not* find waiting for them. They would not find warm inns with cheerful fires in fireplaces already built. They would not find fields ripe with grain, already protected by soundly built fences. On the contrary, they were pursuing an errand into a wilderness. The work of building up cities and homes loomed in front of them as a formidable task. Nearly everything they were to have they would have to build themselves. Climate and environment might well be more hostile than they could withstand. No one man alone could survive. The future depended on their ability to build communities, and to build them in such fashion as would take root and eventually prosper.

While they were very conscious, indeed, of building a new world, and even then were beginning to imagine a new order, our ancestors were far from being indifferent to tradition. They brought books, ideas, artifacts, tools, and goods that they could not at first hope to make for themselves. Even on shipboard, their faces were turned toward the immense tasks of building cities, churches, civic buildings, markets, and even facilities for woodworks, metal shops, brickmakers, ironworkers, glassblowers, and for all the other crafts and trades indispensable for the fairly high levels of common life to which they had been accustomed.

Our ancestors also brought with them a complex heritage of ideas. Some historians of the American experience emphasize the radical break between the ancient, classic tradition of the "liberal" arts and the modern liberal tradition. The first springs from Plato and Aristotle, the second from Hobbes. The first roots itself in natural law, the second in natural rights. The first holds that humans are by nature social animals; the second holds that in "the state of nature" human is to human as wolf to wolf. By its harshness, the second injected perhaps sufficient realism and an ardent desire for checks and balances so as to make a new experiment more likely of success. The first grounded better, perhaps, the hope of genuine human progress and success, as proper to the social constitution of the human heart and mind.

2. The Old and the New

Nevertheless, the conflict between these two visions — that of the ancients and that of the moderns — must not be exaggerated. The formal light under which the ancients looked at nature was different from the formal light under which, for example, Hobbes looked at the "state of nature." The ancients noted the ideal form of human nature, the human capacity for knowing and loving. These capacities are inherently social. Therefore, for the ancients, humans are (ideally, in their capacities, even if not always in their regular constant practice) social animals. Not all the ancients were idealists, however. There have not been many shrewder realists than Aristotle, who said that in politics we must be satisfied to see "some tincture of virtue."[1]

And this, precisely, was Hobbes's starting place. He noted that, apart from civilization, humans showed barely a tincture of virtue. In the pre-civilized state, "nature" shows a barbaric "war of all against all." The formal light through which Hobbes inspects experience is not historical. He does not mean that once upon a time there was a Garden of Evil ("the state of nature"), the experience of which taught humans at a specific date to value civilization. Rather, his formal light was conceptual, and consisted in stressing the antisocial capacities of those human beings who lack all civilizing virtues. Aristotle noted that humans often fall below their true perfection, and in their common life show only a "tincture" of virtue. Hobbes called something like this, but even worse, "the state of nature"— namely the condition in which humans act with even less than a tincture of virtue, evidencing behavior that is purely antisocial. Hobbes thought that this state is always not far away from us, and indeed in our century its teeth have been bared before our eyes many times.

Still, it is much more difficult than Hobbes thinks for humans to be purely evil in all respects. Human evil is perhaps even more awful in its reach than he imagined, as the concentration camps, torture chambers, and gas ovens of the twentieth century have displayed before our eyes. But there is also a broadly shared human revulsion against such evils. It is not "unnatural" for humans to be moved by the torture, pain, and death of others far away. Accordingly, the human rights revolution is slowly affecting nearly all of humankind.[2] In any case, the very scholars who insist upon the sharp divide between the world of Aristotle and the world of Hobbes prize mightily "the better angels of our nature" represented by higher standards of human rights performance.

3. The Contribution of the Catholic Whig Tradition

It is precisely here that the Catholic Whig tradition has a crucial philosophical role to play in bridging the best of the ancient tradition with the best of the modern tradition. In a general way — to state my thesis baldly — the modern "liberal" tradition excelled in devising practical institutional protections for human rights. By contrast, the Great Tradition of the *philosophia perennis* excelled in casting a more accurate light upon those basic philosophical conceptions that undergird liberal institutions. Put another way, the philosophies of Hobbes, Locke, and others among the moderns are less than adequate *as philosophies*. Meanwhile, the philosophies of Aristotle, St. Thomas Aquinas, and others are less than adequate *with regard to the practical institutions* that would incarnate their conceptions in social structures. The present task of the Catholic Whig tradition is to form a new synthesis of philosophical conceptions and practical institutions that do justice, together, to "private rights" and "public happiness." This synthesis must join together the full actualization both of the human person and the human community.

4. The Concept of "Person"

It is obvious that the key conceptions here are "person" and "community." Here the Catholic intellectual tradition, in particular, is able to offer special light. As the German historian of philosophy W. Windelbrand has pointed out, the concept of "person" is richer than the concept of "individual," and arose historically from the efforts of Catholic theologians to do justice to the theological statement that Jesus Christ is human in nature but divine in person.[3] Beyond his human individuality, theologians had to tangle with the concept of his personhood. Therefore, they thought long and hard about the difference between the two concepts, the individual and the person. It is the latter that adequately grounds the dignity and the rights of every man and woman.

The human person, precisely *qua* person, is a foundational source of insight and love; autonomous, autarchic, a hypostatic whole, inviolable, inalienable, an end and not only a means. The human person is called directly to union with the One in whose image each has been created. The person, therefore, can never be treated, even by the community, as a means rather than as an end. The very purpose of a true community is to nourish in its midst the full development of each and every person who is among its members. Conversely, it is in the nature of the human person —an originating source of knowing and of loving—to be in communion with others, who share in his or her knowing and loving. Knowing and loving are inherently acts of communion.

Thus, the classical view, brought in Aquinas to a fullness that was less developed in Aristotle, holds simultaneously that, in one sense, the inherent end of personhood is communion and, in a reciprocal sense, that the inherent end of a true community is full respect for the personhood of each of its members. A human community, therefore, is *sui generis*. It is not like a hive, or a herd, or a mere collective. Each of its members is not merely a member, a part of the whole.[4] On the contrary, each is a whole, wholly worthy of respect in herself or himself. Each must be treated as an end, not solely as a means. Each has an autonomous life of his or her own, worthy of infinite respect as a participant in God's own originating power of knowing and of loving. Each is an agent of reflection and choice. Unless he or she is injuring others, the only way in which a genuine community can approach a rational person is by way of knowing and of loving; that is to say, through rational and civil persuasion, not through coercion, force, or systematic oppression.

Just the same, the classic Catholic tradition, even while working out wonderfully balanced accounts of person and community, tended to tip the balance toward community. Why is this? Perhaps it was because the social, familial, political, and economic institutions that would in later times enlarge the scope of liberty open to the human person remained for many long centuries unknown. Perhaps it was because existing communities were small and their survival was often threatened. (This fact is still visible to us in the thick battlements by which the walled cities of ancient and medieval Europe vainly tried to repel generations of hostile invaders.)

In any case, at least sixty times in his many works, St. Thomas Aquinas articulates one variant or another of a classic dictum that goes back at least to Aristotle: "The good of the many is more godlike than the good of the individual."[5] The example that made this observation cogent to the Great Tradition is the willingness of individuals to die to defend the common good of the city. It is easy to see why the sacrifice of self for the community seemed godlike. But there is also a danger in this formulation. It may suggest to the unwary that the individual is but a means to the survival of the community. Only in extraordinary circumstances, and for a full set of sound reasons, can a community justly ask so much of its citizens.[6] Otherwise, it is wrong to imagine that the individual is always expendable, if only the social whole chooses that expedient. St. Thomas Aquinas did not himself accept this dangerously broad implication. He could not, because of his concept of the human person.

Civilization, Thomas Aquinas liked to say, is constituted by reasoned discourse. The difference between barbarism and civilization consists in this: Barbaric regimes coerce their citizens; civilized regimes approach citizens through their own autonomous capacities for full consent. Persons are treated as persons only when approached through knowing and loving. For free persons, the legitimacy of government lies in the consent of the governed.[7]

The "consent of the governed" is a political principle, clearly articulated in the American Declaration of Independence of 1776. This principle flows from the reality of the human person, an autonomous creature whose essential nature consists in a capacity for reflection and choice. The only appropriate approach to such agents is through reasoned consent.[8] That truth, declared to be self-evident in 1776, was not at that time in fact self-evident to all human beings. But historical experience worldwide, under tyranny and torture, has made that truth increasingly self-evident to all. All the world recognizes today that any approach through tyranny, torture, or coercion—any attempt to treat human beings as part of a mere collective, as ants in an anthill, bees in a hive, sheep in a herd, or animals on an "animal farm"—distorts and oppresses the true capacities of human persons. Any such regime is bound to be as oppressive, uncreative, and unproductive as it is illegitimate. From many sad experiences, the world has learned the hard way that the source of human creativity is the human capacity for reflective choice. "What is socialism [the tyranny of a planned economy]?" a joke in Poland runs. Answer: "The slowest path to a free economy."

One of the contributions of modern thought to ancient thought, therefore, is sharper and more sustained attention to the nature and the rights of the human person. Where ancient and medieval societies tipped the balance toward the common good, modern societies have placed compensating weights — and sometimes more than compensating weights — on the side of the person. Modern institutions make this new emphasis practical, concrete, and consequential.

But where should one draw the line? How should one strike a balance? This debate is more than academic. Push too far in the direction of solidarity, and the outcome is the totalitarian collective. Push too far in the direction of the individual, and the outcome is egotism, moral relativism (subjectivism), and a war of all against all. Even among thinkers determined to avoid both extremes, how exactly to do due justice both to person and to community is not easily discernible — not in daily family life, not in the institutions of religion, not in political action, and not in the business corporation. Thinkers of a moderate bent wish to honor both the person and the community — both the needs of

141

individuals and the needs of social harmony. But how, where, and in what degree?

My aim now is not to answer that question in the abstract. Instead, I take a hint from Tocqueville in *Democracy in America*. Tocqueville suggests that the terms of the ancient debate between the person and the community (between *personalism* and *solidarism*, certain Europeans said in the 1930s) have been changed by the American experience. The New World is different from the Old World. What we mean by "person" is different here, as well as what we mean by "community." And the Novus Ordo has accordingly suggested a fresh historical solution to an ancient conundrum.

5. Tocqueville: The New World Symphony

Alexis de Tocqueville was not only an astute observer, he was also a social scientist of the first rank. And he formulated from what he observed in what he took to be the first people to embody the "new order of the ages" the first "law" of the "new science of politics." His purpose was to alert Europe to a new tide in human history, a tide deep and wide and directed by Providence, that would soon or eventually sweep the whole world.[9] He meant the tide of a new kind of democracy, a democratic republic with an effective respect for the singular human person. A new kind of political-economic-moral order was rising, under the hand of Providence, he thought, and perhaps the most striking thing about this new order is that in it "men have in our time carried to the highest perfection the art of pursuing in common the object of common desires, and have applied this new technique to the greatest number of purposes."[10] Here Tocqueville called attention to a new reality, which can fairly be described neither as individualistic nor, quite, as constituting a full community. This new reality is a new form of social life: the voluntary association.

In America, Tocqueville observed, when citizens discerned new needs or purposes, they voluntarily formed committees or other informal organizations to meet them. What in France citizens turned to the state to do for them, Tocqueville exclaimed, and what in Great Britain they turned to the aristocracy to do, in America they formed their own associations to accomplish. Thus they built great universities, museums, and art galleries; sent missionaries to the antipodes; raised funds for the disabled;

put up public monuments; fed and clothed victims of natural disasters, and the like.[11] This new form of social life — never total enough to constitute a fully defined community, but far beyond the power of individuals alone — called for a new "knowledge of association."

This new "knowledge of association," Tocqueville explains, "is the mother of all other forms of knowledge; on its progress depends that of all the others. . . . Among laws controlling human societies there is one more precise and clearer, it seems to me, than all the others. If men are to remain civilized or to become civilized, the art of association must develop and improve among them at the same speed as equality of conditions spreads."[12]

Why association? Because inherent in respect for the human person is respect for the reflectively chosen forms of association that persons create in order to pursue their common interests. In order to constitute a people out of mere masses or mere mobs, such freely, rationally chosen associations are indispensable.[13]

In an important sense (not only a historical sense, as actually happened in the United States), such freely chosen associations are prior to the state. They are prior philosophically and practically. Philosophically, because they ground the social nature of the human person in reflective and voluntary social life, duly proportioned to the human bodily need of proximity, voice, and active participation. Practically, because human beings need immediate participation in the forming of social consent and they also need social protection, lest in their solitary individual selves they stand naked before the power of an omnipotent state.

In short, "mediating associations" or "mediating institutions," as these voluntarily formed local structures are technically called, are crucial forms of human sociality, and they are prior to the formation of a national society.[14] They are defenses against the state. They are also natural expressions of concrete, fleshly human sociality. Before humans are citizens of states, they are active participants in society.

As Jacques Maritain has stressed, "society" is a far larger and more vital reality than "state."[15] Only a densely active society with many vital civic associations is sufficiently defended against the state, whose tendencies have historically been tyrannous. Only a society with many vital associations fully expresses the social nature of the person. The new science of association, therefore, meets two basic needs of human nature: one positive, one negative. The social nature of humans gives rise to associations not only because individuals need protection from abuse but also because they have a positive need for participation and self-expression.[16] In addition, in a way entirely appropriate to the human person, associations come into being through personal consent.

Tocqueville is surely correct: the principle of association is, in fact, the first law of democracy. Without vital mediating institutions, intermediate between the naked individual and the state, democracy has no muscular social fiber; it is a void within which a mere mob is blown about by demagoguery. The strength of a people, as distinguished from a mob, lies in its capacities for voluntarily forming multiple associations of self-government and social purpose on its own.[17] The social life of a people is rich, complex, and strong even before the question of a national state arises.

Even President Gorbachev in the USSR appears to have grasped this. To make Soviet society creative, he must free Soviet persons (at least a little) through *glasnost*, allowing creative and reflective intellect to flourish. In order to derive legitimacy and creative cooperation from all the people, he must reshape Soviet institutions through *perestroika*. In order to break through the stranglehold of Communist Party members over every sclerotic institution of Soviet life, he must go as far as he dares to empower the creativity of individual citizens. The source of dynamic power in any human community, in short, is the creativity locked within the capacities of individual human persons for insight and choice.

In Latin America, it is sometimes charged that the Anglo-American liberal tradition is excessive in its emphasis upon the individual and deficient in its philosophy of community.[18] That charge is not quite accurate; still, for the sake of argument, let me accept its burden. Suppose that it is true that the *philosophy* of the liberal society is inferior to, say, Catholic social thought on these two points. From that it does not follow that the *institutional praxis* of the liberal society is inferior to the institutional praxis of existing Catholic social orders. It is at least conceivable that a liberal society such as West Germany, Great Britain, France, and the United States pay a more just respect to the rights of persons on the one hand and, on the other hand, to the building up of intermediate social bodies through reflection and choice than do some existing Catholic countries. Explicit philosophy and institutional practice do not always coincide. Indeed, practice may often be better than philosophy. This was the judgment of Jacques Maritain in his *Reflections on America* — namely that American practices are better, deeper, and richer than American ideology.[19]

Let me further propose the Novak rule of philosophical interpretation. Philosophers (and theologians) often stress in their writings exactly what their cultures lack, and are silent about solid habits readily taken for granted. Thus, in Great Britain, where social conformity has long been in fashion, where individuals are supremely sensitive to others around them and have a sort of social conscience internalized within their hearts, British philosophers speak incessantly about the individual. By contrast, in Italy philosophers speak incessantly about *communita* — while practicing an almost medieval and princely self-assertion and exhibiting a fiercely proud individualism bordering on idiosyncrasy. Compare in those two countries the social practice of boarding a bus. In London, citizens patiently and respectfully queue up in social awareness. In Rome, boarding a bus is one of the world's wildest adventures in laissez-faire and one of its most sensuous experiences. In London, where philosophers praise individualism, individuals defer to others; in Rome, where philosophers praise community, it's every man for himself. The Novak rule anticipates this turn.

6. The Co-Definition of Person and Community

In sum, those who in the long run trust realism and the lessons of vivid human experience — and who hold to first principles such as the "self-evident truth" that human persons are appropriately respected solely when their native capacities for reflection and choice are permitted free play — seem to have been vindicated by human history. "The God who gave us life gave us liberty," Thomas Jefferson exclaimed.[20] He made the same point in the text of the Declaration of Independence, for which he wanted posterity to remember him: "That all men are created equal, and endowed by their Creator with inalienable rights." None of the rights he had in mind are American rights; they are human rights. They inhere in persons—they are the properties proper to human persons — because they were conferred on each directly by the Creator, who made all human persons in his image. Catholic thought adds further that as the proper life of God is insight and love, so also is the life proper to human persons. As God is a person, so are humans.

145

It is the distinctive achievement of the modern Catholic Whig tradition to have added to the classical perception of the primacy (in certain respects) of the community the modern perception of the primacy (in other respects) of the person. This achievement permits an unparalleled degree of societal concern for the rights, liberties, and dignity of human persons, *qua* persons (that is, *not* because of their opinions, beliefs, religion, ethnicity, or race). But it also nourishes the achievement of a vastly larger number of voluntary associations, a higher degree of voluntary social cooperation, a broader base of love and gratitude for the commonwealth, and a more explicitly consensual national community than was known in ancient or medieval times.

Not only is it possible to create new social systems — or to reconstitute old ones so that historically unparalleled respect is shown both for individual persons and for the common good. Some three dozen societies on this planet (none of them, of course, saintly or likely to be mistaken for the kingdom of God) have actually shown such respect, in their institutions and in their daily practice. Far from being perfect, each manifesting much to be done before liberty and justice for all are fully served, such societies afford protections for basic rights more broadly and efficaciously than was ever done before in any traditional, pre-modern, pre-capitalist, and pre-republican society.

To my way of thinking, the Whig tradition — and particularly the Catholic Whig tradition — offers the world's best statement of philosophical principles and practical guidelines, concerning how and why free citizens should shape new societies worthy of their human rights and ordered liberties. Such societies, to secure these rights, must give primacy to community. But to build true and authentic communities, these societies must give primacy to persons. Both forms of primacy are important. Each is necessary for the other's definition — and for the other's flourishing.

To secure the rights of the person, give primacy to community. To build a genuinely human community, give primacy to the person. Such is the Catholic Whig tradition, tutored by the experience of the Americas and shocked by the terrors of the twentieth century. And such, now, is most of the world's agenda.

Notes

1. Aristotle, *Nicomachean Ethics*, in *The Basic Works of Aristotle*, edited with an introduction by Richard Mckeon (New York, 1941), Bk. X, Ch. 9 (1179b19).
2. See my "Estructuras de Virtud, Estructuras de Pecado" in *Estudios Publicos*, No. 31 (Invierno, 1988), pp. 231-246; the English version appeared in *America*, Jan. 28, 1989, pp. 54-60.
3. See Wilhelm Windelband, *A History of Philosophy*, Vol. 1 (New York, 1958), p. 257; compare also Franz Mueller, "Person and Society According to St. Thomas Aquinas," *Aquin Papers* (St. Paul, Minn., n.d.), No. 17, Preface.
4. Franz Mueller argues that "there are essentially different reasons for the living together of gregarious animals and that of men." The difference can be traced to man's "personal" as distinguished from his "individual" nature, and man's "personal nature exists only secondarily for the sake of the human race, but primarily for his own sake." It follows that, though St. Thomas "proclaims the primacy of the common weal [over the particular], he confirms at the same time the existence of an individual good and its relative autonomy in its own sphere. There is a certain good proper to every man insofar as he is a single person. . . . There is, on the other hand, another, the common good, which pertains to this one or that one as far as they are parts of some whole, as to the soldier insofar as he is a part of the army, and to the citizen insofar as he is a part of the state" (Ibid., pp. 21, 26). Similarly, Jacques Maritain writes that "it is the human person who enters into society; as an individual, he enters society as a part whose proper good is inferior to the good of the whole (of the whole constituted of persons). But the good of the whole is what it is, and is therefore superior to the private good, only if it benefits the individual persons, is redistributed to them, and respects their dignity." *The Social and Political Philosophy of Jacques Maritain* (New York, 1955), p. 87.
5. Thus St. Thomas quotes this passage from Aristotle, *Nicomachean Ethics*, Bk. I, Ch. 2 (1094b). E. Kurz, O.F.M., has counted up the occurrences of this passage in St. Thomas; see *Individuum und Gemeinschaft beim Hl. Thomas v. Acquin* (Munich, 1933), p. 47.

6. Thomas Aquinas only reluctantly found reasons for calling a war "just." He phrased his question in the negative: "Can war ever be just?" *ST* II-II 40.

7. Lord Acton gave Aquinas credit for this theory in "The History of Freedom in Christianity," *Essays on Freedom and Power,* ed. Gertrude Himmelfarb (Cleveland and New York, 1955), p. 88: he writes that the language found in the "earliest exposition of the Whig theory of the revolution, is taken from the works of St. Thomas Aquinas. . . ."

8. In the very first paragraph of *The Federalist,* Alexander Hamilton called attention to the centrality of reflection and choice: "It has been frequently remarked that it seems to have been reserved to the people of this country, by their conduct and example, to decide the important question, whether societies of men are really capable or not of establishing good government from *reflection* and *choice,* or whether they are forever destined to depend for their political constitutions on accident and force." *The Federalist Papers,* Intro. by Clinton Rossiter (New York, 1961), p. 33 [italics added].

9. "If patient observation and sincere meditation," writes Tocqueville, "have led men of the present day to recognize that both the past and the future of their history consist in the gradual and measured advance of equality, that discovery in itself gives this progress the sacred character of the will of the Sovereign Master. In that case [any] effort to halt democracy appears as a fight against God himself, and nations have no alternative but to acquiesce in the social state imposed by Providence." *Democracy in America,* trans. George Lawrence, ed. by J. P. Mayer (Garden City, N.Y., 1969), p. 12.

10. Ibid., 514; see also p. 189: "Better use has been made of association and this powerful instrument of action has been applied to more varied aims in America than anywhere else in the world."

11. Ibid., 513.

12. Ibid., 517. "It cannot be repeated too often," Tocqueville writes, that "nothing is more fertile in marvels than the art of being free, but nothing is harder than freedom's apprenticeship" (p. 240). Especially in ages of democracy, the defense of freedom requires an arduous education. "A great deal of intelligence, knowledge, and skill are required in these circumstances to organize and maintain secondary powers and to create, among independent but individually weak

citizens, free associations which can resist tyranny without destroying public order'' (p. 676).

13. See n. 17 below.

14. See Peter L. Berger and Richard John Neuhaus, *To Empower People* (Washington, D.C., 1977), Ch. V, ''Voluntary Association.''

15. ''The State,'' writes Maritain in *Man and the State* (Chicago, 1951), p. 24, ''is neither a whole nor a subject of right, or a person. It is a part of the body politic, and, as such, inferior to the body politic as a whole, subordinate to it, and at the service of its common good. The common good of the political society is the final aim of the State, and comes before the immediate aim of the State....'' For a more detailed account see ''The People and the State'' (Ibid., pp. 1-27).

16. ''Precisely because man is a person,'' writes Franz Mueller, ''and because in his consciousness and in his conscience, he can, as it were, converse with himself, he seeks to communicate with others in the order of knowledge and love. Such intercommunication wherein man really gives himself and wherein he is really received is something without which the human person cannot achieve perfection. The spiritual soul, the likeness of God in man, would be stunted without such communication.'' Thus, Mueller concludes, ''man requires the assistance of his fellow men, not primarily because he has been deprived of parts and powers which he needs to be a complete substance, or even because he was created a helpless being, but because it is natural for him to tend toward communion.'' See Franz Mueller, ''Person and Society,'' p. 20.

17. Following Tocqueville, Hannah Arendt notes a crucial distinction between a people and a mob. A mob is approached through the stampeding of its passions, as through a demagogue. A mob is but a collection of individuals, animated not by their autonomous capacities for making choices infused by reflection and reasoned discourse, but rather by their unformed passions swayed by whatever winds may blow. By contrast, a people is an assembly of many smaller assemblies, each with its own forms of reasoned association and reflective consent. A people is a large society of many smaller societies, within which reason holds sway. Thus, Arendt observed a crucial difference between the social condition of North Americans and the social condition of the populations of Europe (France in particular). In America, she noted, there was a people; in France, the masses and the mob. The

149

people of North America had had the good fortune, as Tocqueville had noted, to organize themselves first in villages and other local communities; then in townships; then in counties; then in states; and, only after the passage of one hundred fifty years, in a national federal government. By this time they were neither a mass nor a mob but a people — and, after their consent to the Constitution of 1776, a sovereign people. See Hannah Arendt, *On Revolution* (New York, 1965), pp. 69-73, 88-90, 274, and Tocqueville, *Democracy in America*, "The Need to Study What Happens in the States Before Discussing the Government of the Union," pp. 61-98.

18. Father J. Miquel Ibáñez Langlois, for example, made such a charge against Paul Johnson and me in *El Mercurio* (Santiago, Chile), Sept., 1988, p. E6. Gonzalo Rojas Sanches responded on our behalf in the same pages (Oct. 23, 1988), p. E15.

19. Jacques Maritain, *Reflections on America* (New York, 1958).

20. Thomas Jefferson, "A Summary View of the Rights of British America, 1774," in Adrienne Koch and William Peden, eds., *The Life and Selected Writings of Thomas Jefferson* (New York, 1972), p. 311.

Sources of Community: Reflections on America

Kenneth L. Schmitz, Cambridge Center for the Study of Faith and Culture

American society and American culture are vastly complex so that they defy simple description. Moved by various and often antagonistic forces, American culture holds within itself an astonishing variety: a mixture of received populations, a variety of values, opinions, and styles. As a Canadian I thought — as do other Canadians — that we, among all peoples, are best poised to understand the American fact. We watch their films and television, read their books and journals, buy their products, cheer on their sports' teams, and say "Hi" to them as we come and go across the border. But it took me a good part of two decades living in the U.S. as a permanent resident to discover the misunderstanding that arises from these sources. *There is too much unity in them.* Very little of the quiet but genuine regional and other diversity within the culture comes across, least of all in television, film, and newspapers.

The religious diversity of America is better known, on the other hand. The culture holds within itself a variety of articulate faiths: Christian and Jewish, and more recently Muslim, Hindu, and Buddhist, not to speak of home-grown varieties. But it holds them in a very definite way. It is home to atheists, too, and those defiant of or indifferent to religion in all of its forms. Indeed, there is the odd amalgam entitled "Protestants and Other Americans United for the Separation of Church and State." But of course, the state is not equivalent to the culture, and most Americans take pride in the freedom accorded to the many religions.

The Catholic reality is various, too, embracing within it a variety of peoples, cultures, rites, communities, and callings. For purposes of comparison we may put the matter thus: American culture proudly contains within *its* liberty a plurality of religions, whereas the Catholic religion contains within *its* liberty a variety of cultures. And so, the meeting of Catholicism and Americanism is the meeting of two different liberties. Moreover, both are "ordered liberties." Nor can their different orders be

151

reduced simply the one to the other. Nevertheless, while they are distinct, they cannot remain — if the Catholic is to remain one yet both American and Catholic — simply separate. And indeed, they have grown up together within each American Catholic so that they must be grasped as mutual liberties open to each other. For the Catholic who is American, then, the quest becomes: to find an order among these ordered liberties.

Now, there is unity as well as variety in each of these ordered liberties. Even as the term "Catholic" names a unity of faith, dogma, and cult, so also the term "American" stands for some definite social, political, and cultural unity. In comparison with more traditional cultures, American culture is self-consciously political. During an evening of conversation with Americans it is not uncommon to pass on from talk about sports to talk about politics. Individual and social activism generally receives approval, at least in the abstract. And in actuality democracy and individual initiative flourish within the society. Participation is high, too, although — unless bank-robbing and other violent crimes count as social participation — a considerable degree of alienation is also present.

Still, one who is not American can sense better than define the unity that is characteristically American. It is usually not difficult to spot an American abroad, though occasionally he may be an English-speaking Canadian under false colors. But it is much more difficult to explain the basis of one's recognition. Indeed, it is in attempting to define what is distinctively American that most of us come to grief. And yet, Americans love to define their culture, too. And they do not always do it well — as the distortions of Hollywood and television tell us. Indeed, it remains a puzzle to me to understand how it is that this image-conscious people who invented PR (Public Relations) do such a poor job of portraying themselves to the world at large.

Nevertheless, the culture is attractive to many non-Americans. Some of their political ideas have been borrowed by others, and their technology and business organization, too. In the arts American novels, American painting, and American jazz have their global following. At a popular level, we have only to quake before the wail of "Country" music in Third World bazaars and cafés, need only observe the worldwide cult of blue jeans, and witness the epic battle between Coke and Pepsi for world markets to confirm the still lively presence of America abroad. One suspects that people buying such typically American products often purchase along with them a certain symbolic meaning. If it is not precisely the American dream it is surely a near relative of it.

Here, however, one stumbles upon an ambiguity inherent in reflections on American culture. A rector of a German university once lamented to me that students are now coming to the German universities without a knowledge of Greek. "How do you account for that?" I asked in all innocence. Came the brusque reply: "It's due to the Americanization of the Gymnasium." Now, I have a standard reply to European colleagues who make such complaints: "Whenever there is social change and you approve of it you call it progress, but when you don't, you call it American." For much that we call distinctively American is rather more generally mass industrialization; though, because America was in the forefront of such social changes, its own tastes and styles are often simply reproduced by non-American manufacturers. I mean such products as wash-and-wear fabrics, packaged food, and packaged entertainment. But, in these instances, what is distinctively American is entangled with the more general characteristics of a mass society and mass economy. We have all witnessed the spread of a more general modern culture, into which industrialization has penetrated with a penchant for instrumental solutions, and in which relations between persons rely more and more upon the intervention of a technical device, such as a car or plane, a telephone or television. And America has been in the forefront of this process.

On the plane of ideas, it seems to me that America is more than any of the ideologies that attempt to explain it and to harness its energies; but then, too, it is often less than the idealism it professes. In this entangled plethora of ideas, forces, and influences that make up American culture and American society, I wish to speak of a single strain that has some distinctive American features and that poses something of a problem for the American Catholic. This strain in American culture is only one strain, but it is very prominent and it is at present the dominant strain in most public institutions and in the public media.

American culture rightly places high value upon individual initiative. The meanings of these two words bear scrutiny as they have functioned in the American culture, society, and economy. Americans appreciate individual initiative that has produced a product or more generally brought about a result that had not existed before, and that has been brought about either by a solitary individual or initially by an individual subsequently acting in concert with others. Entrepreneurs, inventors, scientists, engineers, organizers, producers, artists, educators; in a word: persons of ability and sometimes of genius, but above all, persons who out of themselves have made a difference, have left things changed from what they had been before. These people are universally admired, of course, and not only by Americans. But the American culture stresses this value, and if Americans any longer retain the ideal or myth of the hero, it is of just such a person. Many Americans have a special pride and confidence that such inventiveness happens more often in America, and happens because of certain political, social, and cultural advantages in being American. A good deal of this confidence is not misplaced, though many Americans are not so confident as they once were.

It is not unusual to call this combination of initiative and individuality the *liberal* strain in American society and culture. In this broad sense the term "liberal" does not so much name a party or definite position, such as that of the American Civil Liberties Union or Americans for Democratic Action, as it names a more fundamental and pervasive cast of mind. It is characteristic not only of those called "liberal," but of "neo-conservatives" as well. It is in this sense that Alaisdair MacIntyre observes that much of the debate today in America goes on between different kinds of liberals, that is, between conservative liberals, radical liberals, and liberal liberals.[1] Of course, there are other strains in American culture, such as that of the Covenantal Protestantism of the Pilgrim Fathers and the Evangelical Fundamentalism of Sunday morning television and daily AM radio. But the liberal strain I have in mind is also distinctively American, though it arose in part out of a European set of ideas, adapted skillfully to American conditions, and until recently without the confrontational energy that pitted European liberals against traditional believers. European influences did not cease with the founding of the Republic, however, and have continued to play a role even in our own day.

It seems to me that liberalism in its several classical European forms sought to enunciate certain emerging ideals of individual freedom and individual rights in a particular way. Now, these are undoubtedly genuine human values, precious in their fragility and insistent in their durability. A better understanding of the pre-modern period of our culture, however, shows that these values were already coming to articulate prominence in the late Middle Ages with the spread of literacy and the increased accessibility to education, with the "free air" of the towns and the practice of quit-rent in the countryside, with the rise of the merchant classes and the growth of trade, and with the formation of national states and the breakup of a universal Christendom. This was a quite general development open to different interpretations. And so, it is misleading to simply identify these rights as such with liberalism which is a particular interpretation of the process. And it is mistaken to claim them unquestioningly as *liberal* rights so that to oppose liberalism is to oppose these rights. They are not liberal rights; they are initially European, then American, but above all, they have come to be recognized as human rights.

Liberalism is many things, of course, too many to be captured in one short paper in English, or even in a brief introductory sketch in several German volumes. In its various versions liberalism has provided, not so much a theory — for there is more than one liberal theory, ranging from Locke and Spinoza to Kant and beyond — as a range or set of theories with a certain emphasis. The liberal spirit is an attitude toward change which the *literati* and the *philosophes* developed into interpretations of human history. These interpretations share alike an appreciation of the element of novelty in the change. The practicality and conservative temper of many of the American founders qualified and redirected the more extreme tendencies of doctrinaire liberalism, without, however, altering those basic tendencies or providing them with a more fully human foundation and with a more circumspect rational justification.[2]

It may be immodest to attempt to propose a better *rationale* for America than liberalism, but permit me to suggest one. Now, I am Aristotelian enough to accept the broad lines of his analysis of change which balances discontinuity and novelty with continuity and permanence. But I am modern enough to recognize that the Aristotelian analysis may have given too much value to continuity and permanence, if it is to take the measure of the massive shift we call "modernization." On the other hand, the liberal spirit and the liberal ideology gives too little recognition to continuity and permanence. Its account of modern history is partial and reductionist, slighting the past and the stability needed by society. For the liberal spirit and interpretation expresses principally the moment of difference and discontinuity in that massive change. In appreciating what was new, it tended to take for granted or even to depreciate what was old. It heralds the new and, in the various versions of social contract theory or the more abrupt concept of revolution, it celebrates a radical new beginning for society. Once established, it nurtures a tradition of its own by taking its own past up into its search for the new. Its anti-traditional bias is not incidental to it.

It is only fair to recognize that this emphasis undoubtedly played a role in the re-conception of history which lies at the basis of the explosion of the historical disciplines in the nineteenth century. Now, history is not tradition. Unlike the tradition-based confidence of immediate continuity with the past, the new historical consciousness emphasizes the gulf between the present and the past. Instead of stressing the sameness of present and past, it stresses their difference. In compensation it has had to develop a method for the recovery of knowledge about the past. At the same time, the sense of discontinuity and the emphasis upon difference has contributed to some of the excesses of this historical method, especially when applied to realities as traditional as religion and social mores.

No doubt, too, that in its actual development the liberal spirit is closely associated with the rise of modern science and the demise of traditional metaphysics. For the new mechanistic science of the seventeenth century differed from the older physics. The philosophy of nature is a study of mobile being, that is, the study of motion translated into an ontological context, which resolved motion into the principles and causes of being. The new science was a study of motion as such, and motion was initially understood as displacement. With the shift of attention to transitive force, rest was no longer conceived as intransitive activity, and with the abandonment of final causes, rest lost one of its traditional meanings, that is, the sense of complete and perfected being. It became simply the transitory absence of motion. There are good reasons to think, however, that early modern science arose out of a deeper common thrust which also received a particular expression in the social and political ideas that still animate the spirit of liberalism.

In keeping with the emphasis upon motion, the liberty of the individual came to be seen, not simply traditionally as the power to choose, but equally and even primarily as the power to *unchoose*. For where choice is the supreme value, it proves its ultimacy by choosing to disengage from its previous choices. A present-day version of this is found in Bruce Ackerman's forty-year-old "Shifty." We are told that Shifty ought not to have to keep promises he made as a stripling twenty-year-old. If we ask: Why? we are told that Shifty is not at all the same person he was then. Differing as a totality, he is said to differ totally.[3] For liberal choice is not ordered toward a good somehow already inscribed in the nature of things or prescribed for the individual. Liberal choice is directed rather toward itself, toward *the liberty of its liberty*. Liberal choice vindicates itself by its innate power to relinquish its past choices. And in retaining that motility it retains in the mode of liberty the primacy of mobility that is also the supreme interest of the science of nature. This, it seems to me, is what Gabriel Marcel meant when he charged Sartre with a physicalistic conception of freedom. The foundation and force of liberalism lies in the simplicity of the individual's power to move — the impulse to change one's mind and one's place and, where possible, one's world. In this power lies the liberal exaltation of the freedom of the individual.[4] Bella Abzug recently put the matter more succinctly when she insisted that it did not matter *what* one chose, the important point is *that* one does choose.

A résumé of the career of the term *conatus* and its cognates, so prevalent in the seventeenth and eighteenth centuries, provides evidence for this interpretation. Pico della Mirandola's Renaissance *Oration on the Dignity of Man* is a harbinger of the later stress upon liberty. Descartes's proclamation of the infinitude of the will and the liberty of indifference is the translation of a late medieval voluntarism into the modern context.[5] Hobbes's insistence that in the state of nature everyone has a right to everything is a dramatic assertion of primitive striving.[6] Spinoza's maxim that "every natural thing has by nature as much right as it has power to exist and operate" and his rejection of free choice defines freedom in terms of *conatus*.[7] Locke is much more subtle than one first thinks, but his determination of volition as a simple rather than a complex idea may well be a concession to such voluntarism.[8] Hume characterizes passion as "an original existence," which moves the individual prior to rational deliberation, and he insists that it is able to be countered only by another such original impulse.[9] It is operative in Kant, too, in the self-dynamism of the will, but his insistence that it have a kind of rationality *sui generis* transmutes the dynamism into self-legislation according to practical reason.[10]

The understanding of initiative as liberty and liberty as *conatus* found favor among entrepreneurs and intellectuals who sought reform of the social order. The question was where to place the source of that innovative energy. What we generally call "liberalism" has favored the individual as creative source. But I think that the same cast of mind is open to locating it in the body politic itself, in the General Will, for example, so that collectivism is the other side of liberalism. Indeed, modern thought has oscillated between the extremes of anarchy and totalitarianism. This is due, in part at least, it seems to me, because of the primacy of will as impulse and an understanding of unity that does not permit the proper distribution of authority, that is, that inhibits the recognition of the legitimacy of a variety of institutions within society, each with their own authority.

The mechanism that was concomitant with the rise of modern liberalism formed its sense of the basic unit within a predominantly nominalist conception of unity.[11] The search for the basic units of reality was a primary expression of that conception. Nominalism identifies unity with simplicity so that the basic unit is the simplest unit, devoid of intrinsic complexity. This fits well with the understanding of *conatus* as impulse, but it fits ill with the conception of society as an intrinsically structured complex. With such a purview, it is difficult, if not impossible, to locate legitimacy in any other social places than either in individuals or in the state. This accounts for the weak development of institutional rights in American political law, that is, the rights of groups *qua* groups, in distinction from minority rights that inhere in individuals, and from class-action suits that let one individual stand for other similar individuals in securing individual rights. The defense of rights has tended to proceed by resolving any group and its membership back into its individuals. This is evidence, among other things, of a nominalistic conception of unity operative in social practice.

The understanding of the individual as a sort of social atom gave impetus to the understanding of social relations in terms of external connections. By placing the social fact outside the essential meaning of the individual, the primacy of the individual's liberty could be preserved. The various social contract theories that have been spawned by liberal thought would seem strange if taken at face value, since they envisage fully formed adult individuals entering into social life. Of course, in the founding of a new republic it is just this that happens, but even it is not founded anew each generation. Not taken literally, social contract theories have functioned as myths in the sense of Plato's *Laws*, a useful rationalization of a sociopolitical structure and practice. But when we ask: What is it that they justify? the answer seems to be: The liberty of the individual as his primary asset.

This does not prevent a move along the scale from individualism toward collectivism. In the interest of a more equitable society, John Rawls insists that the gifted individual does not have ownership rights to the assets of his own intelligence, family associations, and the like that come to him or her by virtue of birth or other accidents of fortune.[12] And others have argued that advocacy of liberalism does not prohibit advocacy of social democracy.[13] For, since these assets are conceived as externally related to the essential core of the individual, they are detachable from him or her. And in such a "social liberalism," the collective *Individuum* — that is, the same nominalistic individual writ large — asserts its prerogative (in the form of the state) in order to redistribute assets and thus to remedy the received rather than the chosen inequalities among individuals. Insofar as what counts as properly belonging to an individual consists of an incomplex *conatus*, each can be equal to others only if each does not differ from others. Equality becomes the enemy of difference. And significant individuality must be stripped of what it has received, and left without proprietary claim even to those differences that have come about by the individual's will. By "significant individuality," I mean individuality that counts in the social and political order. Thus, for example, Bruce Ackerman permits us to bring the baggage of our opinions and our social conditioning on board his metaphorical "spaceship," and even permits us to adjust the "perfect technology of justice" to meet real conditions, but he then stipulates that "no prior conversation has previously established the legitimacy of any claims to the manna in dispute [his name for the primary goods which we all supposedly want]."[14] He then invites us to what he promises will be an open and neutral dialogue. In any event, however, it turns out to be not unlike an invitation to a nudist camp in which you are advised to divest yourself of your clothes only to arrive at the beach wearing considerably less than your hosts. And you find out too late that they have retained what they regard as indispensable beach wear. Now, one of the vestments I should like to cling to is that rights are not only vested in individuals but also in groups, and not in virtue of their individual members but in virtue of themselves.

If the American community is to be more than a nostalgic sigh for intimacy, it must overcome the one-sided stress on individual rights and become an institutionally differentiated reality with a plurality of *independent* sources of publicly recognized legitimacy. Neither the solitary individual nor the collective *Individuum* in the form of the state can alone provide such differentiation. Nor, I suspect, can the communitarian individual (of which we have recently heard so much), at least not without broadly accepted institutional support. America is noted for its multitude of voluntary associations. These are understood to be essentially private associations whose legitimacy reduces to the rights of association that are guaranteed to the individuals who make up their membership. And it is true that these associations supply a socially differentiated space for much that is creative in American society. Michael Novak[15] rightly insists upon mediating institutions for the protection of the individual over against an overbearing state power, but he seems to envisage these mediating institutions as voluntary associations.[16] Now, such associations rest their realization of community upon individual choice rather than upon the public and legal recognition of their *independent* institutional legitimacy. No doubt for many associations this is true to their character and purpose. But it is not adequate for all communities, and certainly not those which have other grounds than individual choice or state power.

For the Catholic, it seems to me, there are three communities especially that are not associations of choice: the family, the culture, and the Church. It is not that there is no freedom in these communities; indeed, one remains within them freely. But they are more than creations of choice. For want of a better term let me call them "communities of response." Neither the family nor one's culture nor the Church is founded in the way in which a voluntary association comes into being. The foundation of these communities of response does not rest upon the choice of their members. Of course, they are moral communities, and choice is exercised within them, but first and last they are communities of *being* before they are communities of *doing*. To be sure, the family is both the primary natural community and an institution within society, but it does not draw its *own* specific legitimacy from its status as an institution within the society. Nor does it draw it from the state, nor from the rights guaranteed to its individual members.

The family draws its legitimacy from the role the species has given it in the genesis and nourishment of life. The response that is called for by this primary natural association is the acknowledgment of parentage and kinship. Culture is a somewhat more amorphous association, but it is just as deep. The response to culture initially takes form as the infant assimilation of language and mores, then as reaction and only later as deliberate selection, emphasis, and choice within the treasury of that culture. The foundations, however, while in the strict sense voluntary, are nevertheless pre-volitional and occur both before and alongside of deliberate choice.

Even more, for the Catholic, the community that is the Church is founded upon receptivity and response. God moves prior to the moment of choice and to human initiative so that the founding initiative *par excellence* is not the individual's; indeed, it is not human at all: it is grace, the divine initiative. We are called to receive and to respond to grace offered so that receptivity and response come before what we ordinarily call choice. In this sense, then, the relationship is pre-volitional. Or, if you will, the first promptings of the human will are not choice, but recognition and acknowledgment of a gift received. Within the communion of the Church morality rests upon ontology. And this priority needs to be reflected in the structures and values of society. It is not enough that this insight be permitted, it needs to be acknowledged as part of the social fabric. I am not speaking of a "Catholic State," nor even of the justly suspect and rejected "hypothesis." Given the plurality of religions and the non-religions, we neither can nor should expect that the Christian understanding of this priority be the only or even the dominant one. But there are a number of ways to acknowledge the priority of morality over ontology without being unjust to others. Thus, a humanist can acknowledge his or her debt to nature, to family, and to community as something that has not been dependent simply upon his or her choice, nor upon a decision of the state. On the other hand, when such communities of nature or of grace — communities of response — are reduced to voluntary associations, they are situated within a context defined almost exclusively, on the one hand, by the institution of power (I mean the state and its apparatus), and on the other, by the choices of individuals; thus the true nature of these communities of response does not emerge. They are squeezed out of shape. The naturalness of the family gives way to "alternative parenting arrangements." The specificity and regionality of culture gives way to a superficial and generalized everydayness promoted largely by the media. And the Church becomes privatized, driven back into the beliefs and preferences of individuals.

Indeed, we can buttress even properly voluntary associations with something better than voluntarism, if we only look carefully at the actual constitution of the individual. Once again, I am Aristotelian enough to work with his understanding of the individual. It is not the individual unit of nominalism or atomism; rather he always has in mind an internally structured individual of a certain sort (*tode ti*).[17] When we come to the human kind, however, we no longer speak only of what nature has given us as a biological basis, we speak also of the *polis* and its sociality; but we recognize (perhaps better than he did) that human sociality is open to historical development. Both the biological and social constituents of the human individual comprise what he or she has received from nature, family, and other communities so that we may call them *commonalities*. They are constitutive relations in which we participate with others in the mutual formation of ourselves and others, and not only with other persons, but also with things and with the natural environment as well. Now, many of these relationships are entered into by choice, but some are not. Sometimes they come to us, sometimes they are already there before we recognize that they have formed us. All are constitutive of each of us as individuals. Some of them have moral import, but that import does not first wait upon our choice or rejection. It is in this rich sense, then, that a manifold of commonalities are constitutive of the individual.

But the individual is also singular, and this *singularity* is as essential to the individual as the various commonalities. The inherent equality *among* individuals, so prized by liberalism, is not due to the equality of non-difference; it arises rather from the equality of the constitutive factors *within* each individual, since both singularity and commonality are *equally* indispensable in his or her formation. This intrinsic equality of the factors of singularity and commonality within the individual is the true basis of extrinsic social equality, that is, of equality among individuals. Such an ontological equality does not strip individuals bare of their differences; it is instead the equality of integrity that respects those differences.

Our double constitution as individuals calls us to acknowledge what is given and not chosen. We are to acknowledge them, not as Rawls's assets which merely happen to us and are not really ours, but as gifts received from a thousand hands, from the living and the dead. Voluntary

162

associations will receive strength in being rooted in a society that recognizes several independent sources of communal and institutional legitimacy. The Catholic receives this model of community from participation in the Church, but its application is not restricted to communities of faith. It should be argued for on its own merits within the social and political discussion among Americans who seek the improvement of their ordered liberty.

Notes

1. *Whose Justice? Which Rationality?* (Notre Dame, 1988), p. 392.
2. A. Schlesinger, *The Cycles of American History* finds a more balanced interpretation in Frank Bourgin, *The Great Challenge: The Myth of Laissez Faire in the Early Republic* (New York, 1989).
3. *Social Justice in the Liberal State* (New Haven, 1980), pp. 198ff.
4. See Kenneth L. Schmitz, "Is Liberalism Good Enough?" in: *Liberalism and the Good*, eds. G. Mara et al. (London and New York [to appear, Spring, 1990]).
5. *Meditations* IV.
6. *Leviathan* I, 14.
7. *A Theologico-Political Treatise*, c. xvi.
8. *Essay Concerning Human Understanding* II, 6.
9. *Treatise on Human Understanding* II, iii, 3.
10. *The Foundations of the Metaphysics of Morals*; but see also *What is Enlightenment?*
11. Isaiah Berlin in: "The Two Concepts of Liberty," *Four Essays on Liberty* (Oxford, 1969), 1986, p. 129, n. 1, mentions "the valuable discussion" of Michel Villey in: *Lecons d' histiore de la philosophie du droit*, "who traces the embryo of the notion of subjective rights to Occam."
12. *A Theory of Justice* (Cambridge, 1971), pp. 98f., 101f., 179. See also M. Sandel, *Liberalism and the Limits of Justice* (Cambridge, 1982), pp. 70-72.
13. See, for example, John A. Hall, *Liberalism: Politics, Ideology and the Market* (Chapel Hill, 1987), pp. 35-62.
14. Bruce A. Ackerman, *Social Justice in the Liberal State* (New Haven, 1980), p. 25.

15. In this volume and in other publications, especially: *Catholic Social Thought and Liberal Institutions*, 2nd ed., (New Brunswick and Oxford, 1989); and also *Free Persons and the Common Good*.

16. For a somewhat different treatment of mediating institutions, see Kenneth L. Schmitz, "The Authority of Institutions: Meddling or Middling?" in: *Communio* 12 (Spring, 1985), 5-24.

17. See Kenneth L. Schmitz, "Community: The Elusive Unity," in: *Review of Metaphysics* 37 (December, 1983), 245-264; and "Is Liberalism Good Enough?" (n. 4 above).

Response to Michael Novak and Kenneth L. Schmitz

by Mary F. Rousseau, Marquette University

There is a logic that has brought us to this point of the conference. Our general theme is "Nature and Grace: On Being Catholic in America." The theme of this particular session is "The Foundations of Community." We thus come to a question that is crucial to understanding our lives as Catholics in America. The priority of grace over nature tells us that we must be Catholics first and then, to the extent that it is possible, Americans. Our faith requires us to take a critical view of our culture, and to take part in it only to the degree that its values are compatible with our beliefs, and with our life in the Trinity. Political and social life and other voluntary actions can be ways of living the life of grace, but they are not necessarily so. And so, it is an important task of this conference to attempt a critique of American culture, of American social and political life, and of the voluntary associations of Americans, in terms of how communal these are. The question must be to what extent these are ways of living the life of a communal nature elevated by Trinitarian, thus communal, grace, for our God is not a single Person, living in isolated splendor. Our God is three-personed, a unity in which three persons have their very identities as three distinct persons only in relation to, in communion with, one another.

The theme of Mr. Novak's paper is evident in this title: "Priority of Community, Priority of Person." Speaking out of the Catholic Whig tradition, he offers a positive evaluation of American culture in terms of its communal character. We Americans have, to his mind, shown a genius for inventing practical ways to respect these two equal priorities. One of our distinctive and ingenious inventions has been voluntary associations, in which numbers of persons freely choose to collaborate in common goals. These voluntary associations act as buffers between the power of the state and the freedom of individuals. They also actuate the communal nature of individual persons, a nature that is inherently social because of our distinctively human powers of knowing and loving, of insight and choice, of communication.

The theme of Professor Schmitz's paper, "Sources of Community: Reflections on America," is that we American Catholics have to find our own cultural ways of giving correct priority to the ordered liberty of the Church, which is open to many cultures, over the ordered liberty of our culture, which is open to many religions, and, indeed, to the absence of religion. We must be Catholics first, then, and, to the extent that we can be, Americans, participants in our distinctive culture. Catholics in America must be American Catholics, not Catholic Americans.

But the synthesizing of these two liberties is no easy matter. Establishing the priority of Catholic liberty over American liberty means that our relations with one another must be intrinsically and genuinely communal. We must have ontological relations among us that are prior to the choices by which we associate with one another. And our choices, our voluntary associations with one another, must conform to that ontological communality. We have thus reached a focal point of the conference: one who would be Catholic in America must participate in this culture in ways that are genuinely, not just apparently, communal.

It is obvious that anti-communal actions, associations, and cultural institutions are contrary to the Trinitarian grace that is our life as Catholics, and thus sinful and out of bounds as far as our participation is concerned. But falsely communal associations, some of which may have all the alluring appearances of community but really are not, are an equally important hazard. For a Catholic, the social science definition of community will not do. A multitude of individuals joined together in the pursuit of a common goal may or may not be a community, thus may or may not be apt for the enculturation of grace.

To focus the question even more sharply, both of our speakers refer to voluntary associations as worthy of special attention. Mr. Novak sees them as developments of the American practical genius for giving proper priority both to community and to persons as individuals. Professor Schmitz is somewhat critical of them for being constructed, based on the power to choose and the power to unchoose, and thus somewhat arbitrary. They do not deserve the honor of being called communities, because they generate only extrinsic relations among their members and weaken the underlying natural, ontological communities of family, Church, and culture, in which ties among members are intrinsic. These natural communities antedate the liberal tradition. They are not of our own making, but come to us as gifts, as the natural context for our voluntary associations.

The critique of culture, then, is a process of discernment. The question whether an association of human persons is or is not a genuine community is precisely the question whether the relations among its members are intrinsic or extrinsic. And this question, in turn, is the question whether its members are or are not united in their distinctively human powers of knowing and loving. Of these two powers, it is the latter, the power to love, that brings persons into real, as distinct from merely psychological, communion. People who are close in time and space but in no other way, with no communication of their inner selves, are not united at all, but are merely juxtaposed—as, for example, passengers on a crowded bus. Those who are intimate, who do communicate their inner selves (whether or not they are also juxtaposed in time and space) are united, but only psychologically, not existentially. Each possesses, and is thus joined to, the self of the other only through the medium of ideas, images, and feelings, all of which are ontologically his or her own.

Genuine existential community, as St. Thomas argues in his treatise on love, is constituted only by love, love of a very precise kind. It is the love which wishes to another, for that other's sake, his or her fully flourishing existence. St. Thomas gives this love an untranslatable Latin name, *amor amicitiae*, a name in which the noun for love is modified by an adjective derived from the same root, as if to say, "lovingest love," "love in the primary sense of the term." It is characterized by altruistic, rather than egocentric, motivation or intent. The ontological power of the human will is such that when I do will to another person, for that other's sake, his or her fully flourishing existence, that existence, while remaining that of the other person, becomes mine as well. We are thus really, truly, existentially one with each other, in and through our possession of a single good in common — the existence of the one who is loved. No other mode of association, no other kind of love, can constitute genuine community.

All human associations, then, must be judged by this norm, including family, Church, and culture, social and political institutions, and those voluntary associations distinctive of our American practical genius. Community becomes a moral norm because it is the measure of our existential fullness, and existence and goodness coincide. Moral goodness is nothing more, and nothing less, than the fully flourishing existence of human persons in the love that constitutes community. The Church is, of course, always a genuine community, because the Holy Spirit, who is the love of God poured forth in our hearts, binds the existence of all the Church's members into an ontological unity. Members of the Church partake in the holiness that is one of its marks when they first receive the love of God and then love one another so that the existence of each and every individual Catholic belongs in common to all. The Triune God is a *Communio par excellence*. The Church is a *communio* by participation in the Trinity. There is no need, then, to evaluate the Church morally. The Church is holy by its ontological participation in the Triune God. But we do need to evaluate our own voluntary association with the Church. We do that by examining our own love, or lack thereof, in our associations with one another and with Father, Son, and Holy Spirit. The discernment of culture is thus part of that discernment of spirits which has been a mark of Catholic spirituality since the time of St. Anthony of the Desert.

Nature, grace, and culture thus come together in genuine community, or they do not come together at all. Nature, as God's creation, is itself a community, the community of many beings, all of which exist by the creative immanence of the one God. The human members of this community of being can consciously and freely appropriate it, thus forming the community that actuates our nature, with its distinctive powers of knowing and loving. Grace elevates our human communality into a higher unity in the indwelling Spirit of Jesus Christ. And culture? A culture is truly communal only to the extent that those born into it, thus receiving it as a gift, appropriate it in *amor amicitiae*, in that charity which informs all the choices of those whose hearts are pure.

Mr. Novak has said that "the primal American experience is community." It is at least arguable that the primal American experience has been either anti-communal or pseudo-communal. I am thinking, for example, of the violent seizure of this land from its native inhabitants, of the enslavement of black Africans, and of the current slaughter of millions of unborn babies for trivial reasons of convenience. All of these horrors have been perpetrated by voluntary associations, and all of them have been sanctioned, in one way or another, by our institutions.

The abuse of the native Americans continues to this day. My own state of Wisconsin recently made national news because white sports fishermen are calling for abrogation of treaties which allow Indians to spear a certain number of walleyed pike, a staple of the Indian diet. Slaves were defined in our Constitution as fractional persons, and black Americans continue to experience higher than average levels of poverty and unemployment, of disease and infant mortality, of discrimination in housing, education, and the workplace. And abortion on demand has now been the law of our land for more than a decade. It is impossible to see any of these practices as motivated by *amor amicitiae*, or as informed by charity.

My question to our two presenters, then, asks for a critique of American culture, and especially of voluntary associations, in terms of whether or not these are genuine communities.

Faith and the Logic of Intelligence: Secularization and the Academy

David L. Schindler,
University of Notre Dame

The God-centeredness, or God-in-Christ-centeredness, of the cosmos is affirmed throughout the Christian tradition, from Irenaeus to Pope John Paul II.[1] The present paper focuses one expression of this God-in-Christ centeredness: that of the Creed of Nicea as amplified at Constantinople.[2] "We believe in one Lord, Jesus Christ, . . . one in being (*homoousios*) with the Father. Through him all things were made."

What does it mean to say that "Jesus Christ is . . . one in being with the Father?" What does it mean to say in turn that "through him all things were made"? And what do these two affirmations, together, imply in terms of the logic of intelligence?

"Jesus Christ is . . . one in being with the Father." Christ's distinct human nature has its reality, its concrete existence, from the beginning only in the unity of the divine person who is identically the Word who has been with God the Father from all eternity. Christ, in his distinctness as Incarnate Word, is unified with the Father, and this simultaneity of distinctness and unity is what is called relation. The relation is ontological (that is, expresses the logic of his being) rather than moral (that is, a relation first effected by the will).

"Through him all things were made." There is only one *homoousios* (Nicea), only one hypostatic union (Chalcedon). At the same time, however, though this is a truth seen much more clearly in the patristic period than in the modern period, the direct relation of divine and human in the being of Christ is mediated by Christ (in and through the Church by means of the Holy Spirit) to all of created being—to all of the human and natural being of the cosmos—from the beginning of created being's existence. The point, then, is that Christ's relation to the Father is not something which he, as it were, made exclusive or turned in on himself. On the contrary, the relation is one which, in utter freedom and generosity, Christ opens up to all of creation: to every entity and every aspect of every entity in the cosmos. What Christ is by nature all else in the cosmos both is and is to become by adoption and participation.[3]

It needs to be underscored: First, this emphasis upon Christ's sharing of relation to God with all of creation does not entail a denial of the infinite difference between Christ and the rest of creation. What it entails rather is recognition of the radical character of the generosity of God-in-Christ. Secondly, this emphasis upon Christ's sharing of his relation to God does not entail a denial of the fact that the various entities which make up the cosmos share in this relation proportionately, that is, proportionately to their mode or kind of being: conscious and free beings will realize that relation consciously and freely and therefore in ways that rocks, for example, cannot. Finally, this emphasis upon Christ's opening up of relation to God to all created entities from the beginning of their existence does not mean that what is thus "already" is not also a "not yet": the fullness of what is already given in Christ can be realized only in baptism and in faith — which is to say, only by participation in the life of the Church which is the extended body of Christ.

What I mean to suggest here, then, can perhaps be best summed up in the words of Hans Urs von Balthasar, when he says that "God represents and expresses himself in [the world] . . . on the basis of the principle not of pantheistic but of hypostatic union."[4] Thus, on the one hand, the relation to God, the relation of simultaneous distinctness from and unity with God, is not pantheistic: it is not inscribed in the nature of created entities to be unified with God, to be divine. Unity with God, divinization, is exactly infinitely beyond their reach. On the other hand, relation to God is real, that is, in and through the hypostatic union. Relation to God, established in and through God's union with Jesus Christ and his Church, takes its meaning *from* this union with Christ and his Church. And this means a union which is radical: what Christ shares with us, with all of creation, is the reality of his own relation to God and not some other relation. And the point then is that this relation, like Christ's — that is, as utterly freely shared by Christ — is from the depths of being. Every created entity of the cosmos, every aspect of every entity, is, from the beginning of its existence, related to God in Christ.

The creature's relation to God is thus not "substantial": not inscribed in the essence or nature of the creature, such that the divine nature and created nature would be confused — or one or the other eliminated.

171

But that relation likewise is not "accidental": not something which "happens to" the already constituted nature [substantial identity] of the creature, and thus remains extrinsic to that nature. In terms of the Thomistic tradition, that relation is neither substance nor accident after the manner in which *esse* — existential act, the "to be" of things — is neither substance nor accident.

The terminology here can become difficult. The point upon which I wish to insist is twofold: (1) The order of nature is not destroyed but is taken up into the order of grace. The unity of grace and nature does not eliminate their distinctness; but that unity is also (*de facto*, not *de jure*) not after the fact of such distinctness. Grace orients, orders, nature to God in Christ from the beginning of nature's existence. (2) Again, the language of substance and accidents raises profoundly complex questions. The crucial point, whatever terms one wishes to employ, is to recognize that the creature's relation to God runs deeper than its substance (as Augustine and Thomas among others say: God is innermost, is more intimate to me than I am to myself): as deeper than substance, that relation is distinct from, not reducible to, substance; but as deeper than substance, that relation is likewise not "accidental" in the sense of something extrinsic, *added* from *outside*.

All of what I now wish to say about the logic of intelligence I understand to follow by analogy[5] from the *homoousios* and the hypostatic union.

The hypostatic union thus has ontological force: it affects the being of everything.[6] All things have their being only (*de facto*, not *de jure*) as related to God the Father in Jesus Christ (and hence further to one another in God-in-Christ). It follows that the logic of intelligence which takes its origin in a faith rooted in the Creed is a logic of relation. Such a "faithful" logic of intelligence requires understanding the distinct identity of every entity and every aspect of every entity *relationally*. *X*, whatever be the content of *x*, is understood at once to have a distinct identity, and to have that identity only, from the beginning, from within relation. The principles, then, are simultaneously two: things maintain their distinct identity; and they maintain their distinct identity only as always already gathered into relation: to God-in-Christ and to all else in God in Christ.

What this logic of relation requires, then (and this is the thesis proposed in the present argument), is rejection of what may be called *the principle of simple identity.* By the principle of simple identity I mean the principle according to which *x*, whatever be the content of *x*, has its identity in itself, apart from or outside of relation to non-*x*.[7] My suggestion is that it is this principle of simple identity which constitutes the inner meaning of a *secularized* logic of intelligence, at least in the form in which a secularized logic of intelligence has prevailed in the modern West.[8] The basic claim of a Christian logic or, if you will, onto-logic, of relation is that *no simple identities of any sort exist, anywhere.*

My argument, then, is that there are (at least) two logics of intelligence: First, there is a secularized logic whose hallmark is the principle of simple identity, and whose primary features thus are externality and closure (relation of *x* to non-*x* is first external; *x* and non-*x* are first turned in on themselves, closed to each other). These features come to expression in several different ways: causal activity is understood first in terms of *effectivity*, that is, in terms of forceful activity (activity is first and essentially *from outside*); primacy is accorded to the negative or to doubt (psychology of distance), and to control (psychology of mastery and superiority); meaning is first and essentially discrete (*bounded*), and is gotten at most properly by analysis ("breaking up" into ever smaller discrete bits); patterns of thought tend to be dualistic (meaning is gained by the *addition of differences — different identities*); and so on.

In sum, the assumption (however tacit) of the principle of simple identity leads to patterns of thought marked by extroversion (turning outward, staying on the surface), power, domination, and fragmentation.

Second, the logic of intelligence entailed in creedal Christianity in contrast has as its hallmark relation (identities always already in relation). This implies giving primacy to the features of openness and interiority (relation implies openness *from within* of *x* to non-*x*). These features likewise come to expression in several different ways. Causal activity understood first as forceful gives way to activity understood first as interior: to forming and finalizing activities which are from within, and to effective activity now understood first as creative and generous rather than as forceful. The primacy of negation, doubt, and control gives way to a primacy of affirmation, receptivity, and responsiveness (psychology of community and of humility). The meaning of entities is seen from the beginning as relational, and this in turn implies a primacy of "seeing" over analysis (the primitive openness of knower to known and vice versa indicates immediacy of relation just as primitive closure indicates

173

mediacy). Likewise, if meaning is relational, it follows that its fullness is found, not by turning in on itself, but by opening itself to ever larger meanings: each discrete bit of meaning is open from the beginning to ever higher unities of meaning.

In sum, a logic of relation, of identities-in-relation, unfolds into a pattern of thought characterized first and essentially by love: by interiority, by receptivity and response, and by integration.

It is important that the distinction drawn here between these two logics be understood as a distinction, not by way of exclusion, but in terms of what is to be accorded primacy. Either of the logics, to be comprehensive, in some significant sense must include the features of both. For example: a logic of intelligence which would be comprehensive must include both externality and interiority. But it makes all the difference what is presupposed (however tacitly) as the first principle in such an inclusion. Presupposition of the principle of simple identity as a first principle forces inclusion by way of dualistic addition or monistic reduction; presupposition of the principle of relation leads to inclusion by way of integration. Thus, on the presupposition of the principle of simple identity: interiority becomes the "in here" in contrast to the "out there" (external), and hence we have a dualism of private and public or again of subjective and objective; or interiority gets eliminated, simply collapsed into the "out there" (behaviorism). In contrast, on the presupposition of the principle of relation, interiority is revealed *in* what is external, and thus in a way that simultaneously affects the meaning of both interiority and externality (the external has a depth, is a disclosure of depth). The (Cartesian) ghost in the machine becomes rather something like the (Thomistic) incarnated spirit.[9]

The logic of secularization which has as its hallmark the principle of simple identity can perhaps be most aptly termed Cartesian. My suggestion is that it is this logic which has prevailed in the modern West.[10] And the logic of faith which has as its hallmark the principle of relation can, I think, be most aptly termed marian. What Mary's *fiat* teaches us, in the context of all that has been said, is that faithful intellectual activity takes its origin in "letting it be done according to the Word": in letting being be, in helping being to be, according to the Word. Calling that logic of faith marian reminds us that its principle of relation is first theological-christological in meaning: all entities are relational because of — in and through — the relation to God the Father established in Jesus Christ. But

174

that principle of relation is at once ontological in meaning: for the relation to the Father established in Christ has been utterly freely passed on by Christ (through his Church in the Holy Spirit) to all of creation. And thus we have the comprehensiveness of what is indicated by Mary's *fiat*: receptivity and response to the Word entails receptivity and response to all of being in the Word. Mary's *fiat* is a christo-logic which entails an onto-logic.

The preceding argument gives rise to a number of questions. First and perhaps above all: if it is true that what has prevailed in modernity has been a logic of secularization whose central principle is that of simple identity or identification, then it also seems true that the achievements of modernity, notably in medicine and technology — not to mention in the politico-social order with its emergence of liberal democracy — are likewise a function of that same principle. To put it another way, do not these achievements presuppose the kind of specialization which requires assumption of the principle of simple identity, with all that that implies in terms of externality and closure in method and content?

In response it must be made clear that the present argument challenges, not specialization as such, but the *how* of specialization: it challenges the assumption that specialization is coterminous with the fragmented form it has taken in modernity. Specifically: the logic proposed here in the name of a creedal faith does not entail a rejection of the distinctness of the identity of entities required for specialization; it does entail approaching that distinctness as having its proper meaning from the beginning *within* and *not outside of* relation. In a word, the argument presented here establishes the principle for an alternative logic of specialization, and not for a rejection of a logic of specialization. What this alternative logic entails in the concrete detail of its working out is an important issue which must be taken up elsewhere.[11]

But here it must be asked whether such an alternative logic is not required, precisely in the face of the achievements of modernity. Have these achievements been unmixed blessings? Has modernity's assumed logic led to progressively deeper and better understandings of God, of men, of nature, and of their relations? Have developments in medicine and technology improved our ecological understanding and living and sensibility? Has liberal democracy with its inherent tendency to understand politico-social order exhaustively in terms of the self-interest of individual persons and nation-states promoted health and wholeness? And so on. These questions are of course profoundly complex. I raise them only for the purpose of drawing attention to the fact that, if it is the case that the achievements of modernity are in a significant sense linked to a fragmented sort of specialization and thus in turn to an assumed principle of simple identity, then it follows that the problems attendant upon such achievements are likewise linked to this fragmentation and this principle of simple identity. Perhaps then it is worthwhile to consider an alternative logic: one rooted in a more integrated (relational) sense of identity.

In any case, if we as Christians accept the ontological force of the Incarnation, then we *must* consider such an alternative: if things have their being only in relation to Jesus Christ and to all else in Jesus Christ, then of course they can have health and wholeness of being only in relation. They can be properly understood, from the beginning and finally, only in relation.

There is a special form of the preceding question: namely whether the logic which has as its first principle the principle of simple identity can be employed — for practical or pragmatic reasons — merely as a methodological strategy: that is, rather than as a metaphysics. In other words, is it not legitimate to study entities as simple identities, so long as one does not intend to claim thereby that such entities *actually exist* as simple identities? Properly qualified, this question adds nothing significant to the preceding question. For the issue forced by the earlier argument bears not so much (not only) on whether, in the focal study of x (whatever be the content of x), one will remain open to non-x. The issue bears rather (also) on the *how* of that openness. In focusing the distinct identity of x, one does (or can) leave (relation to) non-x unattended to or merely implicit. But the crucial moment comes when one turns to consider (relation to) non-x: if that relation is treated after the manner of an *addition*, or indeed after the manner of a *reduction* (to x or to non-x, or to some third simple entity), then one has presupposed the principle of identity exactly in the sense which requires challenge in the light of the logic of faith sketched above. It thereby becomes irrelevant whether one calls such a procedure merely a strategy or also a metaphysics: for the result in either case is a closure just so far to the truly integrated patterns of thought required by creedal faith. I take it as evident that it is just this sense of procedure which prevails in the academy today.[12]

176

The first two questions concerned a secularized logic of intelligence considered as a logic of specialization. The third question concerns that logic of intelligence precisely in its character as secularized. The question is whether the logic of relation we have sketched in the name of a creedal faith, in challenging what we have called a secularized intelligence, does not effectively eliminate the distinctly secular character of intelligence altogether? Does not a primitive disposition to understand all of being in terms of relation, indeed a disposition whose origin and end is given in Christian faith, of its very nature preempt the inner dynamics of inquiry: not only by indicating in advance (in some significant sense) what is the truth of things (namely their identity-in-relation), but also and especially by insisting that that truth is given most properly in faith, and is thus not accessible, at least in its fullest form, outside of faith?

First, one needs to recognize that it is not only what I have called a "faithful" logic of intelligence which is guided at the outset by some presupposed truth. Quite to the contrary: a secularized logic of intelligence is likewise shaped from the beginning and all along the way (however unwittingly) by a presupposed truth: here, the truth of simple identity. The appropriate question, then, is not *whether* one will weight intellectual inquiry in advance but *how* one will do so.[13]

Secondly, then, and in this connection, it is the case that Christian faith requires assumption of the principle of relation: commits one in advance to the truth of identities-in-relation. And indeed it is the case that this truth to which one is committed in advance has its full and proper meaning only in God as trinity and in Jesus Christ as simultaneously divine and human: and thus in faith. But the pertinent point once again is that this properly Christian meaning has ontological force: *it turns up (also) in the logic of being* — in the various (analogous) ways suggested earlier. The Christian, then, precisely as Christian, is committed to showing the how and where and in what ways relation (openness and interiority) show up *in* the cosmos: *in* the natural and human entities of the cosmos. This requires ontological (cosmological, anthropological) inquiry which is *distinct* from theology, even as it is never to be *separate* from theology. Again, to use the language of grace and nature: nature is truly *related* to grace. Grace thus makes a difference *in* nature, even as it does not thereby absorb or eliminate nature. Hence the Christian is committed at once to showing the difference grace makes, and to showing that difference as turning up *in nature* (as a matter of nature as well as of grace). There follows the legitimacy and indeed requirement in principle of distinctly "natural" inquiry.

Thus one can and must distinguish between a secular and a secularized logic of identity. The difference between them is a difference in their understanding of relation: both logics recognize the distinct identity of entities in the cosmos, but a secular logic does so only as first within relation, while a secularized logic does so only as first outside of relation.

We move, then, to the theme indicated by the subtitle of this paper: "Secularization and the Academy." One of the most widely quoted claims regarding the relation of Catholic faith to the university today is that a Catholic university is a university first and Catholic second: because and in the sense that "university" is the noun or "substance," as it were, and "Catholic" is the adjective or "accident." I take this statement to be a paradigmatic statement of a logic of secularization.

What such a statement typically means is that the Catholic university, as a university first or substantially, is to take over its fundamental logic — the fundamental logic of specialization or of the disciplines — from the university as understood in its conventional sense. My assumption here is that the logic of specialization which is dominant in the contemporary American university is a logic mediated by the principle of simple identity, in all of that principle's implications as sketched earlier. Given this assumption, it follows that the Catholic university which acts consistently with its self-understanding as a university first or substantively is thereby committed to the following two alternatives when it adds its Catholic dimension. On the one hand, if Catholicism is introduced as a matter of logic (substance), and thus as a matter of reason and intelligence, then Catholicism (theology) will and must be introduced in terms of a reason from which relation has already and just so far been removed. On the other hand, Catholicism can be introduced as a matter *not* of logic (not of substance but of accident), and thus not as a matter of reason and intelligence: in which case Catholicism will and must be introduced as a matter of relation without reason (for example, as a matter of will).

In sum, given the self-understanding carried in the above statement one can say of the Catholic university: if a matter of logic or reason, then just so far secularized; if not secularized, then just so far not a matter of logic or reason—rather a matter of will. We have a secularized substance

178

coupled with Catholic accident: a religion of reason without relation conjoined with a religion of relation without reason.

To put the matter more concretely, by secularized substance I mean a Catholic university, for example, wherein theology is taught and researched after the manner of a secularized logic, with all the implications of such a logic in method and content as outlined above.[14]

And by Catholic accident I mean a university, for example, which maintains a high profile on matters of morality and social justice (matters of will): regulation of moral behavior in student dormitories; minority recruitment; establishment of centers for social concern and institutes for peace studies and the like.

Two qualifications are in order here: the burden of my criticism is to challenge the importance neither of a scholarly or "scientific" theology, nor of high standards of moral behavior and sensitivity. These are obviously good, and I have no intention of denying the obvious. The intention is to challenge the *how* of "scientific" theology and of moral commitment: the *way* or *form* of their embodiment in a Catholic university. A Catholic university must be concerned to be Catholic in its *mind*, and not merely to couple a secularized mind with a Catholic will.[15]

Secondly, then, it is of course true that a Catholic university whose assumed principle is "university" first (substantively) and "Catholic" second (adjectively) is sometimes better in practice than that principle, consistently applied, would allow it to be: that is, in adding a Catholic dimension such a university sometimes mixes relation and reason together in a way which could be called integrated. The point is merely that such integration, assuming a first principle as stated, cannot be intentional. That integration has rather the character of a blunder.

In the name of creedal Catholicism, the present paper has challenged the logic of intelligence which has as its first principle the principle of simple identity, and has suggested that that logic has been a dominant (though not the exhaustive) logic of modernity. The very nature of this challenge of course invites comparison with other criticisms of modernity, criticisms which we may loosely call "postmodern."[16] These criticisms (linguistic, pragmatic, hermeneutic, "Deconstructionist"), insofar as they are "postmodern," are all concerned (though in different ways) to challenge the objectivist and power-dominated patterns of thought associated (especially) with Descartes and the Enlightenment. If

I may assume the accuracy of the terms adopted in this paper, what these criticisms thereby can be said to be challenging is the principle of simple identity.

The present paper cannot take up in detail the difference between the criticism proposed here and these other, "postmodern" criticisms. I merely wish to propose that the key to that difference will lie in what one makes of identity: one's criticism of what I have called the principle of simple identity will be decisively different depending on: (a) whether one concedes (however tacitly) that identity is (must be) simple identity, that is, in one's very rejection of identity; or (b) whether one from the beginning challenges the assumption that identity is simple identity, and thereby does not so much reject identity as relationalize identity. The first criticism will invariably reflect the very dualistic patterns of thought it seeks to overcome. (Because its criticism does not penetrate radically enough, it will invariably turn into what it intends to reject.) The second criticism will be marked by an ability to integrate what is deepest in what it rejects.[17]

The criticism of modernity in the present paper, offered in the name of a creedal Christianity, intends an integration of the achievements of modernity, even as such an integration presupposes a reaching to the very roots of modernity: transforming the first principle of the logic which has been dominant in modernity.

The nature of the criticism proposed here thus is radical. Is such a radical criticism in fact really called for, that is, for one who begins from within a creedal faith? The affirmative answer to this question which I have proposed can best be assessed by returning to the three key premises of the argument that have led me to take up the criticism: (1) As affirmed in the *homoousios* and the hypostatic union, Jesus Christ is a relation of unity with the Father from the depths of his being. (2) That relation is passed on to the entire cosmos (in grace; "already" and "not yet"): all entities in the cosmos at once have an irreducibly distinct identity, and have that identity only, from the beginning, from within relation (to God in Jesus Christ; to all else in God in Christ). (3) The logic of intelligence which has prevailed in (though does not account exhaustively for) modernity understands the distinct identity of entities (whatever be their content) as first outside of relation. This logic thereby instantiates a logic of secularization. And thus the burden of my argument: a Catholicism, and a Catholic university, which would be true to the meaning of creedal faith, must just so far challenge this logic of intelligence, which I have called the logic of simple identity.

Notes

1. A selection of "Texts Without Comment" is appended. The selection is of course somewhat arbitrary: a mere sampling of the vast riches of the tradition relative to the theme. It nonetheless serves to direct attention to some of the major sources of the argument, as well as to help fill out the fuller context of the argument.

2. I take it that starting from the creedal text requires no apology. It does, however, carry presuppositions. The presuppositions are two: (a) The creed is normative for Christian thinking (and hence by implication Christian thought has an ecclesiological form). (b) With the *homoousios*, the Church formally introduces an ontological pattern of thinking, in terms of both form and content, into Christianity. The *homoousios* carries a realistic intention: makes explicit a claim about how things are. More precisely, the *homoousios* indicates a logic in and of being ("onto" and "logos"). (See, for example, John Courtney Murray, *The Problem of God* [New Haven, 1964], Ch. 2.)

   These presuppositions are embodied in the present argument, but they are not dealt with formally. Though the presuppositions of course raise profoundly difficult issues in relation to the contemporary theological discussion, their formal examination must be taken up elsewhere.

3. This is the foundation for the conception of holiness among the Fathers as a *theōsis* or *theopoiesis*: a God-becoming or being made into God.

4. See the reference as given in the appended texts.

5. That is, by way of an analogy of being which has its center in the christological dogma of Chalcedon — with its decisive terms *"inconfuse"* (without confusion) and *"inseparabiliter"* (without separation) — and its clarifying development in Lateran IV: "Between the Creator and the creature, no likeness can be noted without there being a greater unlikeness to be noted" (DS 806). There is only one hypostatic union. And there is an infinite difference between a relation of unity with God which is by nature and a relation of unity

with God which is by participation. Nonetheless, it is precisely his relation of unity with the Father which Christ opens up to all of creation. The Chalcedonian dogma as clarified by Lateran IV thereby becomes a kind of formula for understanding the deepest reality of all things.

6. See, for example, the striking statement by Pope John Paul II in *Dominum et Vivificantem* (No. 50), given in the appended texts.

7. What is rejected here, in other words, is not the principle of identity — which would of course be inherently self-defeating — but the principle of identity understood as *simple* identity: where no distinction is allowed between simplicity and unity, where any complexity introduced by relation is seen to fracture internal unity. Perhaps the most straightforward expression of this in the modern West can be found in what goes by the name of mechanism (from *mechanaomai*: what has been brought together arbitrarily). In an important way, though also with important differences which would need to be developed, the principle of identity understood as simple identity seems to me operative in other strains of thought which have had a long career in modernity, and which go, variously, by the names of atomism, liberalism, and nominalism.

8. It bears underscoring: the assumption here is not that what I have called the logic of simple identity is the only form a secularized logic can take. Presumably, secularization can also take the form of a logic of relation: indeed, one could reasonably argue that many of the "postmodern" critics of "modernity" (for example, Jacques Derrida and the like) instantiate just such a secularized logic of relation. The assumption of my paper is merely that the logic of simple identity has had a significant career in the academy in modern times, and, while that logic hardly accounts exhaustively for what we call "modernity," it is nonetheless a distinct and important feature of "modernity."

9. It bears emphasis: what is being proposed here is not another dualism — as though it suffices, for example, to balance a Cartesian *idea clara et distincta* with a Pascalian *logique du coeur*, or again to counter a rationalism with new romanticism, and so on. That would miss the point: which is not to expand the rational by *adding* the irrational or non-rational, but to *transform* rationality (in form and content), by situating it from the beginning within relation.

10. With the qualifiers noted in n. 8 above: it is neither the only logic of

modernity, nor the only factor contributing to what we mean by "modernity."

11. I must remain content here with noting an example only of what an appropriate logic of specialization would look like in theology. The example I would offer is the work of Henri de Lubac and Hans Urs von Balthasar. The "specialized" inquiries of these men are ordered from the beginning in and by relation to the Church, and hence in turn in and by the Christology and trinitarian theology revealed through the Church.

12. Methodological strategies, in other words, are never innocent (of ontological assumptions). What seems a simple matter of analysis or observation and the like will be mediated by some form of the principle of identity: of simple identity or of identity-as-open-to-relation. Consider, for example, the person who studies, say, physical or biological entities, while presupposing for purposes of study the principle of simple identity, and who then turns to consider such entities in terms of their relation to God. Unless such a person now sets aside his assumed principle of simple identity, he will invariably discover a God who is either simply outside of these entities, hence conceived by way of *addition* to them, or exhaustively implicated in them, hence conceived by way of *reduction* to them (or of them to God). His approach to God, in other words, will invariably slide off into some form of deism, atheism, or pantheism. What such a person will never discover (insofar as he or she continues, however tacitly, to presuppose the principle of simple identity), is the transcendent-immanent God of the creedal Christian tradition.

The concern here, then, is merely to stress the non-innocence of methodological strategies. What is often taken by such a person to be a conclusion reached by virtue of innocent methodological strategies is in fact a conclusion already guaranteed by the assumption (of simple identity) which "fills" that strategy. Openness to different conclusions (as noted) can come about only by recognizing this assumption, and then by challenging it.

13. See n. 12.

14. That is, theology is marginalized as another "field of specialization," with little or no concern for integration: either in the sense of allowing an ecclesial dimension to shape its methods and content internally (from within) rather than merely externally (from without), or in the

183

sense of itself shedding a transforming light on the whole range of disciplines, the entire order of knowledge. Again, in lieu of the needed development of the concrete meaning of this suggestion, which must be taken up elsewhere, I refer to the examples of the integrated and integrating theology of Henri de Lubac and Hans Urs von Balthasar.

15. For example, if in hiring, Catholicism is considered not as a matter of how one thinks, but only as a matter of one's moral behavior or juridical affiliation with the Church and the like, then the question is no longer *whether* a university which engages in such a practice will become secularized. It already is secularized: that practice is the logic of secularization. The question which remains is merely how consistently that logic will be carried through.

16. The literature here is of course vast. I mention the works only of Derrida, Foucault, Schürmann, Rorty, and, behind them, of Nietzsche, Heidegger, and Wittgenstein.

17. That is, the logic of its criticism will be the logic of love and generosity, as these are "founded" in Christology and trinitarian theology. For an indication of what is intended here, see Kenneth L. Schmitz, "From Anarchy to Principles: Deconstruction and the Resources of Christian Philosophy," *Communio* 16 (Spring, 1989), 69-88.

Texts Without Comment

Lord, you have made so many things! How wisely you made them all! The earth is filled with your creatures.... All of them depend on you to give them food when they need it. You give it to them, and they eat it; you provide food, and they are satisfied. When you turn away, they are afraid; when you take away your breath, they die and go back to the dust from which they came. But when you give them breath, they are created; and you give new life to the earth (Ps. 104).

* * *

The Lord's spirit fills the entire world, and holds everything in it together ... (Wis. 1:7).

* * *

How clearly the sky reveals God's glory! How plainly it shows what he has done! (Ps. 19:1).

* * *

The Lord loves what is righteous and just; his constant love fills the earth. The Lord created the heavens by his command, the sun, moon, and stars by his spoken word. . . . Worship the Lord, all the earth! (Ps. 33:5-6, 8).

* * *

Let the earth bless the Lord. Praise and exalt him above all forever. Mountains and hills, bless the Lord. Everything growing from the earth, bless the Lord. You springs, bless the Lord. Seas and rivers, bless the Lord. You dolphins and all water creatures, bless the Lord. All you birds of the air, bless the Lord. All you beasts, wild and tame, bless the Lord (Dan. 3:74-81).

* * *

Before the world was created, the Word already existed; he was with God, and he was the same as God. From the very beginning the Word was with God. Through him God made all things; not one thing in all creation was made without him. The Word was the source of life; and this life brought light to mankind (Jn. 1:1-4).

* * *

Yet God is actually not far from any one of us; as someone has said, "In him we live and move and have our being" (Acts 17.27-28).

* * *

God put all things under Christ's feet and gave him to the Church as supreme Lord over all things. The Church is Christ's body, the completion of him who himself completes all things everywhere [or: who is himself completely filled with God's fullness] (Eph. 1:22-23).

* * *

God created the whole universe through (Christ) and for (Christ). Christ existed before all things, and in union with him all things have their proper place (Col. 1:16-17).

* * *

Through creation itself the Word reveals God the Creator. Through the world he reveals the Lord who made the world. Through all that is fashioned he reveals the craftsman who fashioned it all (Irenaeus, *Against Heresies*, Bk. 4, 6, 3.5.6.7).

* * *

He who is the good Word of the good Father produced the order in all creation, joining opposites together, and forming from them one harmonious sound. He is God, one and only-begotten, who proceeds in goodness from the Father as from the fountain of goodness, and gives order, direction, and unity to creation (Athanasius, *Discourse Against the Pagans*, 40-42).

* * *

He was not far from it before, for no part of creation had ever been without him who, while ever abiding in union with the Father, yet fills all things that are (Athanasius, *On the Incarnation*, 8).

* * *

The Word was not hedged in by his body, nor did his presence in the body prevent his being present elsewhere as well. When he moved his body he did not cease also to direct the universe by his mind and might. No. The marvelous truth is, that being the Word, so far from being himself contained by anything, he actually contained all things himself. In creation he is present everywhere, yet is distinct in being from it; ordering, directing, giving life to all, containing all, yet is he himself the uncontained, existing solely in his Father (Athanasius, *On the Incarnation*, 17).

* * *

To the Spirit all creatures turn in their need for sanctification; all living things seek him according to their ability. His breath empowers each to achieve its own natural end . . . . Simple in himself, the Spirit is manifold in his mighty works. The whole of his being is present to each individual; the whole of his being is present everywhere. . . . Through the Spirit we acquire likeness to God; indeed we attain what is beyond our most sublime aspirations — we become God (St. Basil the Great, *On the Holy Spirit*, Ch. 9, 22-23).

* * *

There is one Creator of all things, for in God there is one Father from whom all things have their being. And there is one only-begotten Son, our Lord Jesus Christ, through whom all things exist. And there is one Spirit, the gift who is in all (St. Hilary, *On the Trinity*, Bk. 2, 1.33).

* * *

You have made us for yourself, and our heart is restless until it rests in you (Augustine, *Confessions*, Bk. I, Ch. 1).

* * *

Therefore, my God, I would not be, I would in no wise be, unless you were in me. Or rather, I would not be unless I were in you, "from

186

whom, by whom, and in whom are all things" (Augustine, *Confessions*, Bk. I, Ch. 2).

* * *

You fill all things, and you fill them all with your entire self (Augustine, *Confessions*, Bk. I, Ch. 3).

* * *

Thus uniting created nature with the Uncreated through charity . . . man shows all as one . . . through the power of grace (*charis*). He sees all things in God, first as flowing from God into existence and secondly through them, rising to God as to the end of all moved creatures and the fixed and stable ground of their being, who is the end of every rule and law, the end of every word and mind and of every nature, the infinite and unbounded goal of all things (Maximus the Confessor, *Ambigua*, PG 91, 1307-1308c).

* * *

The creatures of the sense world signify the *invisible attributes of God*, partly because God is the origin, exemplar, and end of every creature, and every effect is the sign of its cause, the exemplification of its exemplar and the path to the end, to which it leads. . . . (Bonaventure, *The Soul's Journey Into God*, Ch. 2, 12).

* * *

These powers lead us to the most blessed Trinity itself in view of their order, origin, and interrelatedness. From memory, intelligence comes forth as its offspring, since we understand when a likeness which is in the memory leaps into the eye of the intellect in the form of a word. From memory and intelligence love is breathed forth as their mutual bond. These three — the generating mind, the word, and love — are in the soul as memory, understanding, and will, which are consubstantial, coequal, and coeval, and interpenetrate each other. If, then, God is a perfect spirit, he has memory, understanding, and will; and he has the Word generated and Love breathed forth, which are necessarily distinct since one is produced by the other — not in the order of essence, not in the order of accident, therefore in the order of persons.

When, therefore, the soul considers itself, it rises through itself as through a mirror to behold the blessed Trinity of the Father, the Word, and Love: three persons, coeternal, coequal, and consubstantial. Thus each one dwells in each of the others; nevertheless one is not the other but the three are one God (Bonaventure, *Journey*, Ch. 3, 5).

187

* * *

It seems amazing when it has been shown that God is so close to our souls that so few should be aware of the First Principle within themselves. Yet the reason is close at hand: for the human mind, distracted by cares, does not enter into itself through memory; clouded by sense images, it does not turn back to itself through intelligence; allured away by concupiscence, it does not turn back to itself through desire for inner sweetness and spiritual joy (Bonaventure, *Journey*, Ch. 4, 1).

* * *

We can contemplate God not only outside us and within us but also above us: outside through his vestiges, within through his image and above through the light which shines upon our minds, which is the light of Eternal Truth, since "our mind by itself is formed immediately by Truth itself" (Bonaventure, *Journey*, Ch. 5, 1).

* * *

Strange, then, is the blindness of the intellect, which does not consider that which it sees first and without which it can know nothing. The eye, concentrating on various differences of color, does not see the very light by which it sees other things; and if it does see this light, it does not advert to it. In the same way, the mind's eye, concentrating on particular and universal being, does not advert to being itself, which is beyond every genus, even though it comes to our minds first and through it we know other things. Hence it is most truly apparent that "as the eye of the bat is in regard to light, so is the eye of our mind in regard to the most evident things of nature." Thus our mind, accustomed to the darkness of beings and the images of the things of sense, when it glimpses the light of the Supreme Being, seems to itself to see nothing. It does not realize that this very darkness is the supreme illumination of our mind (cf. Ps. 138:11), just as when the eye sees pure light, it seems to itself to see nothing (Bonaventure, *Journey*, Ch. 5, 4).

* * *

The Apostle speaks about the existence of God in as far as it is the foundation of the other articles of faith. And this foundation is innate to the nature of man, lest, if the human intellect were to know nothing of God by means of its proper nature, it might excuse itself on grounds of ignorance. And this is what Master Hugh says: "Wherefore from the beginning, God willed to be neither totally manifest to the conscience of man nor totally hidden, lest—if he were totally manifest—faith would have no merit and infidelity would have no place; infidelity would be seen to be erroneous because of the evidence, and faith could not be exercised with respect to the hidden. If he were totally hidden, faith could not be helped by knowledge, and infidelity would be excused of its ignorance. For this reason, it was necessary that God present himself even while remaining hidden, lest, if he were totally hidden, he should be totally unknown; so that even as he manifests himself to be known, he remains hidden lest he be totally manifest; this he does so that man's mind might be stimulated by what is known and challenged by what is hidden (Bonaventure, *Disputed Questions on the Mystery of the Trinity*, q 1 a 1 ad 14).

* * *

... The infinity of the divine being does not exclude causality in accordance with the three types of causes: namely efficient, formal, and final; nor does the infinity in God affirm other modes of causality. Therefore, if it is possible for the three types of causes to coexist, it is likewise possible for a trinity of persons to coexist, especially since there is a mutual correspondence between these in the appropriation of power, wisdom, and goodness, which correspond to the three persons and to the three types of causality (Bonaventure, *Disputed Questions*, q 4 a 1 arg. 1).

* * *

God is in all things, and innermostly (Aquinas, *ST* I 8 a 1).

* * *

As the soul is wholly in every part of the body, so God is wholly in all things and in each one (*ST* I 8 a 2 ad 3).

* * *

Although corporeal things are said to be in something as in that which contains them, nevertheless spiritual beings contain those things in which they are; as the soul contains the body. So, too, God is in things as containing them. Nevertheless, by a certain similitude to corporeal things it is said that all things are in God inasmuch as they are contained by him (*ST* I 8 a 1 ad 2).

* * *

For the higher the cause, the greater its scope and efficacity: the more efficacious the cause, the more deeply does it penetrate into its effect (*On the Power of God*, q 3 a 7).

* * *

But we must not think that God is everywhere in such a way that he is divided in various areas of place, as if one part of him were here and another part there. Rather, his entire being is everywhere (*SCG* III 68).

* * *

Nor is [God's] simplicity something like that of a point which is the terminus of a continuous line and thus has a definite position on this line, with the consequence that one point is impossible unless it be at one, indivisible place (*SCG* III 68).

* * *

All knowers know God implicitly in all that is known (*De Veritate*, q 22 a 2 ad 1).

* * *

The divine Substance is the first intelligible object and the principle of all intellectual cognition (*SCG* III 54).

* * *

The intellect or mind of man is, as it were, a light lit up by the light of the Divine Word (*ST* III 5 a 4 ad 2).

* * *

The Incarnation of God the Son signifies the taking up into unity with God not only of human nature, but in this human nature, in a sense, of everything that is "flesh": the whole of humanity, the entire visible and material world. The Incarnation, then, also has a cosmic significance, a cosmic dimension. The "firstborn of all creation," becoming incarnate in the individual humanity of Christ, unites himself in some way with the entire reality of man, which is also "flesh" — and in this reality with all "flesh," with the whole of creation (John Paul II, *Dominum et Vivificantem*, No. 50).

* * *

If the cosmos as a whole has been created in the image of God that appears — in the First-Born of creation, through him and for him — and if this First-Born indwells the world as its Head through the Church, then in the last analysis the world is a "body" of God, who represents and expresses himself in this body, on the basis of the principle not of pantheistic but of hypostatic union (Hans Urs von Balthasar, *The Glory of the Lord*, Vol. 1, *Seeing the Form* [San Francisco, 1982], p. 679).

* * *

Every human act, whether it is an act of knowledge or an act of the will, rests secretly upon God . . . (Henri de Lubac, *The Discovery of God*, trans. by Alexander Dru [New York, 1960], p. 40).

* * *

We must recognize — in the face of rationalism in all its forms, and all forms of contempt for the certainties of reason — that God is the reality which envelopes, dominates, and measures our thought, and not the reverse (de Lubac, *The Discovery of God*, p. 42).

* * *

Whatever the order in which things are set, God comes before everything. He goes before us on the road, and is always there before us. On whatever plane, it is he who makes himself known to us. It is he who reveals himself to us. The working of reason which carries us to him — not to him so much as to the threshold of his mystery — is never but the second wave of the rhythm which he himself has set in motion. Whatever explanation may be given of knowledge — and St. Thomas's explanation is not in every respect that of St. Augustine or St. Bonaventure, for example — traditional philosophy is unanimous on that point. In the intimacy of the spirit, God is always the "illuminating light" of our "illuminated light" [St. Thomas, *ST* III 5 a 4 ad 2; *De Veritate*, q 16 a 3]. He is "that uncreated Light without which I should not be eye" [Gabriel Marcel, *The Mystery of Being*, II. "Faith and Reality" (1951), p. 178], and unless he pronounced his *fiat lux* upon me, the abyss within me would be dark indeed. He is the hearth from which the souls of men, like so many lamps, take their light [St. Augustine, *De civitate Dei*, 11.27.2 (PL, 41:341)]. He is the *ipse qui illuminat* at the heart of reason [St. Augustine, *Soliloquies*, 1.6.12 (PL, 32:875)] (de Lubac, *The Discovery of God*, pp. 14-15).

* * *

. . . The reality of the divine image in the soul is at the center and principle of all rational activity, which should lead it from knowledge of the world to the affirmation of God (de Lubac, *The Discovery of God*, p. 16).

* * *

[The] mystery of the Trinity has opened up for us an entirely new perspective: the ground of all being is *communio* (de Lubac, *The Christian Faith* [San Francisco, 1986], p. 13).

* * *

In this idea of relativity in word and love, independent of the concept

191

of substance and not to be classified among the "accidents," Christian thought discovered the kernel of the concept of person, which describes something other and infinitely more than the mere idea of the "individual." Let us listen once again to St. Augustine: "In God there are no accidents, only substance and relation." Therein lies concealed a revolution in man's view of the world: the undivided sway of thinking in terms of substance is ended; relation is discovered as an equally valid primordial mode of reality. It becomes possible to surmount what we call today "objectifying thought"; a new plane of being comes into view. It is probably true to say that the task imposed on philosophy as a result of these facts is far from being completed—so much does modern thought depend on the possibilities thus disclosed, but for which it would be inconceivable (Joseph Ratzinger, *Introduction to Christianity* [New York, 1965], p. 132).

* * *

To John "Son" means being-from-another; thus with this word he defines the being of this man as being from another and for others, as a being that is completely open on both sides, knows no reserved area of the mere "I." When it thus becomes clear that the being of Jesus as Christ is a completely open being, a being "from" and "toward," that nowhere clings to itself and nowhere stands on its own, then it is also clear at the same time that this being is pure relation (not substantiality) and, as pure relation, pure unity. This fundamental statement about Christ becomes, as we have seen, at the same time the explanation of Christian existence. To John, being a Christian means being like the Son, becoming a son; that is, not standing on one's own and in oneself, but living completely open in the "from" and "toward" (Ratzinger, *Introduction*, p. 134).

* * *

It is the nature of Christian existence to receive and to live life as relatedness, and thus to enter into that unity which is the ground of all reality and sustains it. This will perhaps make it clear how the doctrine of the Trinity, when properly understood, can become the nodal point of theology and of Christian thought in general (Ratzinger, *Introduction*, p. 135).

* * *

Thus "*logos*"—Christology, as "word"—theology, is once again the opening up of being to the idea of relationship (Ratzinger, *Introduction*, p. 136).

* * *

Thus here again the concept of mere substance (= what stands in itself!) is shattered and it is made apparent how being that truly understands itself grasps at the same time that *in* its self-being it does not belong to itself; that it only comes to itself by moving away from itself and finding its way back as relatedness to its true primordial state (Ratzinger, *Introduction*, p. 137).

* * *

Phenomenology and existential analyses, helpful as they are, cannot suffice for Christology. They do not reach deep enough, because they leave the realm of real "being" untouched (Ratzinger, *Introduction*, p. 170).

* * *

It is openness to the whole, to the infinite, that makes man complete. Man is man by reaching out infinitely beyond himself and he is consequently more of a man the less enclosed he is in himself, the less "limited" he is. For — let me repeat — that man is most man, indeed *the* true man, who is most unlimited, who not only has contact with the infinite — the infinite being! — but who is one with him: Jesus Christ. In him "hominization" has truly reached its goal (Ratzinger, *Introduction*, p. 170).

Response to David L. Schindler

by Robert Slesinski, St. Nicholas of Myra Byzantine Catholic Church, New York

There is little, if anything, in the present paper with which I would disagree. Since I am in agreement with the general thrust of the presentation, I would like to focus my remarks on some of the dimensions of the theme of the intellect, the principle of identity, and the secularization of much of modern thought, as suggested by Professor Schindler's essay.

First of all, the paper offers new avenues for reflection on one of theology's most discussed problems, nay, mysteries, namely the absolute and universal primacy of Christ, the fact that Christ is the ultimate explanation of all things. If, indeed, as St. Paul writes in his Letter to the Colossians (Col. 1:16-17) that every being both in heaven and on earth was created in, through, and for Christ, we cannot but understand man and his intellectual activity in particular as rooted in and ordained to Christ, that is, in other words, as ultimately unintelligible apart from Christ. At the same time, the nature-grace distinction itself, as applied to the life of the intellect, finds a critical context for understanding the true dynamics of the activity of the mind. But the exact "how" of this application is not so readily given. An infusion of grace undoubtedly "perfects" the intellect insofar as the human person *is* one, but obviously there is no simple, verifiable cause-effect relationship obtaining here. An increase in sanctity hardly implies an increase in intelligence. Yet, could not, or does not, the presence of grace have an enabling effect on the intellect? Not enough attention, it would seem, has been devoted to the subject of holiness, the virtuous life, and the life of the intellect. How crippled, indeed, the intellect becomes under the influence of pride, hubris, complacency, lethargy, and other like moral — and intellectual — vices. If the Christian scholar were to level any charge against the secularized intellect, it surely would relate to its limited horizon, to the fact that it cannot soar owing to the pull or "dregs," as it were, of the mundane. More positively put however, can it not be said that the enabling effect of grace precisely relates to *vision*, to the fact that the mind does, indeed, *see* more keenly, more deeply, more expansively? We might even add "more primordially," that is, without the encumbrances of the sin of Adam.

Professor Schindler, in his paper, develops his thoughts on the "engraced" intellect in the light of the *homoousios*, or consubstantiality, of Christ the Son with the Father and the participation of the creature in this consubstantiality *by grace*. The professor adduces that because of the absolute primacy of Christ, the hypostatic union also carries an essential, *ontological* significance for all of creation. Every being has its being precisely in relation to God the Father in Jesus Christ. Thus, we cannot conceive of man as an independent being in and of himself, but only as *in relation*, as created to share in God's life and to be *with* him. Human existence, in other words, is not a closed existence; it is a dynamic existence unintelligible apart from relation, first with God, then with other men. The hypostatic union thus suggests, Professor Schindler remarks, a proper logic of intelligence, a logic which can only be one *of relation*, in contrast with what he calls a "logic of secularization" which prescinds from any consideration of relation. Before specifically discussing this distinction of logics, I would like to draw attention to another era and another context in which a very similar discussion was held and very similar conclusions drawn.

The attempt to address the "crisis of modernity" from a specifically Christian point of view is nothing new. At least since the dawn itself of the Age of the Enlightenment, Christian thinkers have been preoccupied with addressing its challenges with varying degrees of success. One notable attempt to fashion a response to the challenges of the Enlightenment is found in the Slavophile Movement of nineteenth-century Russia culminating in the Silver Age of Russian thought in progress up until the time of the October Revolution. In particular, I am referring to the line of thought initiated by Ivan Kireevsky (1806-1856) and subsequently developed by Aleksei Khomyakov (1804-1860) and Vladimir Soloviev (1853-1900) in the nineteenth century and then, with greater depth, by Pavel Florensky (1882-1937) in the first decades of this century. These thinkers all attempted a critique of what they perceived to be the unilaterally rationalist cast of Western thought, at least, since the dawn of the Modern Age. In contrast to Western rationalism, they speak of "integral knowledge," the attainment of which is not in the exclusive purview of one human faculty alone, specifically the mind, but which is the fruit of the *whole* man, that is, of the mind, the will, and the heart all acting in concert. It is a knowledge that truly attains reality directly and concretely; it is intuitive knowledge that goes beyond the limited perspectives of both empiricism and rationalism, allowing for what Soloviev would label as "mystical knowledge," the object of which is the "living reality of beings in their internal, lived relationships."[1]

Integral knowledge for these thinkers, it is important to note, is a fruit of the "integral life," thus explaining their stress on a lived contact with reality and responsibility to society and for the world. This point is decisive for understanding typically Orthodox approaches to theology and to understanding the standard Orthodox critiques of Catholic and Protestant modes of theology, however incomplete and possibly caricaturizing these may be. Khomyakov set the pattern in this regard in his development of the idea of *sobornost*, or catholicity. He criticizes Western theology for its reliance on what he conceives to be unilaterally external criteria of Church life and thought, namely the appeals to the hierarchy and the magisterium in the case of Catholicism, giving an external unity without freedom, and to the *sola Scriptura* doctrine in the instance of Protestantism, allowing for external freedom without unity. In contrast to these, he finds in Orthodoxy a combination of unity and freedom based in love and thus a true, internal unity and freedom.

Of course, I do not share Khomyakov's analysis in full as he uncritically paves a "high road" for Orthodoxy and a "low road" for Western Christianity. But there is an important kernel of truth underlying his discussion, especially as it applies to theology. Theology, in line with Khomyakov, can never be detached from the commonality of ecclesial life; it can never be a mere "academic discipline," one among many others, but must needs be inserted into the *life* of the Church. As such, theology cannot be "valid" unless it partakes of the fullness of Church life, meaning, in other words, that it must be a *praying* theology, a theology inextricably linked to the worship, or *leitourgia*, of the Church. This is a line of thought not specifically brought out in Professor Schindler's paper as such, but which is, I would say, certainly implied in it, especially in his attempt to overcome a facile substance-accident distinction in understanding what a "Catholic university" really is or should be. If we are to speak of any "triumph of secularism" in our day, it surely relates to the separation of religion from life. Can we not also say this in regard to much of contemporary theology and to the status of

Catholic universities and colleges in general? Whatever has become of the notion of theology as a "living knowledge," as a knowledge *in* a Person, and not just as an abstract knowledge *about* a Person?

In regard to the central line of Professor Schindler's argument regarding a logic of relation, there is a further parallel to be found in the School of Integral Knowledge, specifically as it is developed by Florensky in his search for an ultimate ground for truth. Florensky was one of the most unusual thinkers this century has produced. A man of irreligious background, he gradually came to religion as a student having excelled in mathematics and the positive sciences. Florensky surely shocked his peers when he turned to theology and the priesthood in his search for an all-embracing vision of life and the particular sciences. At the heart of his thought which tries to bring out the organic interrelatedness of the entire created order is his formulation of the principle of dynamic identity by means of which he seeks to supplant the standard understanding of the principle of identity which he deems to be "blind in its immediateness"[2] and evidencing only an empty and lifeless self-identity. Florensky endeavors to delve into the true ground *in being* of the principle of identity, fashioning an understanding of identity that offers a real self-identity, full of content and life, achieved through the dynamic *adoption (usvoenie)* and *assimilation (upodobenie sebe)* of the other than self.[3] Curiously, Florensky's efforts at understanding the principle of identity parallel those of later thinkers in this century, notably Heidegger and Whitehead, who likewise attempt to deepen our understanding and appreciation of self-identity, linking it to self-diversity. Heidegger, for instance, specifically sees the essence of identity in the "event of appropriation,"[4] thus using a terminology surprisingly similar to Florensky's.

With his understanding of the principle of dynamic identity thus fashioned, Florensky goes on to consider all philosophies as either *homoiousian* or *homoousian*, borrowing from dogmatic theology the key concept for delineating all philosophies of rationalism and immobility based on mere similarity, or generic likeness, on the one hand, from what he sees as genuine life-giving philosophy of the type Christian philosophy should be, on the other. If I were to cite any one example of *homoiousian* philosophy in the Modern Age based on static identity and mere similarity, it surely would be Hume's empiricism in which all knowledge of the external world is reduced to mere, atomized sense impressions and on which so much of the modern critique of knowledge depends. Indeed, it is interesting to note that, for Hume, the heart of all knowledge revolves around the principles of association or connection among ideas (resemblance, contiguity, and causation) and that these, in truth, form the "cement of the universe."[5] For Florensky, on the contrary, what is needed is a real metaphysics of participation based on consubstantiality, the focus of which is organic interrelationships and the "cement" of which can be none other than love.

Thus, some remarkable convergences in thought can be found in Professor Schindler's researches and in what I have just presented as a hopefully not tedious digression to the topic at hand. Before I conclude, however, there is one problematic area not addressed by the professor and one when treated by the Russian thinkers I have just mentioned generally does not receive a sympathetic or convincing accounting. I am referring to the thorny issue of ecclesiastical authority and Catholic theology. Certainly from our presentations today, we do want "interior criteria" of authenticity to judge vitality in both theology and ecclesial life. But why is the question of ecclesiastical authority and the magisterium in theology too readily relegated to the sphere of "external criteria" of authenticity? This question cannot be reduced to a mere case of a mechanical "Denziger theology." New insights into the intrinsic dimensions of authority in authentic theology and ecclesial life are rather the call of the hour. If there can be no authentic Catholic theology in the classroom apart from the chapel, there can also, it would seem, not be one divorced from or antagonistic to the life of the whole organism which is the Church.

Notes

1. *Sobranie sochinenii V. S. Solov'eva* (Brussels, 1966), 1:304.
2. Pavel Florensky, *Stolp i utverzhdenie istiny* (The pillar and foundation of truth) (Moscow, 1914), 47.
3. Ibid., 48.
4. Martin Heidegger, *Identity and Difference* (New York, 1969), 39, 103.
5. David Hume, "Abstract" to *A Treatise of Human Nature*, Bk. 1 (Glasgow, 1962), 353.

Response to David L. Schindler

by Walter Nicgorski,
University of Notre Dame

My position on the program, the time now available, and the invitation implicit in David Schindler's subtitle, "Secularization and the Academy," lead me to want to move directly to the practical import of his significant reflections on "faith and the logic of intelligence." I wish then to focus attention on the difference it makes or should make to the scholarly life and to its institutional form in colleges and universities if we would exercise the faith-informed intelligence that has been described. How then might our institutional lives be different if we understand ourselves as thinking and inquiring with this faith-informed logic?

Professor Schindler's presentation does, after all, suggest to us that there is a notable practical import to the logic of intelligence of creedal Christianity. This logic takes being as fundamentally relational and thus gives primacy to openness and interiority. On the other hand, the secularized logic of intelligence that is said to dominate in modernity and in the academies of today is informed by the principle of simple identity — once crisply defined for me, by a good St. Louis Thomist, as the principle that affirms that "a thing is what it is and nothing else." This results in a way of understanding that emphasizes closure of beings to one another and externality and instrumentality as the modes of relationship. Insofar as this secularized logic is implicated with modern medical, technical, and political achievements, Professor Schindler suggests that it may be responsible for the often noted problematic character of those very achievements, for this Cartesian logic of modernity is a logic of specialization that produces "patterns of thought marked by extroversion, power, domination and fragmentation." But the logic of faith, so aptly called marian, leads to intellectual activity marked by receptivity, response, and integration in love.

Just at the point where this sharp contrast of logics begins to give us some sense of practical direction for scholarship and communities of

199

scholars, Professor Schindler's qualified embrace of the modern achievement, so true to the Catholic tradition, enhances the difficulty of grasping the practical import of the logic of faith. The professor's qualified embrace of the modern achievement and its logic is in evidence when he says that "either of the logics, to be comprehensive, in some significant sense must include the features of both." Thus a comprehensive understanding must include both externality and interiority. To be sure, the sounder approach for Professor Schindler, the more genuinely comprehensive and truthful one, is that which would proceed from the logic of faith. The logic of faith can and must integrate what is significant in the logic proceeding from the principle of simple identity. This integration means an acceptance of specialization insofar as there is indeed a "distinctness of the identity of entities." The realm of nature, including the human, must be articulated with its own distinct integrity. Thus Professor Schindler introduces a distinction between a secular and a secularized logic of intelligence; this appears to be a distinction between the secular focus of the logic of faith (that is, nature's integrity) and a simply secularized logic.

Now that the secular focus has been introduced; now that there is set out the task of appropriating what is there to be known about distinct entities, external and instrumental relationships; now that marian receptivity is somehow to integrate with the Cartesian mind or at least the Cartesian strategy — the question of practical import returns with new force and with new contours. It is, to put the matter crudely, easier to expel the devil than to talk with him, work with him, learn from him, and, perhaps, transform him by bringing to the fore his angelic dimensions. What then is to be done in the lives and communities of scholars characterized by the logic of faith in the face of the dominant secularized logic? This problem of practical import to which Professor Schindler's paper leads us has lingered just beneath the surface of often reassuring statements, pastoral and academic, within the Catholic tradition.

Such a statement, important in its own right and, no doubt, a paradigm and source for similar statements from lesser authorities, is that segment (section 36) in Vatican II's *Gaudium et Spes* entitled "The Rightful Independence of Earthly Affairs." The segment consists of five short paragraphs beginning with the following two that I cite in their entirety:

"Now, many of our contemporaries seem to fear that a closer bond between human activity and religion will work against the independence of men, of societies, or of the sciences.

"If by the autonomy of earthly affairs we mean that created things and societies themselves enjoy their own laws and values which must be gradually deciphered, put to use, and regulated by men, then it is entirely right to demand that autonomy. Such is not merely required by modern man, but harmonizes also with the will of the Creator. For by the very circumstance of their having been created, all things are endowed with their own stability, truth, goodness, proper laws, and order. Man must respect these as he isolates them by the appropriate methods of the individual sciences and arts."

Three paragraphs later after specifically cautioning Christians to attend to the rightful independence of science, the Second Vatican Council adds that "the independence of temporal affairs" must not be taken to mean "that created things do not depend on God and that man can use them without any reference to their Creator...." Observing that "without the Creator the creature would disappear," the council concludes the segment on the independence of earthly affairs with the simple and profound truth that "when God is forgotten the creature itself grows unintelligible." The critical eye wants to know what kind of independence this is that is so thoroughly and deeply dependent, and as for the autonomy of the sciences and disciplines, what kind of autonomy is it that if taken seriously produces unintelligibility? The critical eye begins to suspect that faith embraces the modern world at the price of speaking out of both sides of the mouth and that a deep tension, if not contradiction, is involved here. Professor Schindler's argument, we may recall, can seemingly lead us to the same impasse, for he would have us embrace specialization and tend to the distinctness of entities and their external relationships while grounding this all in a logic of faith that escapes the confines of specialization, that affirms the essential relatedness of entities, and that directs us to the interior. What can this mean concretely? To press the question of practical import is to try to see how a logic of faith would lead us to think and work differently from those proceeding from the secularized logic; to press the question of practical import is to try to grasp concretely that the integration and synthesis proposed is a possibility and not the contradiction that our groping language may suggest. I wrote these comments and specifically these last few sentences before hearing Father Walter Kasper and Professor Louis Dupré at this meeting; I now realize that I am pressing for the practical import in the scholarly life of what Professor Dupré spoke of as the dynamic tension in the synthesis of nature and grace and what Father Kasper expressed when he said that God must penetrate the world and yet the world must remain merely world.

There is a mode of reconciliation that at once suggests itself when reflecting on the cited passage from *Gaudium et Spes*. It is commonsensical, and widely in evidence, which is in no way to deny that it has much to commend it. This mode of reconciliation of the light of faith with the work of secularized intelligence proceeds by stressing the first and last things, namely that we and all being are from God the Creator and destined for God. As we exercise our inquiries on the realm of nature, we are to be mindful how we are gifted and turn the fruits of our inquiry to the service of God. To put this concretely, the chemist brings an awe-filled reverence to his unlocking structures within entities and certain interactions between them; he learns to manipulate them for humanly benign results, and he seeks quite selflessly in the service of a loving God to solve medical and environmental problems that beset humankind. Or consider the economist whose understanding embraces laws of a market shaped by vast numbers of self-interested actors who are no model for him but are part of the reality that he must master to endeavor to bring what good he can from it. Or consider the philosopher who would master the intricacies of logical forms and be, in turn, quick to see the structures of argument in important human discourse—ever reducing and clarifying in the interest of a truth-loving God who had so endowed him. Another way to see such scholars concretely is to see them as believing and practicing Catholics who worship regularly and throughout the rhythm of the liturgical year. They are thus kept mindful of the Alpha and Omega and live and ultimately direct their work accordingly. In the workdays of the week (when they are not attending conferences extraordinaire like this one), they are at the business of their disciplines, performing their experiments, examining the data, testing arguments, hustling to their respective professional meetings, conveying their results, and teaching their skills.

These examples seem to meet the mark of lives embracing both their autonomous disciplines of inquiry and the horizons of faith. They work, aware that it is created reality which they study and seek to master; they submit their inquiries and their inventions to the control of moral norms as *Gaudium et Spes* also insists. Perhaps the one indication in the passage on the independence of earthly affairs that the council's ideal is not wholly captured by these examples is there in that last rich statement that "when God is forgotten the creature itself grows unintelligible," for the statement seems also to mean that as God is known, the creature grows ever more intelligible. Movement in such a direction suggests both a continuing effort to know God through all the sources available and a parallel effort to relate to each other in the mode of integration the knowledges, provisional and proximate as they may be, of the Creator and of the various specialized spheres of creation.

Professor Schindler's likely objection to these examples (the chemist, economist, and philosopher) as exemplars of the logic of faith requires no elaborate inference. His paper suggests that he would view these examples as instantiations of a kind of misguided and inadequate effort to add on Catholicism to the secularized logic of intelligence, to relate the Catholic trinitarian faith to other knowledges in the mode of externals, to leave the principle of simple identity in place rather than to transform it. The professor specifically warns against the inclination to believe that one can distance oneself from simple identity as a metaphysical explanation while embracing it "—for practical or pragmatic reasons — merely as a methodological strategy." Allowing, however, that one can focus on distinct identities while leaving relationships unattended or implicit, Professor Schindler claims "the crucial moment" comes when we do turn to consider relation and whether we then do it after the manner of "addition" or after the manner of "reduction," rather than with "the integrated patterns of thought" required by the logic of faith.

To attempt to state positively what Professor Schindler's integration means, what it means to be Catholic in mind, we are drawn to terms like transformation, penetration, determination, renewing, reforming, synthesizing, and uniting in a way that is not merely aggregating. In this respect, I find myself understanding the professor's paper as a deep and probing reflection on that last simple statement of the segment from *Gaudium et Spes* which ties the creature's intelligibility to the Creator. Another statement from the Second Vatican Council supplies another term for "intelligibility"; I have in mind the conciliar document on Christian education and its description of the mission of the Catholic school as one that "strives to relate all human culture eventually to the news of salvation so that the light of faith will illumine the knowledge

203

which students gradually gain of the world, of life, and of mankind." Professor Schindler's paper is an effort to explore the "intelligibility" and the "illumination" that must be the energizing *telos* of the Catholic mind.

To locate what Professor Schindler has done in our pastoral tradition and to appreciate it is not yet to be satisfied on the question of practical import? If not this chemist, economist, and philosopher, then what will the inquirer look like, what will the academy look like that the professor is suggesting to us? It remains a difficulty to articulate what may be felt, or may be intuited, to be a properly Catholic way. I am compelled to leave the question of practical import before us after making two additional sets of comments that might be useful to our discussion. The first set cautions against contributing to a gulf between the Catholic tradition and modernity by throwing down too quickly the gauntlet of fundamental metaphysical difference. These comments may reveal some differences with Professor Schindler. The second set of comments will underscore and emphasize and somewhat extend the professor's own courageous and incisive suggestions near the end of his paper, suggestions on the practical import for the Catholic university.

First, how is it that believers can respect the autonomy of the various sciences and disciplines? How can we participate with the work of inquiry of an often nonbelieving world shaped by modern orientations of inquiry? We are clearly called to do both, in good faith, by the very logic of our great faith. Remembering that the scientific and the rational need not be reductionist, I wonder if the Enlightenment's renewed commitment to truth is not one we can largely share in. Cannot we join the search for truth with the quiet confidence that more honesty, integrity, and effort in the search will lead to more unveiling of what God wills us to know? I am not entirely persuaded that modernity takes up entities outside of relation rather than bracketing relation for the sake of intense scrutiny of the part; I suspect that one can proceed from external relations to the discovery of their indissoluble connection with interiority. I notice a strong dynamic in the secularized world to make sense of things, to look to the whole and the intricate interdependencies throughout the whole. I wonder how much of our academic fragmentation is the result of an intellectual or metaphysical turn, such as Professor Schindler's claim for the modern dominance of the principle of simple identity, and how much is primarily an individual and institutional moral problem. We are over-

204

whelmed with the tasks and rewards of specialization and its concomitant emphasis on limited focus; we know that there is more and that what that more is is critical to our own sense of meaning and, of course, to an integral Christian perspective; but we lack the energy, will, and institutional support to be more steadily concerned with the integral vision.

My second set of comments proceeds from Professor Schindler's important closing theme that the "Catholic" in the idea of Catholic university be understood not as an accidental and secondary modifier but as an essential and characterizing attribute of an academic community seeking and manifesting a "uni-versus," a turning to one, informed by the logic of faith in the Catholic tradition. The practical import of this understanding should, it seems, take at least the following three forms:

First, a dominant campus spirituality of reflection and self-integration in which access to the Catholic tradition and intellectual development meet, and a related consciousness that this spirituality can be enriched but not displaced by programs of social awareness and activism.

Second, central curricular space for the synthetic task of inquiry — in other words, an organization of learning and the steps in it that reflect an institutional concern with that which is unifying and foundational; in this respect graduate education must also come under scrutiny in the hope that there can be some mitigation of our modern tendency to make graduate education but an initiation into academic, secularized fragmentation.

Third, provision for faculty space, in the sense of room and occasion in their lives, for the kind of inquiry and conversation that encourages a faculty's development in coming to possess the Catholic mind; clearly personnel and leadership appointments in the academy should reflect a positive concern with this responsibility of and to the faculty; can one suppose a faculty leading students in the path of integration when they themselves neither have such concern nor manifest in any way such an achievement?

As the faculty is to lead within the university, it is reasonable to expect the university to lead within the culture as a whole. David Schindler's paper, positioned as it is at the end of this conference, brings this responsibility into focus. In November of 1988 Pope John Paul once again put this task of the larger integration before scholars when he wrote of the responsibility of both science and religion to contribute to the integration of human culture. If peoples "are to grow and mature," he

205

wrote, they "cannot continue to live in separate compartments, pursuing totally divergent interests from which they evaluate and judge the world. A divided community fosters a fragmented vision of the world; a community of interchange encourages its members to expand their partial perspectives and form a new unified vision."

Observations

Aquinas on Nature and Grace

Romanus Cessario, O.P., Dominican House of Studies, Washington, D.C.

In this comment, I consider three theological issues which derive from the thought of St. Thomas Aquinas. First, I would like to emphasize the importance of efficient causality in any properly theological approach to nature and grace. Secondly, I would simply recall the classical distinction concerning the diverse ways in which God remains present to his creation. Finally, I think that one should recognize that the threefold grace of Christ remains an indispensable element in Christian deliberation on the relationship between nature and grace. As a *point de départ*, however, I suggest that various kinds of inclusive ontologies, especially those which do not discriminate sufficiently the various levels of efficient causality, have provided a Procrustean bed for contemporary theology. Aquinas, for one, would have experienced certain felt reservations concerning the notion of "grace" as the communication of God's inner being *simpliciter*. Given the importance that he attaches to divine efficient causality, such an exclusive emphasis on formal causality imports a reductionism foreign to his philosophical and theological sensibilities.

Aquinas himself signals the requirements which divine efficient causality imposes on any attempt to set forth, as the *Summa*, for example, purports to do, a teaching about God. In fact, we find efficient cause manifest in the very structure of the *Summa* itself. For example, when Aquinas contemplates our union with God, he envisions the human person as moving between God and God. In this context, grace constitutes the only perfection which makes God exist in the human person as an object known and loved. By this affirmation, Aquinas simply seeks to articulate a theological reason for the divine truth about which St. John speaks: "But to all who received him, who believed in his name, he gave power to become children of God; who were born, not of blood nor of the will of the flesh nor of the will of man, but of God" (Jn. 1:12-13). We can, moreover, easily recognize both formal and efficient causality evident here in the context of finality.

The commentatorial tradition supports this reading of Aquinas. For instance, John of St. Thomas identified the various moments of divine final and efficient cause as the basis for the principal divisions of the *Summa*. In his *Cursus Theologicus*, the author argues that Aquinas divides his material in the *Summa* according to a threefold consideration of divine causality, namely "as effective principle, as finalizing beatitude, as restoring Savior."[1] Thus, in his view, Aquinas combines considerations of efficient and final causality in order to specify three general modes of causation which order the development of theology.[2] Today many theologians distance themselves from this perspective.

But for Aquinas, efficient cause points up a fundamental distinction about God's action *ad extra*. Consider, for example, the divine indwelling. Only in the singular instance of the Incarnation do the three Persons assume an individual human nature to one of themselves, namely the Logos/Son. Yet, in every other individual the blessed Trinity remains present only through the divinely elevated activities of knowledge and love. Customarily we think of this as God coming to dwell in us, as, for instance, in the doctrine of the trinitarian missions. We should, in fact, rather consider the human person as elevated to a share in God's life through knowing and loving each of the divine Persons. This elevation, moreover, represents something distinct from that creative presence of God to every creature which Aquinas titles "*per essentiam, potentiam, et praesentiam.*"[3] In any event, I submit that a discussion of the extrinsic efficient cause must complement analyses of intrinsic formal causality, since efficient cause alone can adequately account for this distinction which remains indispensable for Christian theology.

Finally, the hypostatic union obliges us to speak about the threefold grace of Christ. First of all, the theologian must consider the "grace of union" itself or, to put it differently, what does it mean for an individual human nature to be "personally" united to the Logos? This entails discussions such as those concerning the predestination of Christ and raises questions such as "whether the grace of Christ is infinite." Secondly, Aquinas advances arguments for the created grace of Christ. These seek to reveal the special characteristics of created grace in a human nature personally united to the Logos/Son as well as the effects of that created grace on the human operations of Christ. Given the incommunicability of the *gratia unionis*, theology must attend to these questions in order—for example, to account for the substantial sanctity of Christ, or his "fullness of grace" (cf. Jn. 1:14; Jn. 3:33-35). Thirdly, since Christ possesses the totality of divine gifts, theology must next consider how he communicates these to others. Aquinas, then, speaks about the capital grace of Christ. This brings one to consider the full implications of sharing in Christ's redemptive suffering and the establishment of the Church. All in all, for Aquinas, the person of Christ himself supplies the model for our own adoptive filiation.

Nonetheless, Aquinas makes no apology for talking about the life of one uplifted in grace in the *secunda pars* before he presents Christ, the one mediator of that grace, in the *tertia pars*. He announces that our destiny points to something infinitely above what our natural powers can achieve, nothing less than union with the triune God. Therefore, he argues that the creature requires a *gratia elevans* in order that human capacities can reach out for God. This *gratia elevans* remains the reality which Aquinas properly designates as the grace of the new law: "We say that God exists in any creature in two ways. First of all, by way of an agent cause, and in this way he exists in everything he creates. . . . Secondly, God exists in a special fashion in the rational creature who knows and loves him. . . . God is said to exist in this way in the saint by grace."[4] This distinction, I propose, remains an indispensable one for the present discussion.

In *The Book of Her Life*, St. Teresa of Ávila explains how she came to learn the difference between God's creative presence to the world "according to essence, presence, and power" and his sanctifying presence in grace which terminates in proper relationships with the indwelling Trinity. She writes: "Those who had no learning told me that he was present only by grace. I couldn't believe this, because, as I say, it seemed to me he was present, and so I was troubled."[5] Her Dominican confessor explained the different modes of presence to her. "He told me that God was indeed present and described how he communicated himself to us, which brought me very great comfort."[6] This task remains incumbent on all those who seek to interpret the doctrine of Aquinas on grace and, *a fortiori*, to discover the authentic relationships which exist between grace and nature, even in America.

Notes

1. John of St. Thomas, *Cursus Theologicus* I (Paris, 1883): 191: "Igitur Divus Thomas juxta hanc triplicem considerationem Dei causantis, scilicet ut principium effectivum, ut beatitudo finalizans, ut Salvator reparans, divisit totam doctrinam Summae theologiae, ut patet in initio secundae quaestionis huius primae partis."
2. Ibid., p. 190: "Ex aliis vero duabus causis, scilicet efficienti, et finali, quae Deo conveniunt, considerat Divus Thomas tres generales modos causandi, per quos totum theologiae ordinem partitur." In addition to material causality, John of St. Thomas also excludes the pertinence of formal causality in matters of divine agency ("in quantum causa creaturarum est"), since a formal cause implies either dependence or inferiority with respect to that for which it is a cause. In his view, the perfection of the divine being allows neither relationship to creatures.
3. See *ST* I 8 a 3. In the reply to the fourth argument, Aquinas refers to the distinct causality for which he reserves the term "gratia." In fact, the argument asserts that each divine perfection which changes a person's life should be given a special designation. But Aquinas replies: "Grace is the only perfection added to the substance of things which makes God exist in them as a known and loved object; grace alone then makes God exist in things in a unique way ('*singularem modum*')." Aquinas then acknowledges the special case of the Incarnation: "There is, however, another unique way in which God exists in a man, by union, and we will deal with this in its proper place" (ad 4).
4. See *ST* I 8 a 3.
5. *The Book of Her Life* 18.15 in *The Collected Works of St. Teresa of Ávila*, Vol. 1:121, trans. Kieran Kavanaugh, O.C.D., and Otilio Rodriguez, O.C.D. (Washington, D.C., 1976-1985).
6. E. Allison Peers supposes that the Holy Mother refers to the celebrated Domingo Báñez, O.P. (1528-1604), but also acknowledges that other authors suggest a certain Padre Barron. See his *The Complete Works of Saint Teresa of Jesus*, Vol. 1:111 (New York, 1946). Báñez, of course, would have understood Aquinas's doctrine on grace very well.

An Eastern Catholic View

Archimandrite Boniface (Luykx), Holy Transfiguration Monastery, Redwood Valley, California

This symposium on "Nature, Grace, and Culture" was a great blessing for all who participated in it, and a great event. Let us praise the Lord for it. It was a special blessing to have so many like-minded and competent people together in friendly exchange around this topic which will be so important for the future of Christianity in this country and in the world, helping one another in their search for solutions to so many heavy problems. And let me add that it was a most pleasant surprise to see that all these theologians, who doubtless had their strong personal opinions about many things, basically agreed in all matters proposed or defined by the magisterium of the Church, which was always referred to with respect and submission, in the spirit of the great theologians of the past, and without the rebellion and criticism that characterize some such gatherings.

Yet, as an Eastern theologian, I saw some lacunae which I feel urged to point out in the humble hope that perhaps in the future they could be taken into consideration. I bring them up because I had the same impression at last year's symposium.

First of all, the problems were always approached in their prevailingly horizontal dimension, although religion is primarily a vertical relation with God, as is well known, even though it involves, directly or indirectly, the horizontal values of life as well. So, for example, when Emperor Justinianus I of Constantinople tried to set up the first endeavor in history to build up a Christian culture and commonwealth, his whole codex of laws for taking care of all the human situations was conceived in the vertical perspective of human life in the plan of God, in the image of the Holy Trinity, model of all community and culture.

The Eastern Fathers and theologians see this plan in three continuous stages: creation, incarnation/redemption, and eschatology. Incarnation is built upon creation and fulfills it, on the one hand; on the other hand, it is totally geared to the manifestation of God's glory in Christ's return at the end of time. (Remember the impressive presentation of Hans Urs von Balthasar on the glory of God?) Hence, there is from the outset a dynamic continuity between these three stages and hence also between nature, grace, and culture, so that the final goal of the middle stage (incarnation/redemption) is not only meant to incarnate redemption into the horizontal dimension of life but also to prepare the world for the Lord's return in glory. Now, this dynamic, eschatological orientation was almost entirely absent from the discussion. This lacuna had important side effects. To mention but a few:

In this eschatological perspective, the first task of man and Church is worship. The Church is first of all a worshiping community, praising the Father, celebrating the mysteries of Christ, and interceding for the world in the Holy Spirit. Thus worship anticipates the fulfillment of the kingdom and is the first and strongest generator of culture. ("Cult" and "culture" are from the same root, *colere*: to till the earth, to develop — a dynamic and exchatological concept.) We still see worship as primary in the Eastern Churches where worship is extended into the homes and society in the form of liturgical home customs. Therefore, in our discussions, much more attention should be given to worship, especially in the education of the Christian and in the formation of a Christian society — worship as the generator of grace, of course, but also of culture and of the eschatological dimension in life.

The active agent of God's impact upon person and society is the Spirit of God. He is the One who channels God's uncreated energies into man's history to overcome the heavy, downward weight of sin. In the perspective of Eastern theology, God does this by the constant power of the risen Lord, who is the author of grace and the lever of all human culture. It is the active presence of both the Spirit and the risen Lord that not only drives humanity to create culture as a horizontal incarnation of grace, but also makes us accept the necessary crosses and overcome the inevitable persecutions, the necessary price for this rising with Christ, as Paul wrote in 2 Timothy 3:12: "All those who want to live godly in Christ Jesus, will suffer persecution." This is not just an abstract, pious consideration, but a very practical key to solving a lot of problems in the use of nature and in the building up of a true culture as God intended, and we Christians are the first who have the task to work on this.

This empowerment in the risen Lord will also give us the courage to build up culture in spite of the setbacks. Yet this eschatological perspective will never allow us to forget that we live here on earth as in a foreign land, that our true citizenship is in heaven, as St. Paul reminds us in Philippians 3:20. We are a people on the march, heading for our true homeland, as Hebrews 13:14 teaches us: "We have here no lasting abode; we are searching for the coming one." Who would be so stupid as to invest all of one's efforts, dreams, and money in an enterprise soon to be left behind? Only in the lasting perspective of this eschatological dimension of Christianity will we be able to create a lasting culture, discerning what is of lasting value and what is just passing and passing away.

However, we need that evangelical freedom of the first Christians and that contemplative attitude of the Eastern spirituality to open our eyes to the eschatological contribution that Christianity should make to the world's problems. We also need the necessary detachment that Eastern monasticism could teach us. Western man is perhaps set too much on immediate efficiency and, in general, on all the problems that are linked with efficient causality in the Aristotelian schema of causes; he wants immediate results on the horizontal level, often forgoing the final causality that looks beyond appearances and immediate results to the final goal of the plan, as God saw it in Jesus Christ and his Church, to the only Reality that will last. The only alternative is to proclaim man as the master of himself and of the world, which finally boils down to being his own destroyer and the destroyer of nature, as we see happening, alas, in the ordeal of AIDS and other modern ailments and diseases, environmental destruction, family alienation, abortion, etc. I see no need to hide this terrible alternative that follows from leaving God out of our budget: man must go bankrupt very soon if he doesn't come back to the faith of his fathers (and mothers).

◆ ◆ ◆

Faith and Inculturation
International Theological Commission

[This document was prepared by the International Theological Commission during its plenary session of December, 1987, broadly approved in *forma specifica* during its plenary session of October, 1988, and published with the *placet* of His Eminence, Cardinal Joseph Ratzinger, President of the Commission.]

Introduction

1. The International Theological Commission has had, on several occasions, the opportunity to reflect on the relationship between faith and culture.[1] In 1984 it spoke directly on the inculturation of faith in its study on the mystery of the Church which it produced with a view to the Extraordinary Synod of 1985.[2] For its part, the Pontifical Biblical Commission held its 1979 plenary session on the theme of the inculturation of faith in the light of Scripture.[3]

2. Today the International Theological Commission intends to continue this reflection in a more profound and systematic manner on account of the importance assumed by this theme of the inculturation of faith throughout the Christian world and on account of the insistence with which the Church's magisterium has considered this theme since the Second Vatican Council.

3. The basis is furnished by the conciliar documents and by the synod papers which have continued them. Thus, in Vatican II's *Gaudium et Spes*, the council has shown what lessons and what tasks the Church has drawn from its first experiences of inculturation in the Greco-Roman world.[4] It then devoted an entire chapter of this document to the promotion of culture (*de culturae progressu rite promovendo*).[5] After describing culture as an effort toward a deeper humanity and toward a better plan for the universe, the council considered at length the relationships between culture and the message of salvation. It then enunciated some of

214

the more urgent duties of Christians regarding culture: defense of the right of all to a culture, promotion of an integral culture, and harmonization of the links between culture and Christianity. The Decree on the Church's Missionary Activity and the Declaration on Non-Christian Religions develop some of these positions. Two ordinary synods expressly treated of the evangelization of cultures, that of 1974, on the theme of evangelization,[6] and that of 1976, on catechetical formation.[7] The 1985 synod, which celebrated the twentieth anniversary of the closing of the Second Vatican Council, spoke of inculturation as "the inner transformation of authentic cultural values by their integration into Christianity and the rooting of Christianity in the various human cultures."[8]

4. Pope John Paul II himself has taken to heart in a small manner the evangelization of cultures: in his view, the dialogue of the Church and of cultures assumes a vital importance for the future of the Church and of the world. To assist him in this great work, the Holy Father has created a specialized curial body: the Pontifical Council for Culture.[9] It is moreover with this dicastery that the International Theological Commission is happily in a position to reflect today on the inculturation of faith.

5. Relying on the conviction that "the Incarnation of the Word was also a cultural Incarnation," the pope affirms that cultures—analogically comparable to the humanity of Christ in whatever good they possess— may play a positive role of mediation in the expression and extension of the Christian faith.[10]

6. Two essential themes are bound up with this view. Firstly that of the transcendence of revelation in relation to the cultures in which it finds expression. The Word of God cannot, in effect, be identified or linked in an exclusive manner with the elements of culture which bear it. The gospel quite often demands a conversion of attitudes and an amendment of customs where it establishes itself: cultures must also be purified and restored in Christ.

7. The second major theme of the teaching of John Paul II revolves around the urgency of the evangelization of cultures. This task presupposes that one would understand and penetrate with a critical sympathy particular cultural identities and that, in the interest of a universality corresponding to the truly human reality of all cultures, one would favor exchanges between them. The Holy Father thus bases the evangelization of cultures on an anthropological conception firmly rooted in Christian thought since the Fathers of the Church. Since *culture*, when pure, reveals

and strengthens the *nature* of man, the Christian impregnation presupposes the surpassing of all historicism and relativism in the conception of what is human. The evangelization of cultures should therefore be inspired by the love of man in himself and for himself, especially in those aspects of his being and of his culture which are being attacked or are under threat.[11]

8. *In the light of this teaching, and also of the reflection which the theme of the inculturation of faith has aroused in the Church, we firstly propose a Christian anthropology which situates* — one in relation to the other — nature, culture, and grace. We shall then see the process of inculturation at work in the history of salvation: in ancient Israel, in the life and work of Jesus, and in the early Church. A final section will treat of problems at present posed to faith by its encounter with popular piety, with non-Christian religions, with the cultural traditions in the young Churches, and finally with the various characteristics of modernity.

I
Nature, Culture, and Grace

1. Anthropologists readily return to describe or define culture in terms of the distinction, sometimes even opposition, between nature and culture. The significance of this word *nature* varies moreover with the different conceptions of the natural sciences, of philosophy and of theology. The magisterium understands this word in a very specific sense: the nature of a being is what constitutes it as such, with the dynamism of its tendencies toward its proper ends. It is from God that natures possess what they are, as well as their proper ends. They are from that moment impregnated with a significance in which man, as *the image of God*, is capable of discerning the "creative intention of God."[12]

2. The fundamental inclinations of human nature, expressed by natural law, appear therefore as an expression of the will of the Creator. This natural law declares the specific requirements of *human* nature, requirements which are significative of the design of God for his rational and free creature. Thus all that misunderstanding is avoided which, perceiving nature in a univocal sense, would reduce man to material nature.

3. It is appropriate, at the same time, to consider human nature

according to its unfolding in historical time: that is, to observe what man, endowed with a fallible liberty, and often subjected to his passions, has made of his humanity. This heritage transmitted to new generations includes simultaneously immense treasures of wisdom, art, and generosity, and a considerable share of deviations and perversions. Attention therefore, as a whole, revolves around human nature and the human condition, an expression which integrates existential elements, of which certain ones — sin and grace — affect the history of salvation. If therefore we use the word "culture" in a primarily positive sense — as a synonym of development, for example — as have Vatican II and the recent popes, we will not forget that cultures can perpetuate and favor the choice of pride and selfishness.

4. Culture consists in the extension of the requirements of human nature, as the accomplishment of its ends, as is especially taught in *Gaudium et Spes*: "It is a fact bearing on the very person of man that he can come to an authentic and full humanity only through culture, that is, through the cultivation of natural goods and values. The word *culture* in its general sense indicates all those factors by which man refines and unfolds his manifold spiritual and bodily qualities."[13] Thus the domain of culture is multiple: by knowledge and work, man applies himself to the taming of the universe; he humanizes social life through the progress of customs and institutions; he expresses, communicates, and in short conserves in his works, through the course of time, the great spiritual experiences and aspirations of man in order that they may be of advantage to the progress of many, even of all mankind.

5. The primary constituent of culture is the human person, considered in all aspects of his being. Man betters *himself* — this is the first end of all culture — but he does so, thanks to the *works* of culture and thanks to a cultural memory. Culture also still designates the milieu in which and on account of which persons may grow.

6. The human person is a community being which blossoms in giving and in receiving. It is thus in solidarity with others and across living social relationships that the person progresses. Also, those realities of nation, people, society with their cultural patrimony, constitute for the development of persons "a specific historical environment, from which they draw the values which permit them to promote human and civic culture."[14]

7. Culture, which is always a concrete and particular culture, is open

to the higher values common to all. Thus the originality of a culture does not signify withdrawal into itself but a contribution to the richness which is the good of all. Cultural pluralism cannot therefore be interpreted as the juxtaposition of a closed universe, but as participation in a unison of realities all directed toward the universal values of humanity. The phenomenon of the reciprocal penetration of cultures, frequent in history, illustrates this fundamental openness of particular cultures to the values common to all, and through this their openness one to another.

8. Man is a naturally religious being. The turning toward the Absolute is inscribed in his deepest being. In a general sense, religion is an *integral constituent* of culture, in which it takes root and blossoms. Moreover, all the great cultures include, as the keystone of the edifice they constitute, the religious dimension, the inspiration of the great achievements which have marked the ancient history of civilizations.

9. At the root of the great religions is the transcendent movement of man in search of God. Purified of its deviations and disagreeable aspects, this movement should be the object of sincere respect. It is on this that the Christian faith comes to engraft itself. What distinguishes the Christian faith is that it is free adherence to the proposition of the gratuitous love of God which has been revealed to us, which has given us his only Son to free us from sin and has poured out his Spirit in our hearts. The radical reality of Christianity lies in the gift that God makes of himself to humanity, facing all the aspirations, requests, conquests, and achievements of nature.

10. Therefore, because it transcends the entire natural and cultural order, the Christian faith is, on the one hand, compatible with all cultures insofar as they conform to right reason and goodwill, and, on the other hand, to an eminent degree, is a dynamizing factor of culture. A single principle explains the totality of relationships between faith and culture: grace respects nature, healing in it the wounds of sin, comforting and elevating it. Elevation to the divine life is the specific finality of grace, but it cannot realize this unless nature is healed and unless elevation to the supernatural order brings nature, in the way proper to itself, to the plenitude of perfection.

11. The process of inculturation may be defined as the Church's efforts to make the message of Christ penetrate a given sociocultural milieu, calling on the latter to grow according to all its particular values, as long as these are compatible with the gospel. The term "inculturation"

includes the notion of growth, of the mutual enrichment of persons and groups, rendered possible by the encounter of the gospel with a social milieu. "Inculturation is the incarnation of the gospel in the hereditary cultures, and at the same time, the introduction of these cultures into the life of the Church."[15]

II
Inculturation in the History of Salvation

1. The relationships between nature, culture, and grace shall be considered in the concrete history of the Covenant between God and humanity, that began with a particular people, culminated in a son of this people, who is also Son of God, and extending from him to all the nations of the earth, this history demonstrates the "marvelous 'graciousness' of divine wisdom."[16]

Israel, the People of the Covenant
2. Israel understood itself as formed in an immediate manner by God. And the Old Testament, the Bible of ancient Israel, is the permanent witness of the revelation of the living God to the members of a chosen people. In its written form, this revelation also bears the traces of the cultural and social experiences of the era during which this people and neighboring civilizations encountered each other. Ancient Israel was born in a world which had already given birth to great cultures and progressed together with them.

3. The most ancient institutions of Israel (for example, circumcision, the spring sacrifice, the Sabbath rest) are not particular to it. It borrowed them from the neighboring peoples. A large part of the culture of Israel has a similar origin. However, the people of the Bible subjected these borrowings to profound changes when it incorporated them into its faith and religious practice. It passed them through the screen of a faith in the personal God of Abraham (the free Creator and wise planner of the universe, in whom the source of sin and death is not to be found). It is the encounter with this God, experienced in the Covenant, which permits the understanding of man and woman as personal beings and in consequence the rejection of the inhuman practices inherent in the other cultures.

4. The biblical authors used, while simultaneously transforming, the

cultures of their time to recount, throughout the history of a people, the salvific action which God would cause to culminate in Jesus Christ and to unite the peoples of all cultures, called to form one body of which Jesus is the head.

5. In the Old Testament, cultures, fused and transformed, are placed at the service of the revelation of the God of Abraham, lived in the Covenant and recorded in Scripture. It was a unique preparation, on the social and religious plane, for the coming of Jesus Christ. In the New Testament, the God of Abraham, Isaac, and Jacob, revealed at a deeper level and manifested in the fullness of the Spirit, invites all cultures to allow themselves to be changed by the life, teaching, death, and resurrection of Jesus Christ.

6. If the pagans were "grafted onto Israel,"[17] it must be emphasized that the original plan of God concerns all creation.[18] In fact, a covenant is made through Noah with all the peoples of the earth who are prepared to live in accordance with justice.[19] This covenant is anterior to those made with Abraham and Moses. Beginning from Abraham, Israel is called to communicate the blessings it has received to all the families of the earth.[20]

7. Let us also draw attention to the fact that the various aspects of the culture of Israel do not all maintain the same relationship with divine revelation. Some testify to the resistance to God's Word while others express its acceptance. Among the latter, one must distinguish between the provisional (ritual and judicial prescriptions) and the permanent (universal in scope). Certain elements (in the law of Moses, the prophets, and the psalms[21]) derive their signification from being the prehistory of Christ.

Jesus Christ, Lord and Savior of the World
I. The Transcendence of Jesus Christ in Relation to All Culture

8. One conviction dominates the preaching of Jesus: in Jesus — in his word and in his person — God perfects the gifts he has already made to Israel and to all nations, by transcending them.[22] Jesus is the sovereign light and true wisdom for all nations and all cultures.[23] He shows, in his own activity, that the God of Abraham, already recognized by Israel as creator and Lord,[24] is preparing himself to reign over all those who believe in the gospel, and much more, through Jesus, God already reigns.[25]

9. The teaching of Jesus, notably in the parables, is not afraid to correct, or when the need arises, to challenge a good number of the ideas which history, religion as practiced, and culture had inspired among his contemporaries concerning the nature and action of God.[26]

10. The completely filial intimacy of Jesus with God and the loving obedience which caused him to offer his life and death to his Father[27] show that in him the original plan of God for creation, tainted by sin, has been restored.[28] We are faced with a new creation, a new Adam.[29] Also, the relationships with God are profoundly changed in many respects.[30] The newness is such that the curse which strikes the crucified Messiah becomes a blessing for all peoples,[31] and faith in Jesus as savior replaces the regime of the Law.[32]

11. The death and resurrection of Jesus, on account of which the Spirit was poured out into our hearts, have shown the shortcomings of completely human wisdoms and moralities and even of the Law (nonetheless given by God to Moses), all of which were institutions capable of giving knowledge of the good, but not the force to accomplish it; knowledge of sin, but not the power to extract oneself from it.[33]

II. The Presence of Christ to Culture and Cultures
A. The Uniqueness of Christ, Universal Lord and Savior

12. Since it was fully and historically realized, the incarnation of the Son of God was a cultural incarnation: "Christ himself in virtue of his Incarnation, bound himself to the definite social and cultural conditions of those human beings among whom he dwelt."[34]

13. The Son of God was happy to be a Jew of Nazareth in Galilee, speaking Aramaic, subject to pious parents of Israel, accompanying them to the Temple of Jerusalem where they found him "sitting among the doctors, listening to them and asking them questions."[35] Jesus grew up in a milieu of customs and institutions of first-century Palestine, initiating himself into the trades of his time, observing the behavior of the sinners, peasants, and business people of his milieu. The scenes and countrysides on which the imagination of the future rabbi was nourished are of a very definite country and time.

14. Nourished by the piety of Israel, formed by the teaching of the Law and the prophets, to which a completely singular experience of God as Father added an unheard-of profundity, Jesus may be situated in a

highly specific spiritual tradition, that of Jewish prophecy. Like the prophets of old, he is the mouthpiece of God and calls to conversion. The manner is also quite typical: the vocabulary, literary types, the manner of address also recall the tradition of Elijah and Elisha: the biblical parallelism, the proverbs, paradoxes, admonitions, blessings, right up to the symbolic actions.

15. Jesus is so bound up with the life of Israel that the people and the religious tradition in which he shares acquires in virtue of this liaison a unique place in the history of salvation; this chosen people and the religious tradition which they have left have a permanent significance for humanity.

16. There is nothing improvised about the Incarnation. The Word of God enters into a history which prepares him, announces him, and prefigures him. One could say that the Christ takes flesh in advance with the people God has expressly formed with a view to the gift he would make of his Son. All the words uttered by the prophets are a prelude to the subsistent Word which is the Son of God.

17. Also, the history of the Covenant concluded with Abraham and through Moses with the people of Israel, as also the books which recount and clarify this history, all together hold for the faithful of Jesus, the role of an indispensable and irreplaceable pedagogy. Moreover, the election of this people from which Jesus emerges has never been revoked. "My brethren, my kinsmen by race," writes St. Paul, "they are Israelites, and to them belong the sonship, the glory, the covenants, the giving of the law, the worship and the promises, to them belong the Patriarchs and of their race, according to the flesh is the Christ. God who is over all be blessed for ever. Amen."[36] The cultivated olive has not lost its privileges to the wild olive, which has been grafted onto it.

B. The Catholicity of the Unique Event

18. However historically distinctive the condition of the Word made flesh may be — and consequently of the culture which receives, forms, and continues him — it is not firstly this factor which the Son of God united to himself.[37] It is because he became man that God has also assumed, in a certain way, a race, a country, and a time. "Because in him, human nature was assumed, not absorbed, by that very fact this nature has been raised up to an unequalled dignity in us too. For by his incarnation, the Son of God has united himself in some fashion with every person."[38]

19. The transcendence of Christ does not therefore isolate him above the human family but renders him present to all, beyond all restriction. "He is a stranger nowhere, nor to anyone."[39] "There are no more distinctions between Jew and Greek, slave and free, male and female, but all of you are one in Christ Jesus."[40] Thus Christ is at one with us in the unity we form as in the multiplicity and diversity in which our common nature is realized.

20. However, Christ would not be one with us in the reality of our concrete humanity if he did not affect us as well in the diversity and the complementarity of our cultures. It is in fact cultures—language, history, general attitude to life, diverse institutions, which, for better or worse, receive us into life, form us, accompany us, and survive our passing. If the cosmos as a whole is, in a mysterious sense, the scene of grace and sin, do not our cultures have a similar role in as much as they are both fruits and seeds in the field of our human labors?

21. In the Body of Christ, the cultures, insofar as they are animated and renewed by grace and faith, are moreover complementary. They permit us to see the multiform richness of which the teachings and energies of the same gospel are capable, the same principles of truth, justice, love, and liberty, when they are traversed by the Spirit of Christ.

22. Finally, is it necessary to recall that it is not in virtue of a self-interested strategy that the Church, bride of the Incarnated Word, preoccupies itself with the fate of the various cultures of humanity? The Church wishes to animate from the inside, protect, free from the error and sin with which we have corrupted them, these resources of truth and love which God has placed, as *semina Verbi*, in his creation. The Word of God does not come into a creation which is foreign to it. "All things were created through him and for him. He is before all things and in him all things hold together."[41]

The Holy Spirit and the Church of the Apostles
A. From Jerusalem to the Nations:
The Typical Beginnings of the
Inculturation of the Faith

23. On Pentecost day, the breaking-in of the Holy Spirit inaugurates the relation of the Christian faith and culture as fulfillment in flower: the promise of salvation fulfilled by the risen Christ filled the hearts of

believers by the outpouring of the Holy Spirit himself. "The marvels of God" will from now on be "preached" to all men of every language and culture.[42] While humanity was living under the sign of the division of Babel, the gift of the Holy Spirit was offered to it as the transcendent and now so human the *symphony* of hearts. The divine unification (*koinonia*)[43] recreated a new humanity among people, penetrating, without destroying, the sign of their division: languages.

24. The Holy Spirit does not establish a super culture but is the personal and vital principle which will vivify the new community in working in harness with its members. The gift of the Holy Spirit is not of the order of structures, but the Church of Jerusalem which he fashions is a *koinonia* of faith and of agape, communicating itself in many ways without loss of identity; the Church is the *Body of Christ* whose members are united but with many faces. The first test of *Catholicity* appears when differences of cultural origin (conflicts between Greeks and Hebrews) menace the Communion.[44] The Apostles do not suppress the differences but are concerned with developing an essential function of the ecclesial Body: the *diakonia* at the service of the *koinonia*.

25. In order that the Good News might be announced to the Nations, the Holy Spirit awakens a new perception in Peter and the Jerusalem community, to wit,[45] faith in Christ does not require that new believers abandon their culture to adopt that of the Law of the Jewish people; all peoples are called to be beneficiaries of the Promise and to share the heritage entrusted for them in the People of the Covenant.[46] Therefore "nothing beyond the essentials" is required, according to the decision of the apostolic assembly.[47]

26. Scandal for the Jews, the mystery of the Cross is foolishness to the pagans. Here the inculturation of the faith clashes with the radical sin of *idolatry* which keeps "captive"[48] the truth of a culture which is not assumed by Christ. As long as man is "deprived of the glory of God"[49] all that he "cultivates" is nothing more than the opaque image of himself. The Pauline kerygma begins therefore with creation and the call to the covenant, denounces the moral perversions of blinded humanity, and announces salvation in the crucified and risen Christ.

27. After the testing of Catholicity among culturally different Christian communities, after the resistances of Jewish legalism and those of idolatry, the faith pledges itself to culture in Gnosticism. *The phenomenon begins to appear at the time of the last letters of Paul and*

John; it will fuel the majority of the doctrinal crises of the succeeding centuries. Here, human reason, in its injured state, refuses the folly of the Incarnation of the Son of God and seeks to recover the Mystery by accommodating it to the prevailing culture. Whereas, "faith depends not on human philosophy but on the power of God."[50]

B. The Apostolic Tradition:
Inculturation of Faith and Salvation of Culture

28. *In the "last times" inaugurated at Pentecost, the risen Christ, Alpha and Omega, enters into the history of peoples: from that moment, the sense of history and thus of culture is unsealed*[51] *and the Holy Spirit reveals it by actualizing and communicating it to all. The Church is the sacrament of this revelation and its communication. It recenters* every culture into which Christ is received, placing it in the axis of the "world which is coming" and restores the union broken by the "prince of this world." Culture is thus *eschatologically* situated; it tends toward its completion in Christ, but it cannot be saved except by associating itself with the repudiation of evil.

29. Each local or particular Church is called in the Holy Spirit to the sacrament which manifests Christ, crucified and risen, *enfleshed* in a particular culture.

(a) The culture of a local Church — young or old — participates in the dynamism of cultures and in their vicissitudes. Even if the Church is in the last times it remains subject to trials and temptations.[52]

(b) The Christian "newness" engenders in the local Churches particular expressions stamped by culture (modalities of doctrinal formulations, liturgical symbolisms, models of holiness, canonical directives, etc.). Nevertheless the Communion between the Churches demands constantly that the cultural "flesh" of each does not act as a screen to mutual recognition in the apostolic faith and to solidarity in love.

(c) Every Church sent to the nations witnesses to its Lord only if, having consideration for its cultural attachments, it conforms to him in the first kenosis of his Incarnation and in the final humiliation of his life-giving passion. The inculturation of the faith is one of the expressions of the Apostolic Tradition whose dramatic character is emphasized on several occasions by Paul.[53]

30. The apostolic writings and the patristic witness do not limit their vision of culture to the service of evangelization but integrate it into *the*

totalility of the Mystery of Christ. For them, creation is the reflection of the Glory of God: man is its living icon and it is in Christ that the resemblance with God is seen. Culture is the scene in which man and the world are called to find themselves anew in the glory of God. The encounter is missed or obscured insofar as man is a sinner. Within captive creation is seen the gestation of the "new universe:"[54] The Church is "in labor."[55] In the Church and through it, the creatures of this world are able to live their redemption and their transfiguration.

III
Present Problems of Inculturation

1. The inculturation of the faith, which we have considered firstly from a philosophical viewpoint (nature, culture, and grace), then from the point of view of history and dogma (inculturation in the history of salvation) still poses considerable problems for theological reflection and pastoral action. Thus the questions aroused in the sixteenth century by the discovery of new worlds continue to preoccupy us. How may one harmonize the spontaneous expressions of the religiosity of peoples with faith? What attitude should be adopted in the face of non-Christian religions, especially those "bound up with cultural advancement"?[56] New questions have arisen in our time. How should "young Churches," born in our century of the indigenization of already existing Christian communities, consider both their Christian past and the cultural history of their respective peoples? Finally, how should the gospel animate, purify, and fortify the new world into which we have brought industrialization and urbanization? To us it seems that these four questions should be faced by anyone who reflects on the present conditions of the inculturation of faith.

Popular Piety

2. In the countries which have been affected by the gospel, we normally understand by *popular piety*, on the one hand, the union of Christian faith and piety with the profound culture, and on the other, with the previous forms of religion of populations. It involves those very numerous devotions in which Christians express their religious sentiment in the simple language, among other things, of festival, pilgrimage, dance,

and song. One could speak of *vital synthesis* with reference to this piety, since it unites "body and spirit, ecclesial communion and institution, individual and community, Christian faith and love of one's country, intelligence and affectivity."[57] The quality of the synthesis stems, as one might expect, from the antiquity and profundity of the evangelization, as from the compatibility of its religious and cultural antecedents with the Christian faith.

3. In the Apostolic Exhortation *Evangelii Nuntiandi* Paul VI confirmed and encouraged a new appreciation of popular piety. "For long seen as less pure, sometimes scorned, these particular expressions of the quest for God and the faith today have become practically everywhere the object of a rediscovery."[58]

4. "If well directed, especially by a pedagogy of evangelization," continued Paul VI, "[popular piety] is rich in value. It communicates a thirst of God which only the simple and the poor can understand. It renders capable generosity and sacrifice, even to the level of heroism, when it is a question of manifesting faith. It includes a sharp sense of the profound attributes of God: paternity, providence, loving and constant presence. It engenders internal attitudes, rarely observed elsewhere to a similar degree: patience, sense of the Cross in daily life, detachment, openness to others, devotion."[59]

5. Moreover, the strength and depth of the roots of popular piety clearly manifested themselves in the long period of discredit mentioned by Paul VI. The expressions of popular piety have survived numerous predictions of disappearance of which modernity and the progress of secularity seemed to warn. They have preserved and even increased, in many regions of the globe, the attractions they exercised on the masses.

6. The limits of popular piety have often been condemned. They stem from a certain naïveté, are a source of various deformations of religion, even of superstitions. One remains at the level of cultural manifestations without a true adhesion to faith at the level where this is expressed in service on one's neighbor. Badly directed, popular piety can even lead to the formation of sects and thus place true ecclesial unity in danger. It also risks being manipulated, be it by political powers or by religious forces foreign to the Christian faith.

7. The taking into account of these dangers invites us to practice an intelligent catechesis, won thanks to the merits of an authentic popular

piety and at the same time duly shrewd. A living and adapted liturgy is equally called to play a major role in the integration of a very pure faith and the traditional forms of the religious life of peoples. Without any doubt whatsoever, popular piety can bring an irreplaceable contribution to a Christian cultural anthropology which would permit the reduction of the often tragic division between the faith of Christians and certain socioeconomic institutions, of quite different orientation, which regulate their daily life.

Inculturation of Faith and Non-Christian Religions

8. From its origin, the Church has encountered on many levels the question of the plurality of religions. Even today Christians constitute only about a third of the world's population. Moreover, they must live in a world which expresses a growing sympathy for pluralism in religious matters.

9. Given the great place of religion in culture, a local or particular Church, implanted in a non-Christian sociocultural milieu, must take seriously into account the religious elements of this milieu. Moreover, this preoccupation should be in accordance with the depth and vitality of these religious elements.

10. If we may consider one continent as an example, we shall speak of Asia, which witnessed the birth of several of the world's great religious movements. Hinduism, Buddhism, Islam, Confucianism, Taoism, Shintoism: each of these religious systems certainly located in distinct regions of the continent are deeply rooted in the people and show much vigor. One's personal life, as well as social and community activity, was marked in a decisive manner by these religious and spiritual traditions. In addition the Asian Churches consider the question of non-Christian religions as one of the most important and most urgent. They have even made it the object of that privileged form of relation: the dialogue.

The Dialogue of Religions

11. Dialogue with other religions forms an integral part of Christian life; by exchange, study, and work in common, this dialogue contributes to a better understanding of the religion of the other and to a growth of piety.

12. For Christian faith, the unity of all in their origin and destiny —

that is, in creation and in communion with God in Jesus Christ — is accompanied by the universal presence and action of the Holy Spirit. The Church in dialogue listens and learns. "The Catholic Church rejects nothing which is true and holy in these religions. She looks with sincere respect upon those ways of conduct and of life, those rules and teachings which, though differing in many particulars from what she holds and sets forth, nevertheless often reflects a ray of that Truth which enlightens all men."[60]

13. This dialogue possesses something original, since, as the history of religions testifies, the plurality of religions has often given rise to discrimination and jealousy, fanaticism and despotism, all of which drew on religion the accusation of being a source of division in the human family. The Church, "universal sacrament of salvation" (that is, "sign and instrument of intimate union with God and of the unity of all the human race"[61]), is called by God to be minister and instrument of unity in Jesus Christ for all men and all peoples.

The Transcendence of the Gospel in Relation to Culture

14. We cannot however, forget the transcendence of the gospel in relation to all human cultures in which the Christian faith has the vocation to enroot itself and come to fruition according to all its potentialities. However great the respect should be for what is true and holy in the cultural heritage of a people, this attitude does not demand that one should lend an absolute character to this cultural heritage. No one can forget that, from the beginning, the gospel was a "scandal for the Jews and foolishness for the pagans."[62] Inculturation which borrows the way of dialogue between religions cannot in any way pledge itself to syncretism.

The Young Churches and Their Christian Past

15. The Church prolongs and actualizes the mystery of the Servant of Yahweh who was promised to be "the light of the nations so that salvation might reach the ends of the earth"[63] and to be the "Covenant of the People."[64] This prophecy is realized at the Last Supper, when, on the eve of his Passion, Christ, surrounded by the Twelve, gives his body and blood to his followers as the food and drink of the New Covenant, thus assimilating them into his own body. The Church, people of the New Covenant, was being born. The Church would receive at Pentecost the Spirit of Christ, the Spirit of the Lamb sacrificed from the beginning and

who was already working to fulfill this desire so deeply rooted in human beings: a union the more intense with respect to the intense diversity.

16. In virtue of the Catholic Communion, which unites all the particular Churches in the one history, the young Churches consider the past of the Churches which gives birth to them as part of their own history. However, the major act of interpretation, which is the hallmark of their spiritual maturity, consists in recognizing this precedence as "originatory" and not only as historical. This signifies that in receiving in faith the gospel which their elders announced to them, the young Churches welcomed the "initiator of the faith"[65] and the entire tradition in which the faith is attested, as also the capacity to give birth to new forms in which the unique and common faith would find expression. Equal in dignity, drawing life from the same mystery, authentic sister Churches, the young Churches manifest, in concert with their elders, the fullness of the mystery of Christ.

17. People of the New Covenant: it is insofar as it commemorates the Paschal mystery and ceaselessly announces the return of the Lord that the Church may be called an eschatology that began with the cultural traditions of peoples, on condition, of course, that these traditions had been subjected to the purifying law of death and resurrection in Christ Jesus.

18. Like St. Paul at the Areopagus in Athens, the young Church interprets its ancestral culture in a new and creative manner. When this culture passes through Christ, "the veil falls."[66] At the time of the "incubation" of faith, this Church has discovered Christ as "exegete and exegesis" of the Father in the Spirit;[67] moreover, it does not cease to contemplate him as such. Now it is discovering him as "exegete and exegesis" of man, source and destination of culture. To the unknown God, revealed on the Cross, corresponds unknown man, announced by the young Church as the living Paschal mystery inaugurated by grace in the ancient culture.

19. In the salvation it makes present, the young Church endeavors to locate all the traces of God's care for a particular human group, the *semina Verbi*. What the prologue of the letter to the Hebrews says of the Fathers and the prophets may in relation with Jesus Christ be repeated, in an analogical manner of course, for all human culture insofar as it is right and true and bears wisdom.

Christian Faith and Modernity

20. The technical changes which gave rise to the industrial revolution and subsequently the urban revolution, affected souls of people in depth. They were beneficiaries and also, quite often, the victims of these changes. Therefore believers have the duty, as an urgent and difficult task, to understand the characteristic traits of modern culture, as also its expectations and needs in relation to the salvation wrought by Christ.

21. The Industrial Revolution was also a cultural revolution. Values until then assured were brought into question, such as the sense of personal and community work: the direct relationship of man to nature, membership of a support family, in cohabitation as in work, implantation in local and religious communities of human dimension, participation in traditions, rites, ceremonies, and celebrations which give a sense to the great moment of existence. Industrialization, in provoking a disordered concentrating of populations, seriously affected these age-old values without giving rise to communities capable of integrating new cultures. At a time when the most deprived peoples are in search of a suitable development model, the advantages as also the risks and human costs of industrialization are better perceived.

22. Great progress has been made in many areas of life: diet, health, education, transport, access to all types of consumer goods. Deep misgivings, however, have arisen in the collective subconscious. In many countries, the notion of progress has given way, especially since the Second World War, to disillusion. Rationality as regards production and administration operates against reason, when it forgets the good of persons. The emancipation of communities from a sense of belonging has isolated man in the crowd. The new means of communication destroy to as great an extent as they create. Science, by means of the technical creations which are its fruit, appears simultaneously to be creator and destroyer. In addition some despair of modernity and speak of a new barbarism. Despite many faults and failings, one must hope for a moral uplift of all nations, rich and poor. If the gospel is preached and heard, a cultural and spiritual conversion is possible; it calls to solidarity, in the interest of the whole good of the person, to the promotion of peace and justice, to the adoration of the Father, from whom all good things come.

23. The inculturation of the gospel in modern societies will demand a methodical effort of concerted research and action. This effort will assure

on the part of those responsible for evangelization (1) an attitude of openness and a critical eye; (2) the capacity to perceive the spiritual expectations and human aspirations of the new cultures; (3) the aptitude for cultural analysis, having in mind an effective encounter with the modern world.

24. A receptive attitude is required among those who wish to understand and evangelize the world of our time. Modernity is accompanied by undeniable progress in many cultural and material domains: well-being, human mobility, science, research, education, a new sense of solidarity. In addition the Church of Vatican II has taken a lively account of the new conditions in which the Church must exercise its mission, and it is in the cultures of modernity that the Church of tomorrow will be constructed. The traditional advice applicable to discernment is reiterated by Pius XII. "It is necessary to deepen one's understanding of the civilization and institutions of various peoples and to cultivate their best qualities and gifts. . . . All in the customs of peoples which are not inextricably bound up with superstitions or errors should be examined with benevolence and, if possible, preserved intact."[68]

25. The gospel raises fundamental questions among those who reflect on the behavior of modern man, how should one make this man understand the radical nature of the message of Christ: unconditional love, evangelical poverty, adoration of the Father and constant yielding to his will? How should one educate toward the Christian sense of suffering and death? How should one arouse faith and hope in the event of the resurrection accomplished by Jesus Christ?

26. We must develop a *capacity to analyze cultures* and to gauge their moral and spiritual indicators. A mobilization of the whole Church is called for so that the extremely complex task of the inculturation of the gospel in today's world may be faced with success. We must wed to this topic the preoccupation of John Paul II, "From the beginning of my pontificate I considered that the dialogue of the Church with the cultures of our time was a vital area, whose stake is the fate of the world in this the end of the 20th century."[69]

Conclusion

1. Having said that the important thing was "to affect and to upset, as it were, by the strength of the Gospel, the criteria of judgment,

dominant values, centers of interest, line of thought, the sources of inspiration and models of life which are in contrast with the word of God and the plan of salvation by the strength of the Gospel,'' Paul VI asked that one would ''evangelize, not in any decorative way, by any superficial varnishing as it were, but in a vital manner, in depth and down through the roots — the culture and cultures of man, in the rich and broad sense which these terms possess in *Gaudium et Spes*. . . . The reign announced by the Gospel is lived by men deeply bound to a culture and the building up of the Kingdom cannot but borrow from the elements of human culture and cultures.''[70]

2. ''In this the end of the 20th century,'' as John Paul II affirmed for his part, ''the Church must make itself all things for all men, bringing today's cultures together with sympathy. There still are milieus and mentalities as there are entire countries and regions to evangelize, which supposes a long and courageous process of inculturation so that the Gospel may penetrate the soul of living cultures, respond to their highest expectations and make them grow in the dimension of Christian faith, hope and charity. Sometimes cultures have only been touched superficially and in any case, to continuously transform themselves, they demand a renewed approach. In addition, new areas of culture appear, with diverse objectives, methods and languages.''[71]

Notes

1. See the documents of the International Theological Commission on Theological Pluralism (1972), Human Promotion and Christian Salvation (1976), Catholic Doctrine on the Sacrament of Marriage (1977), Selected Questions on Christology (1979), in the collection of the International Theological Commission, ''Texts and Documents'' (1969-1985) (Paris, 1988).

2. ''Themes chosen from ecclesiology on the occasion of the twentieth anniversary of the closure of the Second Vatican Council,'' International Theological Commission (1984), in the collection referred to in the previous note, pp. 336-340.

3. Pontifical Biblical Commission, ''Fede e cultura alla luce della Bibbia, Foi et Culture à la lumière de la Bible'' (Torino, 1981).

4. Vatican II, Pastoral Constitution *Gaudium et Spes* on the Church in the modern world, No. 44.

5. Ibid., Nos. 53-62.

6. Paul VI, Apostolic Exhortation *Evangelii Nuntiandi* on evangelization in the modern world, Nos. 18-20, in "Documentation Catholique," 73, January 4, 1976, p. 45.

7. John Paul II, Apostolic Exhortation *Catechesi Tradendae* on catechesis in our time, No. 53, in "Documentation Catholique," 76, November 4, 1979, p. 914.

8. Extraordinary Synod for the twentieth anniversary of the closing of the Second Vatican Council, final report voted by the Fathers, December 7, 1985, in "Documentation Catholique," 83, January 5, 1986, p. 41.

9. John Paul II, Letter of foundation of the Pontifical Council for Culture, May 20, 1982, *Acta Apostolicae Sedis* 74 (1983), 683-688; "Documentation Catholique," 79, June 20, 1982, pp. 604-606.

10. John Paul II, Speech to the University of Coimbra (May 15, 1982) in "Documentation Catholique," A, June 6, 1982, p. 549. Speech to the bishops of Kenya (May 7, 1980), in "Documentation Catholique," 77, June 1, 1980, p. 534.

11. John Paul II, Discourse to the members of the Pontifical Council for Culture (January 18, 1983), in "Documentation Catholique," 80, February 6, 1983, p. 147.

12. Paul VI, Encyclical letter *Humanae Vitae* on birth control, in "Documentation Catholique," 65, September 1, 1968, p. 1447.

13. Vatican II, Pastoral Constitution *Gaudium et Spes* on the Church in the modern world, No. 53.

14. Ibid.

15. John Paul II, Encyclical letter *Slavorum Apostoli* for the eleventh centenary of the work of evangelization of SS. Cyril and Methodius, June 2, 1985, No. 21, in "Documentation Catholique," June 2, 1985, p. 724.

16. Vatican II, Dogmatic Constitution *Dei Verbum* on divine revelation, No. 13.

17. Cf. Rom. 11:11-24.

18. Gen. 1:12, 4a.

19. Cf. Gen. 9:1-17; Sir. 44:17-18.

20. Gen. 12:1-5; Jn. 4:2; Sir. 44:21.

21. Lk. 24:27-44.
22. Mk. 13:10; Mt. 12:21; Lk. 2:32.
23. Mt. 11:19; Lk. 7:35.
24. Ps. 93:1-4; Is. 6:1.
25. Mk. 1:15; Mt. 12:28; Lk. 11:20; 17:21.
26. Mt. 20:1-16; Lk. 15:11-32; 18:9-14.
27. Mk. 14:36.
28. Mk. 1:14-45; 10:2-9; Mt. 5:21-48.
29. Rom. 5:12-19; 1 Cor. 15:20-22.
30. Mk. 8:27-33; 1 Cor. 1:18-25.
31. Gal. 3:13; Dt. 21:22-23.
32. Gal. 3:12-14.
33. Rom. 7:16ff.; 3:20; 7:7; 1 Tim. 1:8.
34. Vatican II, Decree *Ad Gentes* on the Church's missionary activity, No. 10.
35. Lk. 2:46.
36. Rom. 9:3-5.
37. Rom. 11:24.
38. Vatican II, Pastoral Constitution *Gaudium et Spes* on the Church in the modern world, No. 22.
39. Vatican II, Decree *Ad Gentes* on the Church's missionary activity, No. 8.
40. Gal. 3:28.
41. Col. 1:16-17.
42. Acts 2:11.
43. Acts 2:42.
44. Acts 6:1ff.
45. Acts 10 and 11.
46. Eph. 2:14-15.
47. Acts 15-28.
48. Rom. 1:18.
49. Rom. 3:23.
50. 1 Cor. 2:4ff.
51. Rev. 5:1-5.
52. Cf. Rev. 2 and 3.
53. 1 and 2 Cor. passim.
54. Rev. 21:5.
55. Cf. Rom. 8:18-25.

56. Vatican II, Declaration *Nostra Aetate* on the relationship of the Church to non-Christian religions, No. 2.

57. Third general conference of the bishops of Latin America, The Evangelization of Latin America in the Present and in the Future, No. 448.

58. Paul VI, Apostolic Exhortation *Evangelii Nuntiandi* on evangelization in the modern world, December 8, 1975, No. 48.

59. Ibid.

60. Vatican II, Declaration *Nostra Aetate* on the relationship of the Church to non-Christian religions, No. 2.

61. Vatican II, Dogmatic Constitution *Lumen Gentium* on the Church, No. 1.

62. 1 Cor. 1:23.

63. Is. 49:6.

64. Is. 49:8.

65. Heb. 12:2.

66. 2 Cor. 3:16.

67. Cf. Henri de Lubac "Exégèse medievale," coll. *Thèologie*, n. 41 (Paris, 1959), t. 1, pp. 322-324.

68. Pius XII, Encyclical letter *Summi Pontificatus* on the feast of Christ the King, October 20, 1939, in "Documentation Catholique," 40, December 5, 1939, c. 1261.

69. John Paul II, Letter of foundation of the Pontifical Council for Culture, May 20, 1982, in "Documentation Catholique," 79, June 20, 1982, p. 604.

70. Paul VI, Apostolic Exhortation *Evangelii Nuntiandi* on evangelization in the modern world, Nos. 19-20, in "Documentation Catholique," 73, January 4, 1976, p. 4.

71. John Paul II, Discourse to the members of the Pontifical Council for Culture, January 18, 1983, in "Documentation Catholique," 80, February 6, 1983, p. 147.